WHY WOULD ANYONE EDIT THE NEW TESTAMENT?

"To add to the image, the spirit, and the message of THE GOOD NEWS ABOUT JESUS, I decided to adapt and rearrange the Acts of the Apostles, the thirteen letters of Paul, the eight New Testament books called the General Letters, and The Revelation to John in a manner that would blend with the edited, continuous narrative of the four Gospels. The decision to edit these books was difficult indeed. To include them in their entirety would have detracted from the basic theme of the work. It should be noted that the abridged and rearranged treatment of these books does not in any way affect the inspiring and edifying accounts which are in the complete version. To read these books in the present format is to grasp the heart and mind of the simple, courageous, loving followers of Christ who unite their forces so they can give substance and fruition to the message of the Gospel."

—Frank Dell'Isola
from the Preface

"This life story of Jesus Christ in the words of contemporary Scripture is thrilling reading."
—Robert Schuller

THOMAS MERTON:	
A BIBLIOGRAPHY	1956
THE GOOD-MAN JESUS	1959
THE OLD TESTAMENT FOR EVERYMAN	1968
THOMAS MERTON: A BIBLIOGRAPHY	1975
THE GOOD NEWS ABOUT JESUS	1975

The Good News About Jesus

THE NEW TESTAMENT
IN TODAY'S ENGLISH VERSION

Edited and Rearranged
in a Continuous Narrative
by FRANK DELL'ISOLA

TRUMPET BOOKS
published by
A. J. HOLMAN COMPANY
Division of J. B. Lippincott Company
Philadelphia and *New York*

Published by Pillar Books for A. J. Holman Company

This arrangement © 1975 by Frank Dell'Isola

All rights reserved.

Printed in the United States of America

ISBN-0-87981-076-9

Trumpet Books edition published May 1977

The Bible text in this publication is from *Today's English Version* of the New Testament. Copyright © American Bible Society 1966, 1971. Used by permission.

The Scriptures throughout The Good News About Jesus *are presented without note or comment.*

PREFACE

The measure and wealth of the new covenant, which is the story of the fulfillment of the prophecies of Old Testament, can best be summed up in these words:

> Everyman,
> I will go with thee,
> And be thy guide.
> In thy most need
> To go by thy side.

The above quotation from the play *Everyman* was the driving force behind the making of *The Good News About Jesus*. The present work is an attempt to arrange the gospel texts of Matthew, Mark, Luke, and John in chronological sequence so that the reader may have a unified view of the life of Christ as recorded in the four Gospels. Originally, my purpose was to present only the words of Jesus that are found in the New Testament, but such a method would have failed to give a rounded and balanced portrait of the Son of God. Ultimately I decided to group selected passages from the four evangelists (as Tatian did in his *Diatessaron*) into a chronological order so as to give a consecutive account of the Messiah's earthly life in the words of the Gospels themselves. Where more than one evangelist reports a certain incident, I have used the one best suited to the development of the narrative.

To add to the image, the spirit, and the message of the *The Good News About Jesus,* I decided to adapt and rearrange the Acts of the Apostles, the thirteen letters of Paul, the eight New Testament books called the General Letters, and The Revelation to John in a manner that would blend with the edited, continuous narrative of the four Gospels. The decision to edit these books was difficult indeed. To include them in their entirety would have detracted from the basic theme of the work. It should be noted that the abridged and rearranged treatment of these books does not in any way affect the inspiring and edifying accounts which are in the complete version. To read these books in the present format is to grasp the heart and mind of the simple, courageous, loving followers of Christ who unite their forces so they can give substance and fruition to the message of the gospel.

Despite major editing, *The Good News About Jesus* has, I believe, the overall effect of an even, balanced rhythm which gives it the impact of an absorbing story with a beginning, a middle, and an ending.

And as the reader reads the inspired message of the Good News, he gradually begins to realize that "Holy writ is set before the eye of the mind like a kind of mirror, that we may see our inward face in it; for therein we learn the deformities, therein we learn the beauties that we possess; there we are made sensible what progress we are making, there too how far we are from proficiency" (Pope Saint Gregory I).

In order to make the work as effective as possible, it was necessary to find the best-suited modern English translation of the New Testament. After studying a number of modern translations, I selected *Today's English Version* of the New Testament, a new translation from the Greek New Testament. The TEV is an outstanding rendering that highlights with clearness and poignancy the message of the Good News; a message from which today's modern man could profit beyond measure if he were to take the time and the effort to put it into practice; his life would be richer for it.

I hope the arrangement of *The Good News About Jesus* accomplishes this and much more: that the reading of it will impel man, who is constantly searching for peace of mind, to go further and read the entire New Testament so that he may discover for himself the truth of Paul's words: "All Scripture is inspired by God and is useful for teaching the truth, rebuking error, correcting faults, and giving instruction for right living, so that the man who serves God may be fully qualified and equipped to do every kind of good work" (2 Timothy 3:16-17).

CONTENTS

PREFACE ... 7

PART 1. THE MESSIAH'S EARTHLY LIFE ... 15

PROLOGUE ... 17

CHAPTER ONE
　The Dawn of the Good News ... 19

CHAPTER TWO
　The Baptist Prepares the Way for the Son of God ... 29

CHAPTER THREE
　The Early Ministry of Jesus ... 37

CHAPTER FOUR
　Jesus Speaks with Authority ... 46

CHAPTER FIVE
　Miracles and Parables ... 53

CHAPTER SIX
　Coming Events Cast Their Shadows ... 81

CHAPTER SEVEN
　"To Search Out and to Save What Was Lost" ... 102

CHAPTER EIGHT
　"And Now My Soul Is Distressed. What Am I to Say?" ... 132

CHAPTER NINE
　Final Preaching of Jesus; His Betrayal and Arrest ... 149

CHAPTER TEN
    The Trial of Jesus; His Crucifixion,
    Death, and Triumph 164

EPILOGUE 181

PART 2. THE REST OF THE NARRATIVE 183

CHAPTER ELEVEN
    The Plight and Struggle of the Believers 185

CHAPTER TWELVE
    The Followers of Christ Preach
    the Good News 224

CHAPTER THIRTEEN
    "Let Us Come Near to God" 254

CHAPTER FOURTEEN
    The Better Part 281

CHAPTER FIFTEEN
    "A Revelation of Things That Were, Are,
    and Will Be" 293

SCRIPTURAL REFERENCES 305

You have made us for yourself, O Lord, and our hearts are restless till they rest in you.

Saint Augustine, Book 1:i

PART I

The Messiah's Earthly Life

PROLOGUE

The Word of Life
Before the world was created, the Word already existed; he was with God, and he was the same as God. From the very beginning, the Word was with God. Through him God made all things; not one thing in all creation was made without him. The Word was the source of life, and this life brought light to men. The light shines in the darkness, and the darkness has never put it out.

God sent his messenger, a man named John, who came to tell people about the light. He came to tell them, so that all should hear the message and believe. He himself was not the light; he came to tell about the light. This was the real light, the light that comes into the world and shines on all men.

The Word, then, was in the world. God made the world through him, yet the world did not know him. He came to his own country, but his own people did not receive him. Some, however, did receive him and believed in him; so he gave them the right to become God's children. They did not become God's children by natural means, by being born as the children of a human father; God himself was their Father.

The Word became a human being and lived among us. We saw his glory, full of grace and truth. This was the glory which he received as the Father's only Son.

John told about him. He cried out, "This is the one I was talking about when I said, 'He comes after me, but he is greater than I am, because he existed before I was born.' "

Out of the fulness of his grace he has blessed us all,

giving us one blessing after another. God gave the Law through Moses; but grace and truth came through Jesus Christ. No one has ever seen God. The only One, who is the same as God and is at the Father's side, he has made him known.

Introduction
Dear Theophilus: Many have done their best to write a report of the things that have taken place among us. They wrote what we have been told by those who saw these things from the beginning and proclaimed the message. And so, your Excellency, because I have carefully studied all these matters from their beginning, I thought it good to write an orderly account for you. I do this so that you will know the full truth of all those matters which you have been taught.

One

THE DAWN OF THE GOOD NEWS

The Birth of John the Baptist Announced
During the time when Herod was king of the land of Israel, there was a priest named Zechariah, who belonged to the priestly order of Abijah. His wife's name was Elizabeth; she also belonged to a priestly family. They both lived good lives in God's sight, and obeyed fully all the Lord's commandments and rules. They had no children because Elizabeth could not have any, and she and Zechariah were both very old.

One day Zechariah was doing his work as a priest before God, taking his turn in the daily service. According to the custom followed by the priests, he was chosen by lot to burn the incense on the altar. So he went into the temple of the Lord, while the crowd of people outside prayed during the hour of burning the incense. An angel of the Lord appeared to him, standing at the right side of the altar where the incense was burned. When Zechariah saw him, he was troubled and felt afraid. But the angel said to him, "Don't be afraid, Zechariah! God has heard your prayer, and your wife Elizabeth will bear you a son. You are to name him John. How glad and happy you will be, and how happy many others will be when he is born! He will be a great man in the Lord's sight. He must not drink any wine or strong drink. From his very birth he will be filled with the Holy Spirit. He will bring back many of the people of Israel to the Lord their God. He will go ahead of him, strong and mighty like the prophet Elijah. He will bring fathers and children together again; he will turn the disobedient people back to the way of thinking of the righteous; he will get the Lord's people ready for him."

Zechariah said to the angel, "How shall I know if this is so? I am an old man and my wife also is old."

"I am Gabriel," the angel answered. "I stand in the presence of God, who sent me to speak to you and tell you this good news. But you have not believed my message, which will come true at the right time. Because you have not believed you will be unable to speak; you will remain silent until the day my promise to you comes true."

In the meantime the people were waiting for Zechariah, wondering why he was spending such a long time in the temple. When he came out he could not speak to them, and so they knew that he had seen a vision in the temple. Unable to say a word, he made signs to them with his hands.

When his period of service in the temple was over, Zechariah went back home. Some time later his wife Elizabeth became pregnant, and did not leave the house for five months. "Now at last the Lord has helped me in this way," she said. "He has taken away my public disgrace!"

The Birth of Jesus Announced
In the sixth month of Elizabeth's pregnancy God sent the angel Gabriel to a town in Galilee named Nazareth. He had a message for a girl promised in marriage to a man named Joseph, who was a descendant of King David. The girl's name was Mary. The angel came to her and said, "Peace be with you! The Lord is with you, and has greatly blessed you!"

Mary was deeply troubled by the angel's message, and she wondered what his words meant. The angel said to her, "Don't be afraid, Mary, because God has been gracious to you. You will become pregnant and give birth to a son, and you will name him Jesus. He will be great and will be called the Son of the Most High God. The Lord God will make him a king, as his ancestor David was, and he will be the king of the descendants of Jacob forever; his kingdom will never end!"

Mary said to the angel, "I am a virgin. How, then, can this be?"

The angel answered, "The Holy Spirit will come on you, and God's power will rest upon you. For this reason the holy child will be called the Son of God. Remember your relative Elizabeth. It is said that she cannot have children; but she herself is now six months pregnant, even though she is very old. For there is not a thing that God cannot do."

"I am the Lord's servant," said Mary; "may it happen to me as you have said." And the angel left her.

Mary Visits Elizabeth

Soon afterward Mary got ready and hurried off to the hill country, to a town in Judea. She went into Zechariah's house and greeted Elizabeth. When Elizabeth heard Mary's greeting, the baby moved within her. Elizabeth was filled with the Holy Spirit, and spoke in a loud voice, "You are the most blessed of all women, and blessed is the child you will bear! Why should this great thing happen to me, that my Lord's mother comes to visit me? For as soon as I heard your greeting, the baby within me jumped with gladness. How happy are you to believe that the Lord's message to you will come true!"

Mary's Song of Praise

Mary said, "My heart praises the Lord; my soul is glad because of God my Savior, because he has remembered me, his lowly servant! From now on all people will call me happy, because of the great things the Mighty God has done for me. His name is holy; he shows mercy to those who fear him, from one generation to another. He stretched out his mighty arm and scattered the proud with all their plans. He brought down mighty kings from their thrones, and lifted up the lowly. He filled the hungry with good things, and sent the rich away with empty hands. He kept the promise he made to our ancestors, and came to the help of his servant Israel; he remembered to show mercy to Abraham and to all his descendants forever!"

Mary stayed about three months with Elizabeth, and then went back home.

The Birth of John the Baptist

The time came for Elizabeth to have her baby, and she gave birth to a son. Her neighbors and relatives heard how wonderfully good the Lord had been to her, and they all rejoiced with her.

When the baby was a week old they came to circumcise him; they were going to name him Zechariah, his father's name. But his mother said, "No! His name will be John."

They said to her, "But you don't have any relative with that name!" Then they made signs to his father, asking him what name he would like the boy to have.

Zechariah asked for a writing pad and wrote, "His name is John." How surprised they all were! At that moment Zechariah was able to speak again, and he started praising God. The neighbors were all filled with fear, and the news about these things spread through all the hill country of Judea. Everyone who heard of it thought about it and asked, "What is this child going to be?" It was plain that the Lord's power was with him.

Zechariah's Prophecy

John's father Zechariah was filled with the Holy Spirit, and he spoke God's message, "Let us praise the Lord, the God of Israel! He came to the help of his people and set them free. He provided a mighty Savior for us, who is a descendant of his servant David. Long ago by means of his holy prophets he said this: he promised to save us from our enemies, and from the power of all those who hate us. He said he would show mercy to our ancestors, and remember his sacred covenant. He made a solemn promise to our ancestor Abraham, and vowed that he would rescue us from our enemies, and allow us to serve him without fear; to be holy and righteous before him, all the days of our life.

"You, my child, will be called a prophet of the Most High God. You will go ahead of the Lord to prepare his road for him; to tell his people that they will be saved, by having their sins forgiven. Our God is merciful and tender. He will cause the bright dawn of salvation to rise on us, and shine from heaven on all those who live in the dark shadow of death, to guide our steps into the path of peace."

The child grew and developed in body and spirit. He lived in the desert until the day when he would appear publicly to the people of Israel.

The Birth of Jesus Christ

This was the way that Jesus Christ was born. His mother Mary was engaged to Joseph, but before they were married she found out that she was going to have a baby by the Holy Spirit. Joseph, to whom she was engaged, was a man who always did what was right; but he did not want to disgrace Mary publicly, so he made plans to break the engagement secretly. While he was thinking about this an angel of the Lord appeared to him in a dream and said, "Joseph, descendant of David, do not be afraid to take Mary to be your wife. For it is by the Holy Spirit that she has conceived. She will give birth to a son and you will name him Jesus—because he will save his people from their sins."

Now all this happened in order to make come true what the Lord had said through the prophet, "The virgin will become pregnant and give birth to a son, and he will be called Emmanuel" (which means, "God is with us").

So when Joseph woke up he did what the angel of the Lord had told him to do and married Mary. But he had no sexual relations with her before she gave birth to her son. And Joseph named him Jesus.

At that time Emperor Augustus sent out an order for all the citizens of the Empire to register themselves for the census. When this first census took place, Quirinius was the governor of Syria. Everyone, then, went to register himself, each to his own town.

Joseph went from the town of Nazareth, in Galilee, to Judea, to the town named Bethlehem, where King David was born. Joseph went there because he was a descendant of David. He went to register himself with Mary, who was promised in marriage to him. She was pregnant, and while they were in Bethlehem, the time came for her to have her baby. She gave birth to her first son, wrapped him in cloths and laid him in a manger—there was no room for them to stay in the inn.

The Shepherds and the Angels
There were some shepherds in that part of the country who were spending the night in the fields, taking care of their flocks. An angel of the Lord appeared to them, and the glory of the Lord shone over them. They were terribly afraid, but the angel said to them, "Don't be afraid! I am here with good news for you, which will bring great joy to all the people. This very day in David's town your Savior was born—Christ the Lord! What will prove it to you is this: you will find a baby wrapped in cloths and lying in a manger."

Suddenly a great army of heaven's angels appeared with the angel, singing praises to God, "Glory to God in the highest heaven, and peace on earth to those with whom he is pleased!"

When the angels went away from them back into heaven, the shepherds said to one another, "Let us go to Bethlehem and see this thing that has happened, that the Lord has told us."

So they hurried off and found Mary and Joseph, and saw the baby lying in the manger. When the shepherds saw him they told them what the angel had said about this child. All who heard it were filled with wonder at what the shepherds told them. Mary remembered all these things and thought deeply about them. The shepherds went back, singing praises to God for all they had heard and seen; it had been just as the angel had told them.

Jesus Is Named
A week later, when the time came for the baby to be circumcised, he was named Jesus, the name which the angel had given him before he had been conceived.

Jesus Is Presented in the Temple
The time came for Joseph and Mary to do what the Law of Moses commanded and perform the ceremony of purification. So they took the child to Jerusalem to present him to the Lord, as it is written in the law of the

Lord, "Every firstborn male shall be dedicated to the Lord." They also went to offer a sacrifice of a pair of doves or two young pigeons, as required by the law of the Lord.

Now there was a man living in Jerusalem whose name was Simeon. He was a good and God-fearing man, and was waiting for Israel to be saved. The Holy Spirit was with him, and he had been assured by the Holy Spirit that he would not die before he had seen the Lord's promised Messiah. Led by the Spirit, Simeon went into the temple. When the parents brought the child Jesus into the temple to do for him what the Law required, Simeon took the child in his arms, and gave thanks to God:

"Now, Lord, you have kept your promise, and you may let your servant go in peace. With my own eyes I have seen your salvation, which you have prepared in the presence of all peoples: A light to reveal your way to the Gentiles, and bring glory to your people Israel."

The child's father and mother were amazed at the things Simeon said about him. Simeon blessed them and said to Mary, his mother, "This child is chosen by God for the destruction and the salvation of many in Israel. He will be a sign from God which many people will speak against, and so reveal their secret thoughts. And sorrow, like a sharp sword, will break your own heart."

There was a prophetess named Anna, daughter of Phanuel, of the tribe of Asher. She was an old woman who had been married for seven years, and then she had been a widow for eighty-four years. She never left the temple; day and night she worshiped God, fasting and praying. That very same hour she arrived and gave thanks to God, and spoke about the child to all who were waiting for God to redeem Jerusalem.

When they had finished doing all that was required by the law of the Lord, they returned to Galilee, to their home town of Nazareth.

Visitors from the East

Jesus was born in the town of Bethlehem, in the land of Judea, during the time when Herod was king. Soon afterwards some men who studied the stars came from the east to Jerusalem and asked, "Where is the baby born to be the king of the Jews? We saw his star when it came up in the east, and we have come to worship him."

When King Herod heard about this he was very upset, and so was everyone else in Jerusalem. He called together all the chief priests and the teachers of the Law and asked them, "Where will the Messiah be born?"

"In the town of Bethlehem, in Judea," they answered. "This is what the prophet wrote, 'Bethlehem, in the land of Judah, you are by no means the least among the rulers of Judah: for from you will come a leader who will guide my people Israel.'"

So Herod called the visitors from the east to a secret meeting and found out from them the exact time the star had appeared. Then he sent them to Bethlehem with these instructions: "Go and make a careful search for the child, and when you find him let me know, so that I may go and worship him too."

With this they left, and on their way they saw the star—the same one they had seen in the east—and it went ahead of them until it came and stopped over the place where the child was. How happy they were, what joy was theirs, when they saw the star! They went into the house and saw the child with his mother Mary. They knelt down and worshiped him: then they opened their bags and offered him presents: gold, frankincense, and myrrh.

God warned them in a dream not to go back to Herod; so they went back to their country by another road.

The Escape to Egypt

After they had left, an angel of the Lord appeared in a dream to Joseph and said, "Get up, take the child and his mother and run away to Egypt, and stay there until I tell you to leave. Herod will be looking for the child to kill him."

Joseph got up, took the child and his mother, and left during the night for Egypt, where he stayed until Herod died.

This was done to make come true what the Lord had

said through the prophet, "I called my Son out of Egypt."

The Killing of the Children
When Herod realized that the visitors from the east had tricked him, he was furious. He gave orders to kill all the boys in Bethlehem and its neighborhood who were two years old and younger—in accordance with what he had learned from the visitors about the time when the star had appeared.

In this way what the prophet Jeremiah had said came true: "A sound is heard in Ramah, the sound of bitter crying and weeping. Rachel weeps for her children; she weeps and will not be comforted, because they are all dead."

The Return from Egypt
After Herod had died, an angel of the Lord appeared in a dream to Joseph, in Egypt, and said, "Get up, take the child and his mother, and go back to the land of Israel, because those who tried to kill the child are dead." So Joseph got up, took the child and his mother, and went back to Israel.

When he heard that Archelaus had succeeded his father Herod as king of Judea, Joseph was afraid to settle there. He was given more instructions in a dream, and so he went to the province of Galilee and made his home in a town named Nazareth. He did this to make come true what the prophets had said, "He will be called a Nazarene."

The Boy Jesus in the Temple
The child grew and became strong; he was full of wisdom, and God's blessings were with him.

Every year the parents of Jesus went to Jerusalem for the Feast of Passover. When Jesus was twelve years old, they went to the feast as usual. When the days of the feast were over, they started back home, but the boy Jesus stayed in Jerusalem. His parents did not know this; they thought that he was with the group, so they traveled a whole day, and then started looking for him among their relatives and friends. They did not find him, so they went back to Jerusalem looking for him. On the third day they found him in the temple, sitting with the Jewish teachers, listening to them and asking questions. All who heard him were amazed at his intelligent answers. His parents were amazed when they saw him, and his mother said to him, "Son, why have you done this to us? Your father and I have been terribly worried trying to find you."

He answered them, "Why did you have to look for me? Didn't you know that I had to be in my Father's house?" But they did not understand what he said to them.

So Jesus went back with them to Nazareth, where he was obedient to them. His mother treasured all these things in her heart. And Jesus grew, both in body and in wisdom, gaining favor with God and men.

Two

THE BAPTIST PREPARES THE WAY FOR THE SON OF GOD

The Preaching of John the Baptist
At that time John the Baptist came and started preaching in the desert of Judea. "Turn away from your sins," he said, "because the Kingdom of heaven is near!" John was the one that the prophet Isaiah was talking about when he said, "Someone is shouting in the desert, 'Get the Lord's road ready for him; make a straight path for him to travel!' "

John's clothes were made of camel's hair; he wore a leather belt around his waist, and ate locusts and wild honey. People came to him from Jerusalem, from the whole province of Judea, and from all the country around the Jordan River. They confessed their sins and he baptized them in the Jordan.

When John saw many Pharisees and Sadducees coming to him to be baptized, he said to them, "You snakes—who told you that you could escape from God's wrath that is about to come? Do the things that will show that you have turned from your sins. And don't think you can excuse yourselves by saying, 'Abraham is our ancestor.' I tell you that God can take these rocks and make descendants for Abraham! The ax is ready to cut down the trees at the roots; every tree that does not bear good fruit will be cut down and thrown in the fire."

The people asked him, "What are we to do then?"

He answered, "Whoever has two shirts must give one to the man who has none, and whoever has food must share it."

Some tax collectors came to be baptized, and they asked him, "Teacher, what are we to do?"

"Don't collect more than is legal," he told them.

Some soldiers also asked him, "What about us? What are we to do?"

He said to them, "Don't take money from anyone by force or accuse anyone falsely. Be content with your pay."

The Baptism of Jesus

At that time Jesus went from Galilee to the Jordan, and came to John to be baptized by him. But John tried to make him change his mind. "I ought to be baptized by you," John said, "yet you come to me!"

But Jesus answered him, "Let it be so for now. For in this way we shall do all that God requires."

So John agreed. As soon as he was baptized, Jesus came up out of the water. Then heaven was opened to him, and he saw the Spirit of God coming down like a dove and lighting on him. And then a voice said from heaven, "This is my own dear Son, with whom I am well pleased."

The Temptation of Jesus

Then the Spirit led Jesus into the desert to be tempted by the Devil. After spending forty days and nights without food, Jesus was hungry. The Devil came to him and said, "If you are God's Son, order these stones to turn into bread."

Jesus answered, "The scripture says, 'Man cannot live on bread alone, but on every word that God speaks.'"

Then the Devil took Jesus to the Holy City, set him on the highest point of the temple, and said to him, "If you are God's Son, throw yourself down to the ground; because the scripture says, 'God will give orders to his angels about you; they will hold you up with their hands, so that not even your feet will be hurt on the stones.'"

Jesus answered, "But the scripture also says, 'You must not put the Lord your God to the test.'"

Then the Devil took Jesus to a very high mountain

and showed him all the kingdoms of the world, in all their greatness. "All this I will give you," the Devil said, "if you kneel down and worship me."

Then Jesus answered, "Go away, Satan! The scripture says, 'Worship the Lord your God and serve only him!'"

Then the Devil left him; and angels came and helped Jesus.

John the Baptist's Message

The Jewish authorities in Jerusalem sent priests and Levites to John, to ask him, "Who are you?"

John did not refuse to answer, but spoke out openly and clearly. This is what he said, "I am not the Messiah."

"Who are you, then?" they asked. "Are you Elijah?"

"No, I am not," John answered.

"Are you the Prophet?" they asked.

"No," he replied.

"Tell us who you are," they said. "We have to take an answer back to those who sent us. What do you say about yourself?"

John answered, "This is what I am: 'The voice of one who shouts in the desert: Make a straight path for the Lord to travel!'" (This is what the prophet Isaiah had said.)

The messengers had been sent by the Pharisees. They asked John, "If you are not the Messiah, nor Elijah, nor the Prophet, why do you baptize?"

John answered, "I baptize with water; among you stands the one you do not know. He is coming after me, but I am not good enough even to untie his sandals."

All this happened in Bethany, on the east side of the Jordan River, where John was baptizing.

The next day John saw Jesus coming to him, and said, "Here is the Lamb of God, who takes away the sin of the world! This is the one I was talking about when I said, 'A man is coming after me, but he is greater than I am, because he existed before I was born.' I did not know who he would be, but I came baptizing with water in order to make him know to Israel."

This is the testimony that John gave: "I saw the

Spirit come down like a dove from heaven and stay on him. I still did not know him, but God, who sent me to baptize with water, said to me, 'You will see the Spirit come down and stay on a man; he is the one who baptizes with the Holy Spirit.' I have seen it," said John, "and I tell you that he is the Son of God."

The First Disciples of Jesus

The next day John was there again with two of his disciples, when he saw Jesus walking by. "Here is the Lamb of God!" he said.

The two disciples heard him say this and went with Jesus. Jesus turned, saw them following him, and asked, "What are you looking for?"

They answered, "Where do you live, Rabbi?" (This word, translated, means "Teacher.")

"Come and see," he answered. So they went with him and saw where he lived, and spent the rest of that day with him. (It was about four o'clock in the afternoon.)

One of the two who heard John, and went with Jesus, was Andrew, Simon Peter's brother. At once Andrew found his brother Simon and told him, "We have found the Messiah." (This word means "Christ.") Then he took Simon to Jesus.

Jesus looked at him and said, "You are Simon, the son of John. Your name will be Cephas." (This is the same as Peter, and means "Rock.")

The next day Jesus decided to go to Galilee. He found Philip and said to him, "Come with me!" (Philip was from Bethsaida, the town where Andrew and Peter lived.) Philip found Nathanael and told him, "We have found the one of whom Moses wrote in the book of the Law, and of whom the prophets also wrote. He is Jesus, the son of Joseph, from Nazareth."

"Can anything good come from Nazareth?" Nathanael asked. "Come and see," answered Philip.

When Jesus saw Nathanael coming to him, he said about him, "Here is a real Israelite; there is nothing false in him!"

Nathanael asked him, "How do you know me?"

Jesus answered, "I saw you when you were under the fig tree, before Philip called you."

"Teacher," answered Nathanael, "you are the Son of God! You are the King of Israel!"

Jesus said, "Do you believe just because I told you I saw you when you were under the fig tree? You will see much greater things than this!" And he said to them, "I tell you the truth: you will see heaven open and God's angels going up and coming down on the Son of Man."

The Wedding at Cana

Two days later there was a wedding in the town of Cana, in Galilee. Jesus' mother was there, and Jesus and his disciples had also been invited to the wedding. When all the wine had been drunk, Jesus' mother said to him, "They are out of wine."

"You must not tell me what to do, woman," Jesus replied. "My time has not yet come."

Jesus' mother then told the servants, "Do whatever he tells you."

The Jews have religious rules about washing, and for this purpose six stone water jars were there, each one large enough to hold between twenty and thirty gallons. Jesus said to the servants, "Fill these jars with water." They filled them to the brim, and then he told them, "Now draw some water out and take it to the man in charge of the feast." They took it to him, and he tasted the water, which had turned into wine. He did not know where this wine had come from (but the servants who had drawn out the water knew); so he called the bridegroom and said to him, "Everyone else serves the best wine first, and after the guests have drunk a lot he serves the ordinary wine. But you have kept the best wine until now!"

Jesus performed this first of his mighty works in Cana of Galilee; there he revealed his glory, and his disciples believed in him.

After this, Jesus and his mother, brothers, and disciples went to Capernaum, and stayed there a few days.

Jesus Goes to the Temple

It was almost time for the Jewish Feast of Passover, so Jesus went to Jerusalem. In the temple he found men selling cattle, sheep, and pigeons, and also the moneychangers sitting at their tables. He made a whip from cords and drove all the animals out of the temple, both the sheep and the cattle; he overturned the tables of the moneychangers and scattered their coins; and he ordered the men who sold the pigeons, "Take them out of here! Do not make my Father's house a market place!" His disciples remembered that the scripture says, "My devotion to your house, God, burns in me like a fire."

The Jewish authorities came back at him with a question, "What miracle can you perform to show us that you have the right to do this?"

Jesus answered, "Tear down this house of God and in three days I will build it again."

"You are going to build it again in three days?" they asked him. "It has taken forty-six years to build this temple!"

But the temple Jesus spoke of was his body.

Jesus and Nicodemus

There was a man named Nicodemus, a leader of the Jews, who belonged to the party of the Pharisees. One night he went to Jesus and said to him, "We know, Rabbi, that you are a teacher sent by God. No one could do the mighty works you are doing unless God were with him."

Jesus answered, "I tell you the truth: no one can see the Kingdom of God unless he is born again."

"How can a grown man be born again?" Nicodemus asked. "He certainly cannot enter his mother's womb and be born a second time!"

"I tell you the truth," replied Jesus, "that no one can enter the Kingdom of God unless he is born of water and the Spirit. A man is born physically of human parents, but he is born spiritually of the Spirit. Do not be surprised because I tell you, 'You must all be born again.' The wind blows wherever it wishes; you hear the sound it makes, but you do not know where it comes from or where it is going. It is the same way with everyone who is born of the Spirit."

"How can this be?" asked Nicodemus.

Jesus answered, "You are a great teacher of Israel, and you don't know this? I tell you the truth: we speak of what we know, and tell what we have seen, yet none of you is willing to accept our message. You do not believe me when I tell you about the things of this world; how will you ever believe me, then, when I tell you about the things of heaven? And no one has ever gone up to heaven except the Son of Man, who came down from heaven."

As Moses lifted up the bronze snake on a pole in the desert, in the same way the Son of Man must be lifted up, so that everyone who believes in him may have eternal life. For God loved the world so much that he gave his only Son, so that everyone who believes in him may not die but have eternal life. For God did not send his Son into the world to be its Judge, but to be its Savior.

Whoever believes in the Son is not judged; whoever does not believe has already been judged, because he has not believed in God's only Son. This is how the judgment works: the light has come into the world, but men love the darkness rather than the light, because they do evil things. Anyone who does evil things hates the light and will not come to the light, because he does not want his evil deeds to be shown up. But whoever does what is true comes to the light, in order that the light may show that he did his works in obedience to God.

Jesus and the Baptist

After this, Jesus and his disciples went to the province of Judea. He spent some time with them there, and baptized. John also was baptizing in Aenon, not far from Salim, because there was plenty of water there. People were going to him and he was baptizing them. (John had not yet been put in prison.)

Some of John's disciples began arguing with a Jew about the matter of religious washing. So they went to John and told him, "Teacher, you remember the man who was with you on the other side of the Jordan, the one you spoke about? Well, he is baptizing now, and everyone is going to him!"

John answered, "No one can have anything unless God gives it to him. You yourselves are my witnesses that I said, 'I am not the Messiah, but I have been sent ahead of him.' The bridegroom is the one to whom the bride belongs; the bridegroom's friend stands by and listens, and he is glad when he hears the bridegroom's voice. This is how my own happiness is made complete. He must become more important, while I become less important."

He Who Comes from Heaven
He who comes from above is greater than all; he who is from the earth belongs to the earth and speaks about earthly matters. He who comes from heaven is above all. He tells what he has seen and heard, but no one accepts his message. Whoever accepts his message proves by this that God is true. The one whom God has sent speaks God's words, because God gives him the fulness of his Spirit. The Father loves his Son and has put everything in his power. Whoever believes in the Son has eternal life; whoever disobeys the Son will never have life, but God's wrath will remain on him forever.

Three

THE EARLY MINISTRY OF JESUS

Jesus and the Woman of Samaria

The Pharisees heard that Jesus was winning and baptizing more disciples than John. (Actually, Jesus himself did not baptize anyone; only his disciples did.) When Jesus heard what was being said, he left Judea and went back to Galilee; on his way there he had to go through Samaria.

He came to a town in Samaria named Sychar, which was not far from the field that Jacob had given to his son Joseph. Jacob's well was there, and Jesus, tired out by the trip, sat down by the well. It was about noon.

A Samaritan woman came to draw some water, and Jesus said to her, "Give me a drink of water." (His disciples had gone into town to buy food.)

The woman answered, "You are a Jew and I am a Samaritan—how can you ask me for a drink?" (Jews will not use the same dishes that Samaritans use.)

Jesus answered, "If you only knew what God gives, and who it is that is asking you for a drink, you would ask him and he would give you living water."

"Sir," the woman said, "you don't have a bucket and the well is deep. Where would you get living water? Our ancestor Jacob gave us this well; he, his sons, and his flocks all drank from it. You don't claim to be greater than Jacob, do you?"

Jesus answered, "Whoever drinks this water will get thirsty again; but whoever drinks the water that I will give him will never be thirsty again. The water that I will give him will become in him a spring which will provide him with living water, and give him eternal life."

"Sir," the woman said, "give me this water! Then I will never be thirsty again, nor will I have to come here and draw water."

"Go call your husband," Jesus told her, "and come back here."

"I don't have a husband," the woman said.

Jesus replied, "You are right when you say you don't have a husband. You have been married to five men, and the man you live with now is not really your husband. You have told me the truth."

"I see you are a prophet, sir," the woman said. "My Samaritan ancestors worshiped God on this mountain, but you Jews say that Jerusalem is the place where we should worship God."

Jesus said to her, "Believe me, woman, the time will come when men will not worship the Father either on this mountain or in Jerusalem. You Samaritans do not really know whom you worship; we Jews know whom we worship, because salvation comes from the Jews. But the time is coming, and is already here, when the real worshipers will worship the Father in spirit and in truth. These are the worshipers the Father wants to worship him. God is Spirit, and those who worship him must worship in spirit and in truth."

The woman said to him, "I know that the Messiah, called Christ, will come. When he comes he will tell us everything."

Jesus answered, "I am he, I who am talking with you."

At that moment Jesus' disciples returned; and they were greatly surprised to find him talking with a woman. But none of them said to her, "What do you want?" or asked him, "Why are you talking with her?"

Then the woman left her water jar, went back to town, and said to the people there, "Come and see the man who told me everything I have ever done. Could he be the Messiah?" So they left the town and went to Jesus.

In the meantime the disciples were begging Jesus, "Teacher, have something to eat!"

But he answered, "I have food to eat that you know nothing about."

So the disciples started asking among themselves, "Could somebody have brought him food?"

"My food," Jesus said to them, "is to obey the will of him who sent me and finish the work he gave me to do. You have a saying, 'Four more months and then the harvest.' I tell you, take a good look at the fields; the crops are now ripe and ready to be harvested! The man who reaps the harvest is being paid and gathers the crops for eternal life; so that the man who plants and the man who reaps will be glad together. The saying is true, 'One man plants, another man reaps.' I have sent you to reap a harvest in a field where you did not work; others worked there, and you profit from their work."

Many of the Samaritans in that town believed in Jesus because the woman had said, "He told me everything I have ever done." So when the Samaritans came to him they begged him to stay with them, and Jesus stayed there two days.

Many more believed because of his message, and they told the woman, "We believe now, not because of what you said, but because we ourselves have heard him, and we know that he is really the Savior of the world."

Jesus Heals an Official's Son

After spending two days there, Jesus left and went to Galilee. For Jesus himself had said, "A prophet is not respected in his own country." When he arrived in Galilee the people there welcomed him, because they had gone to the Passover Feast in Jerusalem and had seen everything that he had done during the feast.

So Jesus went back to Cana of Galilee, where he had turned the water into wine. There was a government official there whose son in Capernaum was sick. When he heard that Jesus had come from Judea to Galilee, he went to him and asked him to go to Capernaum and heal his son, who was about to die. Jesus said to him, "None of you will ever believe unless you see great and wonderful works."

"Sir," replied the official, "come with me before my child dies."

Jesus said to him, "Go, your son will live!"

The man believed Jesus' words and went. On his way home his servants met him with the news, "Your boy is going to live!"

He asked them what time it was when his son got better, and they said, "It was one o'clock yesterday afternoon when the fever left him." The father remembered, then, that it was at that very hour when Jesus had told him, "Your son will live." So he and all his family believed.

This was the second mighty work that Jesus did after coming from Judea to Galilee.

The Healing at the Pool

After this, there was a Jewish religious feast, and Jesus went to Jerusalem. There is in Jerusalem, by the Sheep Gate, a pool with five porches: in the Hebrew language it is called Bethzatha. A large crowd of sick people were lying on the porches—the blind, the lame, and the paralyzed. [They were waiting for the water to move, because every now and then an angel of the Lord went down into the pool and stirred up the water. The first sick person to go into the pool after the water was stirred up was healed from whatever disease he had.] A man was there who had been sick for thirty-eight years. Jesus saw him lying there, and he knew that the man had been sick for such a long time; so he said to him, "Do you want to get well?"

The sick man answered, "Sir, I don't have anyone here to put me in the pool when the water is stirred up; while I am trying to get in, somebody else gets there first."

Jesus said to him, "Get up, pick up your mat, and walk." Immediately the man got well; he picked up his mat, and walked.

The day this happened was a Sabbath, so the Jewish authorities told the man who had been healed, "This is a Sabbath, and it is against our Law for you to carry your mat."

He answered, "The man who made me well told me, 'Pick up your mat and walk.' "

They asked him, "Who is this man who told you to pick up your mat and walk?"

But the man who had been healed did not know who he was, because there was a crowd in that place and Jesus had slipped out.

Afterward, Jesus found him in the temple and said, "Look, you are well now. Quit your sins, or something worse may happen to you."

Then the man left and told the Jewish authorities that it was Jesus who had healed him. For this reason they began to persecute Jesus, because he had done this healing on a Sabbath. Jesus answered them, "My Father works always, and I too must work."

This saying made the Jewish authorities all the more determined to kill him; not only had he broken the Sabbath law, but he had said that God was his own Father, and in this way had made himself equal with God.

The Authority of the Son

So Jesus answered them, "I tell you the truth: the Son does nothing on his own; he does only what he sees his Father doing. What the Father does, the Son also does. For the Father loves the Son and shows him all that he himself is doing. He will show him even greater things than this to do, and you will all be amazed. Even as the Father raises the dead and gives them life, in the same way the Son gives life to those he wants to. Nor does the Father himself judge anyone. He has given his Son the full right to judge, so that all will honor the Son in the same way as they honor the Father. Whoever does not honor the Son does not honor the Father who sent him.

"I tell you the truth: whoever hears my words, and believes in him who sent me, has eternal life. He will not be judged, but has already passed from death to life. I tell you the truth: the time is coming—the time has already come—when the dead will hear the voice of the Son of God, and those who hear it will live. Even as the Father is himself the source of life, in the same way he has made his Son to be the source of life. And he has given the Son the right to judge, because he is the Son of Man. Do not be surprised at this; the time is coming when all the dead in the graves will hear his voice, and they will come out of their graves: those who have done good will rise and live, and those who have done evil will rise and be condemned."

Witnesses to Jesus
"I can do nothing on my own; I judge only as God tells me, so my judgment is right, because I am not trying to do what I want, but only what he who sent me wants.

"If I testify on my own behalf, what I say is not to be accepted as real proof. But there is someone else who testifies on my behalf, and I know that what he says about me is true. You sent your messengers to John, and he spoke on behalf of the truth. It is not that I must have a man's witness; I say this only in order that you may be saved. John was like a lamp, burning and shining, and you were willing for a while to enjoy his light. But I have a witness on my behalf even greater than the witness that John gave: the works that I do, the works my Father gave me to do, these speak on my behlaf and show that the Father has sent me. And the Father, who sent me, also testifies on my behalf. You have never heard his voice, or seen his face, and you do not keep his message in your hearts, because you do not believe in the one whom he sent. You study the Scriptures because you think that in them you will find eternal life. And they themselves speak about me! Yet you are not willing to come to me in order to have life.

"I am not looking for praise from men. But I know you; I know that you have no love for God in your hearts. I have come with my Father's authority, but you have not received me; when someone comes with his own authority, you will receive him. You like to have praise from one another, but you do not try to win praise from the only God; how, then, can you believe? Do not think, however, that I will accuse you to my Father. Moses is the one who will accuse you—Moses, in whom you have hoped. If you had really believed Moses, you would have believed me, because he wrote about me. But since you do not believe what he wrote, how can you believe what I say?"

Jesus Rejected at Nazareth
Then Jesus went to Nazareth, where he had been brought up, and on the Sabbath day he went as usual to the synagogue. He stood up to read the Scriptures, and was handed the book of the prophet Isaiah. He unrolled the scroll and found the place where it is written, "The Spirit of the Lord is upon me, because he has chosen me to preach the Good News to the poor. He has sent me to proclaim liberty to the captives, and recovery of sight to the blind; to set free the oppressed, and announce the year when the Lord will save his people."

Jesus rolled up the scroll, gave it back to the attendant, and sat down. All the people in the synagogue had their eyes fixed on him. He began speaking to them, "This passage of scripture has come true today, as you heard it being read."

They were all well impressed with him, and marveled at the beautiful words that he spoke. They said, "Isn't he the son of Joseph?"

He said to them, "I am sure that you will quote this proverb to me, 'Doctor, heal yourself.' You will also say to me, 'Do here in your own home town the same things we were told happened in Capernaum.' I tell you this," Jesus added. "A prophet is never welcomed in his own home town. Listen to me: it is true that there were many widows in Israel during the time of Elijah, when there was no rain for three and a half years and there was a great famine throughout the whole land. Yet Elijah was not sent to a single one of them, but only to a widow of Zarephath, in the territory of Sidon. And there were many lepers in Israel during the time of the prophet Elisha; yet not one of them was made clean, but only Naaman the Syrian."

All the people in the synagogue were filled with anger when they heard this. They rose up, dragged Jesus out of town, and took him to the top of the hill on which their town was built, to throw him over the cliff. But he walked through the middle of the crowd and went his way.

Jesus Calls Four Fishermen

After John had been put in prison, Jesus went to Galilee and preached the Good News from God. "The right time has come," he said, "and the Kingdom of God is near! Turn away from your sins and believe the Good News!"

As Jesus walked by Lake Galilee, he saw two fishermen, Simon and his brother Andrew, catching fish in the lake with a net. Jesus said to them, "Come with me and I will teach you to catch men." At once they left their nets and went with him.

He went a little farther on and saw two other brothers, James and John, the sons of Zebedee. They were in their boat getting their nets ready. As soon as Jesus saw them he called them; they left their father Zebedee in the boat with the hired men and went with Jesus.

A Man with an Evil Spirit

They came to the town of Capernaum, and on the next Sabbath day Jesus went into the synagogue and began to teach. The people who heard him were amazed at the way he taught. He wasn't like the teachers of the Law; instead, he taught with authority.

Just then a man with an evil spirit in him came into the synagogue and screamed, "What do you want with us, Jesus of Nazareth? Are you here to destroy us? I know who you are: you are God's holy messenger!"

Jesus commanded the spirit, "Be quiet, and come out of the man!"

The evil spirit shook the man hard, gave a loud scream, and came out of him. The people were all so amazed that they started saying to each other, "What is this? Some kind of new teaching? This man has authority to give orders to the evil spirits, and they obey him!"

And so the news about Jesus spread quickly everywhere in the region of Galilee.

They left the synagogue and went straight to the home of Simon and Andrew; and James and John went with them.

Very early the next morning, long before daylight,

Jesus got up and left the house. He went out of town to a lonely place, where he prayed. But Simon and his companions went out searching for him; when they found him they said, "Everyone is looking for you."

But Jesus answered, "We must go on to the other villages around here. I have to preach in them also, because that is why I came."

So he traveled all over Galilee, preaching in the synagogues and driving out demons.

Four

JESUS SPEAKS WITH AUTHORITY

The Sermon on the Mount
Jesus saw the crowds and went up a hill, where he sat down. His disciples gathered around him, and he began to teach them:

"Happy are those who know they are spiritually poor; the Kingdom of heaven belongs to them! Happy are those who mourn; God will comfort them! Happy are the meek; they will receive what God has promised! Happy are those whose greatest desire is to do what God requires; God will satisfy them fully! Happy are those who are merciful to others; God will be merciful to them! Happy are the pure in heart; they will see God! Happy are those who work for peace among men; God will call them his sons! Happy are those who are persecuted because they do what God requires; the Kingdom of heaven belongs to them!

"Happy are you when men insult you, and persecute you, and tell all kinds of evil lies against you because you are my followers. Be glad and happy, because a great reward is kept for you in heaven. This is how men persecuted the prophets who lived before you."

"You are like salt for all mankind. But if salt loses its taste, there is no way to make it salty again. It has become worthless, so it is thrown away and people walk on it.

"You are like light for the whole world. A city built on a hill cannot be hid. No one lights a lamp to put it under a bowl; instead he puts it on the lampstand, where it gives light for everyone in the house. In the same way your light must shine before people, so they will see the good things you do and give praise to your Father in heaven."

"Do not think that I have come to do away with the law of Moses and the teachings of the prophets. I have not come to do away with them, but to make their teachings, come true. Remember this! As long as heaven and earth last, the least point or the smallest detail of the Law will not be done away with—not until the end of all things. So then, whoever disobeys even the smallest of the commandments, and teaches others to do the same, will be least in the Kingdom of heaven. On the other hand, whoever obeys the Law, and teaches others to do the same, will be great in the Kingdom of heaven. I tell you, then, that you will be able to enter the Kingdom of heaven only if you are more faithful than the teachers of the Law and the Pharisees in doing what God requires."

"You have heard that men were told in the past, 'Do not murder; anyone who commits murder will be brought before the judge.' But now I tell you: whosever is angry with his brother will be brought before the judge; whoever calls his brother 'You good-for-nothing!' will be brought before the Council; and whoever calls his brother a worthless fool will be in danger of going to the fire of hell. So if you are about to offer your gift to God at the altar and there you remember that your brother has something against you, leave your gift there in front of the altar and go at once to make peace with your brother; then come back and offer your gift to God.

"If a man brings a lawsuit against you and takes you to court, be friendly with him while there is time, before you get to court; once you are there he will turn you over to the judge, who will hand you over to the police, and you will be put in jail. There you will stay, I tell you, until you pay the last penny of your fine."

"You have heard that it was said, 'Do not commit adultery.' But now I tell you: anyone who looks at a woman and wants to possess her is guilty of committing adultery with her in his heart. So if your eye causes you to sin, take it out and throw it away! It is much better for you to lose a part of your body than to have your whole body thrown into hell. If your right hand causes you to sin, cut it off and throw it away! It is much better for you to lose one of your limbs than to have your whole body go off to hell."

"It was also said, 'Anyone who divorces his wife must give her a written notice of divorce.' But now I tell you: if a man divorces his wife, and she has not been unfaithful, then he is guilty of making her commit adultery if she marries again; and the man who marries her also commits adultery."

"You have also heard that men were told in the past, 'Do not break your promise, but do what you have sworn to the Lord to do.' But now I tell you; do not use any vow when you make a promise; do not swear by heaven, because it is God's throne; nor by earth, because it is the resting place for his feet; nor by Jerusalem, because it is the city of the great King. Do not even swear by your head, because you cannot make a single hair white or black. Just say 'Yes' or 'No'—anything else you have to say comes from the Evil One."

"You have heard that it was said, 'An eye for an eye, and a tooth for a tooth.' But now I tell you: do not take revenge on someone who does you wrong. If anyone slaps you on the right cheek, let him slap your left cheek too. And if someone takes you to court to sue you for your shirt, let him have your coat as well. And if one of the occupation troops forces you to carry his pack one mile, carry it another mile. When someone asks you for something, give it to him; when someone wants to borrow something, lend it to him."

"You have heard that it was said, 'Love your friends, hate your enemies.' But now I tell you: love your enemies, and pray for those who persecute you, so that you will become the sons of your Father in heaven. For he makes his sun to shine on bad and good people alike, and gives rain to those who do good and those who do evil. Why should God reward you if you love only the people who love you? Even the tax collectors do that! And if you speak only to your friends, have you done anything out of the ordinary! Even the pagans do that! You must be perfect—just as your Father in heaven is perfect."

"Be careful not to perform your religious duties in public so that people will see what you do. If you do these things publicly you will not have any reward from your Father in heaven.

"So when you give something to a needy person, do not make a big show of it, as the hypocrites do in the synagogues and on the streets. They do it so that people will praise them. Remember this! They have already been paid in full. But when you help a needy person, do it in such a way that even your closet friend will not know about it, but it will be a private matter. And your Father, who sees what you do in private, will reward you."

"When you pray, do not be like the hypocrites! They love to stand up and pray in the synagogues and on the street corners so that everyone will see them. Remember this! They have already been paid in full. But when you pray, go to your room and close the door, and pray to your Father, who is unseen. And your Father, who sees what you do in private, will reward you.

"In your prayers do not use a lot of meaningless words, as the pagans do, who think that God will hear them because of their long prayers. Do not be like them; your Father already knows what you need before you ask him. This, then, is how you should pray: 'Our Father in heaven: May your holy name be honored; may your Kingdom come; may your will be done on earth as it is in heaven. Give us today the food we need. Forgive us the wrongs that we have done, as we forgive the wrongs that others have done us. Do not bring us to hard testing, but keep us safe from the Evil One.'

"If you forgive others the wrongs they have done you, your Father in heaven will also forgive you. But if you do not forgive the wrongs of others, then your Father in heaven will not forgive the wrongs you have done."

"And when you fast, do not put on a sad face as the hypocrites do. They go around with a hungry look so that everyone will see that they are fasting. Remember this! They have already been paid in full. When you go without food, wash your face and comb your hair, so that others cannot know that you are fasting—only your Father, who is unseen, will know. And your Father, who sees what you do in private, will reward you."

"Do not save riches for yourselves here on earth, where moths and rust destroy, and robbers break in and steal. Instead, save riches for yourselves in heaven, where moths and rust cannot destroy, and robbers cannot break in and steal. For your heart will always be where your riches are."

"The eyes are like a lamp for the body. If your eyes are clear, your whole body will be full of light; but if your eyes are bad, your body will be in darkness. So if the light in you is darkness, how terribly dark it will be!"

"No one can be a slave to two masters: he will hate one and love the other; he will be loyal to one and despise the other. You cannot serve both God and money.

"This is why I tell you: do not be worried about the food and drink you need to stay alive, or about clothes for your body. After all, isn't life worth more than food? And isn't the body worth more than clothes? Look at the birds flying around: they do not plant seeds, gather a harvest, and put it in barns; your Father in heaven takes care of them! Aren't you worth much more than birds? Which one of you can live a few more years by worrying about it?

"And why worry about clothes? Look how the wild flowers grow: they do not work or make clothes for themselves. But I tell you that not even Solomon, as rich as he was, had clothes as beautiful as one of these flowers. It is God who clothes the wild grass—grass that is here today, gone tomorrow, burned up in the oven. Won't he be all the more sure to clothe you? How little faith you have! So do not start worrying: 'Where will my food come from? or my drink? or my clothes?" (These are the things the heathen are always concerned about.) Your Father in heaven knows that you need all these things. Instead, be concerned above everything else with his Kingdom and with what he requires, and he will provide you with all these other things. So do not worry about tomorrow; it will have enough worries of its own. There is no need to add to the troubles each day brings."

"Do not judge others, so that God will not judge you—because God will judge you in the same way you judge others, and he will apply to you the same rules you apply to others. Why, then, do you look at the speck in your brother's eye, and pay no attention to the log in your own eye? How dare you say to your brother, 'Please, let me take that speck out of your eye,' when you have a log in your own eye? You hypocrite! Take the log out of your own eye first, and then you will be able to see and take the speck out of your brother's eye.

"Do not give what is holy to dogs—they will only turn and attack you; do not throw your pearls in front of pigs—they will only trample them underfoot."

"Ask, and you will receive; seek, and you will find; knock, and the door will be opened to you. For everyone who asks will receive, and he who seeks will find, and the door will be opened to him who knocks. Would any of you who are fathers give your son a stone, when he asks you for bread? Or would you give him a snake, when he asks you for fish? As bad as you are, you know how to give good things to your children. How much more, then, your Father in heaven will give good things to those who ask him!

"Do for others what you want them to do for you: this is the meaning of the Law of Moses and the teaching of the prophets."

"Go in through the narrow gate, because the gate is wide and the road is easy that leads to hell, and there are many who travel it. The gate is narrow and the way is hard that leads to life, and few people find it."

"Watch out for false prophets; they come to you looking like sheep on the outside, but they are really like wild wolves on the inside. You will know them by the way they act. Thorn bushes do not bear grapes, and briers do not bear figs. A healthy tree bears good fruit, while a poor tree bears bad fruit. A healthy tree cannot bear bad fruit, and a poor tree cannot bear good fruit. Any tree that does not bear good fruit is cut down and thrown in the fire. So, then, you will know the false prophets by the way they act."

"Not everyone who calls me 'Lord, Lord,' will enter into the Kingdom of heaven, but only those who do what my Father in heaven wants them to do. When that Day comes, many will say to me, 'Lord, Lord! In your name we spoke God's message, by your name we drove out many demons and performed many miracles!' Then I will say to them, 'I never knew you. Away from me, you evildoers!' "

"So then, everyone who hears these words of mine and obeys them will be like a wise man who built his house on the rock. The rain poured down, the rivers flooded over, and the winds blew hard against that house. But it did not fall, because it had been built on the rock.

"But everyone who hears these words of mine and does not obey them will be like a foolish man who built his house on the sand. The rain poured down, the rivers flooded over, the winds blew hard against that house, and it fell. What a terrible fall that was!"

Jesus finished saying these things, and the crowd was amazed at the way he taught. He wasn't like their teachers of the Law; instead, he taught with authority.

Five

MIRACLES AND PARABLES

Jesus Makes a Leper Clean

Jesus came down from the hill, and large crowds followed him. Then a leper came to him, knelt down before him, and said, "Sir, if you want to, you can make me clean."

Jesus reached out and touched him. "I do want to," he answered. "Be clean!" At once he was clean from his leprosy. Then Jesus said to him, "Listen! Don't tell anyone, but go straight to the priest and let him examine you; then offer the sacrifice that Moses ordered, to prove to everyone that you are now clean."

But the man went away and began to spread the news everywhere. Indeed, he talked so much that Jesus could not go into a town publicly. Instead, he stayed out in lonely places, and people came to him from everywhere.

Jesus Calls the First Disciples

One time Jesus was standing on the shore of Lake Gennesaret while the people pushed their way up to him to listen to the word of God. He saw two boats pulled up on the beach; the fishermen had left them and were washing the nets. Jesus got into one of the boats—it belonged to Simon—and asked him to push off a little from the shore. Jesus sat in the boat and taught the crowd.

When he finished speaking, he said to Simon, "Push the boat out further to the deep water, and you and your partners let your nets down for a catch."

"Master," Simon answered, "we worked hard all night long and caught nothing. But if you say so, I will let down the nets." They let the nets down and caught such a large number of fish that the nets were about to break. So they motioned to their partners in the other boat to come and help them. They came and filled both boats so full of fish that they were about to sink. When Simon Peter saw what had happened, he fell on his knees before Jesus and said, "Go away from me, Lord! I am a sinful man!"

He and the others with him were all amazed at the large number of fish they had caught. The same was true of Simon's partners, James and John, the sons of Zebedee. Jesus said to Simon, "Don't be afraid; from now on you will be catching men."

They pulled the boats on the beach, left everything, and followed Jesus

Jesus Heals a Paralyzed Man

A few days later Jesus came back to Capernaum, and the news spread that he was at home. So many people came together that there wasn't any room left, not even out in front of the door. Jesus was preaching the message to them.

Some men came carrying a paralyzed man on a bed, and they tried to take him into the house and lay him before Jesus. Because of the crowd, however, they could find no way to take him in. So they carried him up on the roof, made an opening in the tiles, and let him down on his bed into the middle of the group in front of Jesus. When Jesus saw how much faith they had, he said to the man, "Your sins are forgiven you, my friend."

The teachers of the Law and the Pharisees began to say to themselves, "Who is this man who speaks against God in this way? No man can forgive sins; God alone can!"

Jesus knew their thoughts and said to them, "Why do you think such things? Is it easier to say, 'Your sins are forgiven you,' or to say, 'Get up and walk'? I will prove to you, then, that the Son of Man has authority on earth to forgive sins." So he said to the paralyzed man, "I tell you, get up, pick up your bed, and go home!"

At once the man got up before them all, took the bed he had been lying on, and went home, praising God. They were all completely amazed! Full of fear, they praised God, saying, "What marvelous things we have seen today!"

Jesus Calls Levi

After this, Jesus went out and saw a tax collector named Levi, sitting in his office. Jesus said to him, "Follow me." Levi got up, left everything, and followed him.

Then Levi had a big feast in his house for Jesus, and there was a large number of tax collectors and other people at the table with them. Some Pharisees and teachers of the Law who belonged to their group complained to Jesus' disciples. "Why do you eat and drink with tax collectors and outcasts?" they asked.

Jesus answered them, "People who are well do not need a doctor, but only those who are sick. I have not come to call the respectable people to repent, but the outcasts."

The Question About Fasting

Some people said to Jesus, "The disciples of John fast frequently and offer up prayers, and the disciples of the Pharisees do the same; but your disciples eat and drink."

Jesus answered, "Do you think you can make the guests at a wedding party go without food as long as the bridegroom is with them? Of course not! But the time will come when the bridegroom will be taken away from them, and they will go without food in those days."

Jesus told them this parable also, "No one tears a piece off a new coat to patch up an old coat. If he does, he will have torn the new coat, and the piece of new cloth will not match the old. Nor does anyone pour new wine into used wineskins. If he does, the new wine will burst the skins, the wine will pour out, and the skins will be ruined. No! New wine should be poured into fresh skins! And no one wants new wine after drinking old wine. 'The old is better,' he says."

The Question About the Sabbath

Not long afterward Jesus was walking through the wheat fields on a Sabbath day. His disciples were hungry, so they began to pick heads of wheat and eat the grain. When the Pharisees saw this, they said to Jesus, "Look, it is against our Law for your disciples to do this on the Sabbath!"

Jesus answered, "Have you never read what David did that time when he and his men were hungry? He went into the house of God, and he and his men ate the bread offered to God, even though it was against the Law for them to eat that bread—only the priests were allowed to eat it. Or have you not read in the Law of Moses that every Sabbath the priests in the temple actually break the Sabbath law, yet they are not guilty? There is something here, I tell you, greater than the temple. The scripture says, 'I do not want animal sacrifices, but kindness.' If you really knew what this means, you would not condemn people who are not guilty; because the Son of Man is Lord of the Sabbath."

Jesus left that place and went to one of their synagogues. A man was there who had a crippled hand. They were some men present who wanted to accuse Jesus of wrongdoing; so they asked him, "Is it against our Law to cure on the Sabbath?"

Jesus answered, "What if one of you has a sheep and it falls into a deep hole on the Sabbath? Will you not take hold of it and lift it out? And a man is worth much more than a sheep! So then, our Law does allow us to help someone on the Sabbath." Then he said to the man, "Stretch out your hand."

He stretched it out, and it became well again, just like the other one. The Pharisees left and made plans against Jesus to kill him.

When Jesus heard about it, he went away from that place; and many people followed him. He healed all the sick, and gave them orders not to tell others about him.

Jesus and Beelzebul

Jesus was driving out a demon that could not talk; when the demon went out, the man began to talk. The crowds were amazed, but some of the people said, "It is Beelzebul, the chief of the demons, who gives him the power to drive them out."

Others wanted to trap him, so they asked him to perform a miracle to show God's approval. But Jesus knew their thoughts and said to them, "How can Satan drive out Satan? If a country divides itself into groups that fight each other, that country will fall apart. If a family divides itself into groups that fight each other, that family will fall apart. So if Satan's kingdom divides into groups, it cannot last, but will fall apart and come to an end.

"No one can break into a strong man's house and take away his belongings unless he ties up the strong man first; then he can plunder his house.

"Remember this! Men can be forgiven all their sins and all the evil things they may say. But whoever says evil things against the Holy Spirit will never be forgiven, because he has committed an eternal sin." (Jesus said this because some had said, "He has an evil spirit in him.")

Jesus Chooses the Twelve Apostles

At that time Jesus went up a hill to pray, and spent the whole night there praying to God. When day came he called his disciples to him and chose twelve of them, whom he named apostles: Simon (whom he also named Peter) and his brother Andrew; James and John, Philip and Bartholomew, Matthew and Thomas, James, the son of Alphaeus, and Simon (who was called the Patriot), Judas, the son of James, and Judas Iscariot, who became the traitor.

"I have chosen you to be with me," he told them; "I will also send you out to preach, and you will have authority to drive out demons."

Jesus Teaches and Heals

Coming down from the hill with them, Jesus stood on a level place with a large number of his disciples. A great crowd of people was there from all over Judea, and from Jerusalem, and from the coast cities of Tyre and Sidon; they came to hear him and to be healed of their diseases. Those who were troubled by evil spirits also came and were healed. All the people tried to touch him, for power was going out from him and healing them all.

Jesus looked at his disciples and said, "Happy are you poor; the Kingdom of God is yours! Happy are you who are hungry now; you will be filled! Happy are you who weep now; you will laugh!

"Happy are you when men hate you, and reject you, and insult you, and say that you are evil, because of the Son of Man! Be glad when that happens, and dance for joy, because a great reward is kept for you in heaven. For their ancestors did the very same things to the prophets.

"But how terrible for you who are rich now; you have had your easy life! How terrible for you who are full now; you will go hungry! How terrible for you who laugh now; you will mourn and weep!

"How terrible when all men speak well of you; because their ancestors said the very same things to the false prophets.

"But I tell you who hear me: Love your enemies, do good to those who hate you, bless those who curse you, and pray for those who mistreat you. If anyone hits you on one cheek, let him hit the other one too; if someone takes your coat, let him have your shirt as well. Give to everyone who asks you for something, and when someone takes what is yours, do not ask for it back. Do for others just what you want them to do for you.

"If you love only the people who love you, why should you receive a blessing? Even sinners love those who love them! And if you do good only to those who do good to you, why should you receive a blessing? Even sinners do that! And if you lend only to those from whom you hope to get it back, why should you receive a blessing? Even sinners lend to sinners, to get back the same amount! No! Love your enemies and do good to them; lend and expect nothing back. You will have a great reward, and you will be sons of the Most High God. For he is good to the ungrateful and the wicked. Be merciful, just as your Father is merciful.

"Do not judge others, and God will not judge you; do

not condemn others, and God will not condemn you; forgive others, and God will forgive you. Give to others, and God will give to you: you will receive a full measure, a generous helping, poured into your hands—all that you can hold. The measure you use for others is the one God will use for you."

And Jesus told them this parable, "One blind man cannot lead another one; if he does, both will fall into a ditch. No pupil is greater than his teacher; but every pupil, when he has completed his training, will be like his teacher.

"Why do you look at the speck in your brother's eye, but pay no attention to the log in your own eye? How can you say to your brother, 'Please, brother, let me take that speck out of your eye,' yet not even see the log in your own eye? You hypocrite! Take the log out of your own eye first, and then you will be able to see and take the speck out of your brother's eye.

"A healthy tree does not bear bad fruit, nor does a poor tree bear good fruit. Every tree is known by the fruit it bears; you do not pick figs from thorn bushes, or gather grapes from bramble bushes. A good man brings good out of the treasure of good things in his heart; a bad man brings bad out of his treasure of bad things. For a man's mouth speaks what his heart is full of.

"Why do you call me, 'Lord, Lord,' and don't do what I tell you? Everyone who comes to me, and listens to my words, and obeys them—I will show you what he is like. He is like a man who built a house; he dug deep and laid the foundation on the rock. The river flooded over and hit that house but could not shake it, because it had been well built. But the one who hears my words and does not obey them is like a man who built a house on the ground, without laying a foundation; when the flood hit that house it fell at once—what a terrible crash that was!"

Jesus Heals a Roman Officer's Servant
When Jesus entered Capernaum, a Roman officer met him and begged for help: "Sir, my servant is at home, sick in bed, unable to move and suffering terribly."

"I will go and make him well," Jesus said.

"Oh no, sir," answered the officer. "I do not deserve to have you come into my house. Just give the order and my servant will get well. I, too, am a man under the authority of superior officers, and I have soldiers under me. I order this one, 'Go!' and he goes; and I order that one, 'Come!' and he comes; and I order my slave, 'Do this!' and he does it."

Jesus was surprised when he heard this, and said to the people who were following him, "I tell you, I have never seen such faith as this in anyone in Israel. Remember this! Many will come from the east and the west and sit down at the table in the Kingdom of heaven with Abraham, Isaac, and Jacob. But those who should be in the Kingdom will be thrown out into the darkness outside, where they will cry and gnash their teeth." And Jesus said to the officer, "Go home, and what you believe will be done for you."

And the officer's servant was healed that very hour.

Jesus Raises a Widow's Son

Soon afterward Jesus went to a town named Nain; his disciples and a large crowd went with him. Just as he arrived at the gate of the town, a funeral procession was coming out. The dead man was the only son of a woman who was a widow, and a large crowd from the city was with her. When the Lord saw her his heart was filled with pity for her and he said to her, "Don't cry." Then he walked over and touched the coffin, and the men carrying it stopped. Jesus said, "Young man! Get up, I tell you!" The dead man sat up and began to talk, and Jesus gave him back to his mother.

Everyone was filled with fear, and they praised God, "A great prophet has appeared among us!" and, "God has come to save his people!"

This news about Jesus went out through all the country and the surrounding territory.

The Messengers from John the Baptist

When John the Baptist heard in prison about Christ's works, he sent some of his disciples to him. "Tell us," they asked Jesus, "are you the one John said was going to come, or should we expect someone else?"

Jesus answered, "Go back and tell John what you are hearing and seeing: the blind can see, the lame can walk, the lepers are made clean, the deaf hear, the dead are raised to life, and the Good News is preached to the poor. How happy is he who has no doubts about me!"

After John's messengers had left, Jesus began to speak about John to the crowds, "When you went out to John in the desert, what did you expect to see? A blade of grass bending in the wind? What did you go out to see? A man dressed up in fancy clothes? Really, those who dress like that and live in luxury are found in palaces! Tell me, what did you go out to see? A prophet? Yes, I tell you—you saw much more than a prophet. For John is the one of whom the scripture says, 'Here is my messenger, says God; I will send him ahead of you to open the way for you.' I tell you," Jesus added, "John is greater than any man ever born; but he who is least in the Kingdom of God is greater than he."

All the people and the tax collectors heard him; they were the ones who had obeyed God's righteous demands and had been baptized by John. But the Pharisees and the teachers of the Law rejected God's purpose for themselves, and refused to be baptized by John.

"Now, to what can I compare the people of this day? What are they like? They are like children sitting in the market place. One group shouts to the other, 'We played wedding music for you, but you would not dance! We sang funeral songs, but you would not cry!' John the Baptist came, and he fasted and drank no wine, and you said, 'He has a demon in him!' The Son of Man came, and he ate and drank, and you said, "Look at this man! He is a glutton and wine-drinker, a friend of tax collectors and outcasts!' God's wisdom, however, is shown to be true by all who accept it."

The Unbelieving Towns
Then Jesus began to reproach the towns where he had performed most of his miracles, because the people had not turned from their sins. "How terrible it will be for you, Chorazin! How terrible for you too, Bethsaida! If the miracles which were performed in you had been performed in Tyre and Sidon, long ago the people there

would have put on sackcloth, and sprinkled ashes on themselves to show they had turned from their sins! Remember, then, that on the Judgment Day God will show more mercy to the people of Tyre and Sidon than to you! And as for you, Capernaum! You wanted to lift yourself up to heaven? You will be thrown down to hell! If the miracles which were performed in you had been performed in Sodom, it would still be in existence today! Remember, then, that on the Judgment Day God will show more mercy to Sodom than to you!"

At that time Jesus said, "Father, Lord of heaven and earth! I thank you because you have shown to the unlearned what you have hidden from the wise and learned. Yes, Father, this was done by your own choice and pleasure.

"My Father has given me all things. No one knows the Son except the Father, and no one knows the Father except the Son, and those to whom the Son wants to reveal him.

"Come to me, all of you who are tired from carrying your heavy loads, and I will give you rest. Take my yoke and put it on you, and learn from me, because I am gentle and humble in spirit; and you will find rest. The yoke I will give you is easy, and the load I will put on you is light."

Jesus at the Home of Simon the Pharisee

A Pharisee invited Jesus to have dinner with him. Jesus went to his house and sat down to eat. There was a woman in that town who lived a sinful life. She heard that Jesus was eating in the Pharisee's house, so she brought an alabaster jar full of perfume and stood behind Jesus, by his feet, crying and wetting his feet with her tears. Then she dried his feet with her hair, kissed them, and poured the perfume on them. When the Pharisee who had invited Jesus saw this, he said to himself, "If this man really were a prophet, he would know who this woman is who is touching him; he would know what kind of sinful life she leads!"

Jesus spoke up and said to him, "Simon, I have something to tell you."

"Yes, Teacher," he said, "tell me."

"There were two men who owed money to a moneylender," Jesus began; "one owed him five hundred dollars and the other one fifty dollars. Neither one could pay him back, so he canceled the debts of both. Which one, then, will love him more?"

"I suppose," answered Simon, "that it would be the one who was forgiven more."

"Your answer is correct," said Jesus. Then he turned to the woman and said to Simon, "Do you see this woman? I came into your home, and you gave me no water for my feet, but she has washed my feet with her tears and dried them with her hair. You did not welcome me with a kiss, but she has not stopped kissing my feet since I came. You provided no oil for my head, but she has covered my feet with perfume. I tell you, then, the great love she has shown proves that her many sins have been forgiven. Whoever has been forgiven little, however, shows only a little love."

Then Jesus said to the woman, "Your sins are forgiven."

The others sitting at the table began to say to themselves, "Who is this, who even forgives sins?"

But Jesus said to the woman, "Your faith has saved you; go in peace."

Jesus and Beelzebul

Then some people brought to Jesus a man who was blind and could not talk because he had a demon. Jesus healed the man, so that he was able to talk and see. The crowds were all amazed. "Could he be the Son of David?" they asked.

When the Pharisees heard this they replied, "He drives out demons only because their ruler Beelzebul gives him power to do so."

Jesus knew what they were thinking and said to them, "Any country that divides itself into groups that fight each other will not last very long. And any town or family that divides itself into groups that fight each other will fall apart. So if one group is fighting another in Satan's kingdom, this means that it is already divided into groups and will soon fall apart! You say that I drive out demons because Beelzebul gives me the power to do so. Well, then, who gives your followers the power to drive them out? Your own followers prove that you are wrong! No, it is God's Spirit who gives me the power to drive out demons, which proves that the Kingdom of God has already come upon you.

"No one can break into a strong man's house and take away his belongings unless he ties up the strong man first; then he can plunder his house.

"Anyone who is not for me is really against me; anyone who does not help me gather is really scattering. For this reason I tell you: men can be forgiven any sin and any evil thing they say; but whoever says evil things against the Holy Spirit will not be forgiven. Anyone who says something against the Son of Man can be forgiven; but whoever says something against the Holy Spirit will not be forgiven—now or ever.

"To have good fruit you must have a healthy tree; if you have a poor tree you will have bad fruit. For a tree is known by the kind of fruit it bears. You snakes—how can you say good things when you are evil? For the mouth speaks what the heart is full of. A good man brings good things out of his treasure of good things; a bad man brings bad things out of his treasure of bad things.

"I tell you this: on the Judgment Day everyone will have to give account of every useless word he has ever spoken. For your words will be used to judge you, either to declare you innocent or to declare you guilty."

Then some teachers of the Law and some Pharisees spoke up. "Teacher," they said, "we want to see you perform a miracle."

"How evil and godless are the people of this day!" Jesus exclaimed. "You ask me for a miracle? No! The only miracle you will be given is the miracle of the prophet Jonah. In the same way that Jonah spent three days and nights in the belly of the big fish, so will the Son of Man spend three days and nights in the depths of the earth. On the Judgment Day the people of Nineveh will stand up and accuse you, because they turned from their sins when they heard Jonah preach; and there is something here, I tell you, greater than Jonah! On the Judgment Day the Queen from the South will stand up and accuse you, because she traveled halfway around the world to listen to Solomon's wise teaching; and there is something here, I tell you, greater than Solomon!

"When an evil spirit goes out of a man, it travels over dry country looking for a place to rest. If it can't find one, it says to itself, 'I will go back to my house which I left.' So it goes back and finds the house empty, clean, and all fixed up. Then it goes out and brings along seven other spirits even worse than itself, and they come and live there. So that man is in worse shape, when it is all over, than he was at the beginning. This is the way it will happen to the evil people of this day."

Jesus' Mother and Brothers
Jesus was still talking to the people when his mother and brothers arrived. They stood outside, asking to speak with him. So one of the people there said to him, "Look, your mother and brothers are standing outside, and they want to speak with you."

Jesus answered, "Who is my mother? Who are my brothers?" Then he pointed to his disciples and said, "Look! Here are my mother and my brothers! Whoever does what my Father in heaven wants him to do is my brother, my sister, my mother."

Jesus Teaches in Parables
Again Jesus began to teach by Lake Galilee. The crowd that gathered around him was so large that he got into a boat and sat in it. The boat was out in the water, while the crowd stood on the shore, at the water's edge. He used parables to teach them many things, and in his teaching said to them,

"Listen! There was a man who went out to sow. As he scattered the seed in the field, some of it fell along the path, and the birds came and ate it up. Some of it fell on rocky ground, where there was little soil. The seeds soon sprouted, because the soil wasn't deep. Then when the sun came up it burned the young plants, and because the roots had not grown deep enough the plants soon dried up. Some of the seed fell among thorns, which grew up and choked the plants, and they didn't bear grain. But some seeds fell in good soil, and the plants sprouted, grew, and bore grain: some had thirty grains, others sixty, and others one hundred."

And Jesus concluded, "Listen, then, if you have ears to hear with!"

When Jesus was alone, some of those who had heard him came to him with the twelve disciples and asked him to explain the parables. "You have been given the secret of the Kingdom of God," Jesus answered. "But the others, who are on the outside, hear all things by means of parables, so that, 'They may look and look, yet not see, they may listen and listen, yet not understand; for if they did, they would turn to God and he would forgive them.' "

Then Jesus asked them, "Don't you understand this parable? How, then, will you ever understand any parable? The sower sows God's message. Sometimes the message falls along the path; these people hear it, but as soon as they hear it Satan comes and takes away the message sown in them. Other people are like the seeds that fall on rocky ground. As soon as they hear the message they receive it gladly. But it does not sink deep into them, and they don't last long. So when trouble or persecution comes because of the message, they give up at once. Other people are like the seeds sown among the thorns. These are the ones who hear the message, but the worries about this life, the love for riches, and all other kinds of desires crowd in and choke the message, and they don't bear fruit. But other people are like the seeds sown in good soil. They hear the message, accept it, and bear fruit: some thirty, some sixty, and some one hundred."

Jesus continued, "Does anyone ever bring in a lamp and put it under a bowl or under the bed? Doesn't he put it on the lampstand? Whatever is hidden away will be brought out into the open, and whatever is covered up will be uncovered. Listen, then, if you have ears to hear with!"

He also said to them, "Pay attention to what you hear! The same rules you use to judge others will be used by God to judge you—but with even greater severity. The man who has something will be given more; the man who has nothing will have taken away from him even the little he has."

Jesus went on to say, "The Kingdom of God is like a man who scatters seed in his field. He sleeps at night, is up and about during the day, and all the while the seeds are sprouting and growing. Yet he does not know how it happens. The soil itself makes the plants grow and bear fruit: first the tender stalk appears, then the head, and finally the head full of grain. When the grain is ripe the man starts working with his sickle, because harvest time has come."

Jesus told them another parable, "The Kingdom of heaven is like a mustard seed, which a man takes and sows in his field. It is the smallest of all seeds, but when it grows up it is the biggest of all plants. It becomes a tree, so that the birds come and make their nests in its branches."

Jesus told them another parable, "The Kingdom of heaven is like yeast. A woman takes it and mixes it with a bushel of flour, until the whole batch of dough rises."

Jesus told them another parable, "The Kingdom of heaven is like a man who sowed good seed in his field. One night, when everyone was asleep, an enemy came and sowed weeds among the wheat, and went away. When the plants grew and the heads of grain began to form, then the weeds showed up. The man's servants came to him and said, 'Sir, it was good seed you sowed in your field; where did the weeds come from?' 'It was some enemy who did this,' he answered. 'Do you want us to go and pull up the weeds?' they asked him. 'No,' he answered, 'because as you gather the weeds you might pull up some of the wheat along with them. Let the wheat and the weeds both grow together until harvest, and then I will tell the harvest workers: Pull up the weeds first and tie them in bundles to throw in the fire; then gather in the wheat and put it in my barn.'"

Jesus used parables to tell all these things to the crowds; he would not say a thing to them without using a parable.

The Parables Explained

Then Jesus left the crowd and went indoors. His disciples came to him and said, "Tell us what the parable of the weeds in the field means."

Jesus answered, "The man who sowed the good seed is the Son of Man; the field is the world; the good seed is the people who belong to the Kingdom; the weeds are the people who belong to the Evil One; and the enemy who sowed the weeds is the Devil. The harvest is the end of the age, and the harvest workers are angels. Just as the weeds are gathered up and burned in the fire, so it will be at the end of the age: the Son of Man will send out his angels and they will gather up out of his Kingdom all who cause people to sin, and all other evildoers, and throw them into the fiery furnace, where they will cry and gnash their teeth. Then God's people will shine like the sun in their Father's Kingdom. Listen, then, if you have ears!

"The Kingdom of heaven is like a treasure hidden in a field. A man happens to find it, so he covers it up again. He is so happy that he goes and sells everything he has, and then goes back and buys the field.

"Also, the Kingdom of heaven is like a buyer looking for fine pearls. When he find one that is unusually fine, he goes and sells everything he has, and buys the pearl.

"Also, the Kingdom of heaven is like a net thrown out in the lake, which catches all kinds of fish. When it is full, the fishermen pull it to shore and sit down to divide the fish: the good ones go into their buckets, the worthless ones are thrown away. It will be like this at the end of the age: the angels will go out and gather up the evil people from among the good, and throw them into the fiery furnace. There they will cry and gnash their teeth.

"Do you understand these things?" Jesus asked them.

"Yes," they answered.

So he replied, "This means, then, that every teacher of the Law who becomes a disciple in the Kingdom of heaven is like a homeowner who takes new and old things out of his storage room."

Jesus preached his message to the people, using many

other parables like these; he told them as much as they could understand. He would not speak to them without using parables; but when he was alone with his disciples he would explain everything to them.

Jesus Calms a Storm

On the evening of that same day Jesus said to his disciples, "Let us go across to the other side of the lake." So they left the crowd; the disciples got into the boat that Jesus was already in, and took him with them. Other boats were there too. A very strong wind blew up and the waves began to spill over into the boat, so that it was about to fill with water. Jesus was in the back of the boat, sleeping with his head on a pillow. The disciples woke him up and said, "Teacher, don't you care that we are about to die?"

Jesus got up and commanded the wind, "Be quiet!" and said to the waves, "Be still!" The wind died down, and there was a great calm. Then Jesus said to his disciples, "Why are you frightened? Are you still without faith?"

But they were terribly afraid, and began to say to each other, "Who is this man? Even the wind and the waves obey him!"

Jesus Heals a Man with Demons

They sailed on over to the territory of the Gergesenes, which is across the lake from Galilee. As Jesus stepped ashore, he was met by a man from the town who had demons in him. He had gone for a long time without clothes, and would not stay at home, but spent his time in the burial caves. When he saw Jesus he gave a loud cry, fell down before him, and said in a loud voice, "Jesus, Son of the Most High God! What do you want with me? I beg you, don't punish me!" He said this because Jesus had ordered the evil spirit to go out of him. Many times it had seized him, and even though he was kept a prisoner, his hands and feet tied with chains, he would break the chains and be driven by the demon out into the desert.

Jesus asked him, "What is your name?"

"My name is 'Mob,' " he answered—because many

demons had gone into him. The demons begged Jesus not to send them into the abyss.

A large herd of pigs was near by, feeding on the hillside. The demons begged Jesus to let them go into the pigs, and he let them. So the demons went out of the man and into the pigs; the whole herd rushed down the side of the cliff into the lake and were drowned.

The men who were taking care of the pigs saw what happened, so they ran off and spread the news in the town and among the farms. People went out to see what had happened. They came to Jesus and found the man from whom the demons had gone out sitting at the feet of Jesus, clothed, and in his right mind; and they were all afraid. Those who had seen it told the people how the man had been cured. Then all the people from the territory of the Gergesenes asked Jesus to go away, because they were terribly afraid. So Jesus got into the boat and left. The man from whom the demons had gone out begged Jesus, "Let me go with you."

But Jesus sent him away, saying, "Go back home and tell what God has done for you."

The man went through the whole town telling what Jesus had done for him.

Jairus' Daughter and the Woman Who Touched Jesus' Cloak

Jesus went back across to the other side of the lake. There at the lakeside a large crowd gathered around him. Jairus, an official of the local synagogue, came up, and when he saw Jesus he threw himself down at his feet and begged him with all his might, "My little daughter is very sick. Please come and place your hands on her, so that she will get well and live!"

Then Jesus started off with him. So many people were going along with him that they were crowding him from every side.

There was a woman who had suffered terribly from severe bleeding for twelve years, even though she had been treated by many doctors. She had spent all her money, but instead of getting better she got worse all the time. She had heard about Jesus, so she came in the crowd behind him. "If I touch just his clothes," she said to herself, "I shall get well."

She touched his cloak and her bleeding stopped at once; and she had the feeling inside herself that she was cured of her trouble. At once Jesus knew that power had gone out of him. So he turned around in the crowd and said, "Who touched my clothes?"

His disciples answered, "You see how the people are crowding you; why do you ask who touched you?"

But Jesus kept looking around to see who had done it. The woman realized what had happened to her; so she came, trembling with fear, fell at his feet, and told him the whole truth. Jesus said to her, "My daughter, your faith has made you well. Go in peace, and be healed from your trouble."

While Jesus was saying this, some messengers came from Jairus' house and told him, "Your daughter has died. Why should you bother the Teacher any longer?"

Jesus paid no attention to what they said, but told him, "Don't be afraid, only believe." Then he did not let anyone else go on with him except Peter and James and his brother John. They arrived at the official's house, where Jesus saw the confusion and heard all the loud crying and wailing. He went in and said to them, "Why all this confusion? Why are you crying? The child is not dead—she is only sleeping!"

They started making fun of him, so he put them all out, took the child's father and mother, and his three disciples, and went into the room where the child was lying. He took her by the hand and said to her, *"Talitha, koum,"* which means, "Little girl! Get up, I tell you!"

She got up at once and started walking around. (She was twelve years old.) When this happened they were completely amazed! But Jesus gave them strict orders not to tell anyone, and said, "Give her something to eat."

Jesus Heals Two Blind Men
Jesus left that place, and as he walked along two blind men started following him. "Have mercy on us, Son of David!" they shouted.

When Jesus had gone indoors, the two blind men came to him and he asked them, "Do you believe that I can do this?"

"Yes, sir!" they answered.

Then Jesus touched their eyes and said, "May it happen, then, just as you believe!"—and their sight was restored. Jesus spoke harshly to them, "Don't tell this to anyone!"

Jesus Has Pity for the People

So Jesus went around visiting all the towns and villages. He taught in their synagogues, preached the Good News of the Kingdom, and healed people from every kind of disease and sickness. As he saw the crowds, his heart was filled with pity for them, because they were worried and helpless, like sheep without a shepherd. So he said to his disciples, "There is a large harvest, but few workers to gather it in. Pray to the owner of the harvest that he will send out workers to gather in his harvest."

Jesus Sends Out the Twelve Disciples

Then Jesus went to the villages around there, teaching the people. He called the twelve disciples together and sent them out two by two. He gave them authority over the evil spirits and ordered them, "Don't take anything with you on the trip except a walking stick; no bread, no beggar's bag, no money in your pockets. Wear sandals, but don't wear an extra shirt." He also told them, "Wherever you are welcomed, stay in the same house until you leave that town. If you come to a place where people do not welcome you or will not listen to you, leave it and shake the dust off your feet. This will be a warning to them!"

The Mission of the Twelve

Jesus sent these twelve men out with the following instructions: "Do not go to any Gentile territory or any Samaritan towns. Go, instead, to the lost sheep of the people of Israel. Go and preach, 'The Kingdom of heaven is near!' Heal the sick, raise the dead, make the lepers clean, drive out demons. You have received without paying, so give without being paid. Do not carry any gold, silver, or copper money in your pockets; do not carry a beggar's bag for the trip, or an extra shirt, or shoes, or a walking stick. A worker should be given what he needs.

"When you come to a town or village, go in and look for someone who is willing to welcome you, and stay with him until you leave that place. When you go into a house say, 'Peace be with you.' If the people in that house welcome you, let your greeting of peace remain; but if they do not welcome you, then take back your greeting. And if some home or town will not welcome you or listen to you, then leave that place and shake the dust off your feet. Remember this! On the Judgment Day God will show more mercy to the people of Sodom and Gomorrah than to the people of that town!

"Listen! I am sending you just like sheep to a pack of wolves. You must be as cautious as snakes and as gentle as doves. Watch out, for there will be men who will arrest you and take you to court, and they will whip you in their synagogues. You will be brought to trial before rulers and kings for my sake, to tell the Good News to them and to the Gentiles. When they bring you to trial, do not worry about what you are going to say or how you will say it; when the time comes, you will be given what you will say. For the words you speak will not be yours; they will come from the Spirit of your Father speaking in you.

"Men will hand over their own brothers to be put to death, and fathers will do the same to their children; children will turn against their parents and have them put to death. Everyone will hate you, because of me. But whoever holds out to the end will be saved. And when they persecute you in one town, run away to another one. I tell you, you will not finish your work in all the towns of Israel before the Son of Man comes.

"No pupil is greater than his teacher; no slave is greater than his master. So a pupil should be satisfied to become like his teacher, and a slave like his master. If the head of the family is called Beelzebul, the members of the family will be called by even worse names!

"Do not be afraid of men, then. Whatever is covered up will be uncovered, and every secret will be made known. What I am telling you in the dark you must repeat in broad daylight, and what you have heard in private you must tell from the housetops. Do not be afraid of those who kill the body but cannot kill the soul; rather be afraid of God, who can destroy both body and soul in hell. You can buy two sparrows for a penny; yet not a single one of them falls to the ground without your Father's consent. As for you, even the hairs of your head have all been counted. So do not be afraid; you are worth much more than many sparrows!

"Whoever declares publicly that he belongs to me, I will do the same for him before my Father in heaven. But whoever denies publicly that he belongs to me, then I will deny him before my Father in heaven.

"Do not think that I have come to bring peace to the world; no, I did not come to bring peace, but a sword. I came to set sons against their fathers, daughters against their mothers, daughters-in-law against their mothers-in-law; a man's worst enemies will be the members of his own family.

"Whoever loves his father or mother more than me is not worthy of me; whoever loves his son or daughter more than me is not worthy of me. Whoever does not take up his cross and follow in my steps is not worthy of me. Whoever tries to gain his own life will lose it; whoever loses his life for my sake will gain it.

'Whoever welcomes you, welcomes me; and whoever welcomes me, welcomes the one who sent me. Whoever welcomes God's messenger because he is God's messenger will share in his reward; and whoever welcomes a truly good man, because he is that, will share in his reward. And remember this! Whoever gives even a drink of cold water to one of the least of these my followers, because he is my follower, will certainly receive his reward."

So they went out and preached that people should turn away from their sins. They drove out many demons, and rubbed oil on many sick people and healed them.

The Death of John the Baptist

Now King Herod heard about all this, because Jesus' reputation had spread everywhere. Some people were saying, "John the Baptist has come back to life! That is why these powers are at work in him."

Others, however, said, "He is Elijah."

Others said, "He is a prophet, like one of the prophets of long ago."

When Herod heard it he said, "He is John the Baptist! I had his head cut off, but he has come back to life!" Herod himself had ordered John's arrest, and had him tied up and put in prison. Herod did this because of Herodias, whom he had married, even though she was the wife of his brother Philip. John the Baptist kept telling Herod, "It isn't right for you to marry your brother's wife!"

So Herodias held a grudge against John and wanted to kill him, but she could not because of Herod. Herod was afraid of John because he knew that John was a good and holy man, and so he kept him safe. He liked to listen to him, even though he became greatly disturbed every time he heard him.

Finally Herodias got her chance. It was on Herod's birthday, when he gave a feast for all the top government officials, the military chiefs, and the leading citizens of Galilee. The daughter of Herodias came in and danced, and pleased Herod and his guests. So the king said to the girl, "What would you like to have? I will give you anything you want." With many vows he said to her, "I promise that I will give you anything you ask for, even as much as half my kingdom!"

So the girl went out and asked her mother, "What shall I ask for?"

"The head of John the Baptist," she answered.

The girl hurried back at once to the king and demanded, "I want you to give me right now the head of John the Baptist on a plate!"

This made the king very sad; but he could not refuse her, because of the vows he had made in front of all the guests. So he sent off a guard at once with orders to bring John's head. The guard left, went to the prison, and cut John's head off; then he brought it on a plate and gave it to the girl, who gave it to her mother. When John's disciples heard about this, they came and got his body and laid it in a grave.

Herod said, "I had John's head cut off; but who is this man I hear these things about?" And he kept trying to see Jesus.

Jesus Feeds the Five Thousand

The apostles returned and met with Jesus, and told him all they had done and taught. There were so many people coming and going that Jesus and his disciples didn't even have time to eat. So he said to them, "Let us go off by ourselves to some place where we will be alone and you can rest a while." So they started out in the boat by themselves to a lonely place.

Many people, however, saw them leave and knew at once who they were; so they went from all the towns and ran ahead by land and got to the place ahead of Jesus and his disciples.

Jesus looked around and saw that a large crowd was coming to him, so he said to Philip, "Where can we buy enough food to feed all these people?" (He said this to test Philip; actually he already knew what he would do.)

Philip answered, "For everyone to have even a little, it would take more than two hundred dollars' worth of bread."

Another one of his disciples, Andrew, Simon Peter's brother, said, "There is a boy here who has five loaves of barley bread and two fish. But what good are they for all these people?"

"Make the people sit down," Jesus told them. (There was a lot of grass there.) So all the people sat down; there were about five thousand men. Jesus took the bread, gave thanks to God, and distributed it to the people who were sitting there. He did the same with the fish, and they all had as much as they wanted. When they were all full, he said to his disciples, "Pick up the pieces left over; let us not waste a bit." So they took them all up, and filled twelve baskets with the pieces left over from the five barley loaves which the people had eaten.

Jesus Walks on the Water

Then Jesus made the disciples get into the boat and go ahead of him to the other side of the lake, while he sent the people away. After sending the people away, he went up a hill by himself to pray. When evening came, Jesus was there alone; by this time the boat was far out in the lake, tossed about by the waves, because the wind was blowing against it. Between three and six o'clock in the morning Jesus came to them, walking on the water. When the disciples saw him walking on the water they were terrified. "It's a ghost!" they said, and screamed with fear.

Jesus spoke to them at once. "Courage!" he said. "It is I. Don't be afraid!"

Then Peter spoke up. "Lord," he said, "if it is really you, order me to come out on the water to you."

"Come!" answered Jesus. So Peter got out of the boat and started walking on the water to Jesus. When he noticed the wind, however, he was afraid, and started to sink down in the water. "Save me, Lord!" he cried.

At once Jesus reached out and grabbed him and said, "How little faith you have! Why did you doubt?"

They both got into the boat, and the wind died down. The disciples in the boat worshiped Jesus. "Truly you are the Son of God!" they exclaimed.

Jesus the Bread of Life

Next day the crowd which had stayed on the other side of the lake saw that only one boat was left there. They knew that Jesus had not gone in the boat with his disciples, but that they had left without him. Other boats, from Tiberias, came to shore near the place where the crowd had eaten the bread, after the Lord had given thanks. When the crowd saw that Jesus was not there, nor his disciples, they got into boats and went to Capernaum, looking for him.

When the people found Jesus on the other side of the lake they said to him, "Teacher, when did you get here?"

Jesus answered, "I tell you the truth: you are looking for me because you ate the bread and had all you wanted, not because you understood my works of power. Do not work for food that spoils; instead, work for the food that lasts for eternal life. This food the Son of Man will give you, because God, the Father, has put his mark of approval on him."

So they asked him, "What can we do in order to do God's works?"

Jesus answered, "This is the work God wants you to do: believe in the one he sent."

They replied, "What sign of power will you perform so that we may see it and believe you? What will you do? Our ancestors ate manna in the desert, just as the scripture says, 'He gave them bread from heaven to eat.'"

"I tell you the truth," Jesus said. "What Moses gave you was not the bread from heaven; it is my Father who gives you the real bread from heaven. For the bread that God gives is he who comes down from heaven and gives life to the world."

"Sir," they asked him, "give us this bread always."

"I am the bread of life," Jesus told them. "He who comes to me will never be hungry; he who believes in me will never be thirsty. Now, I told you that you have seen me but will not believe. Everyone whom my Father gives me will come to me. I will never turn away anyone who comes to me, because I have come down from heaven to do the will of him who sent me, not my own will. He who sent me wants to do this: that I should not lose any of all those he has given me, but that I should raise them all to life on the last day. For what my Father wants is this: that all who see the Son and believe in him should have eternal life; and I will raise them to life on the last day."

The Jews started grumbling about him, because he said, "I am the bread that came down from heaven." So they said, "This man is Jesus the son of Joseph, isn't he? We know his father and mother. How, then, does he now say he came down from heaven?"

Jesus answered, "Stop grumbling among yourselves.

MIRACLES AND PARABLES

No one can come to me unless the Father who sent me draws him to me; and I will raise him to life on the last day. The prophets wrote, 'All men will be taught by God.' Everyone who hears the Father and learns from him comes to me. This does not mean that anyone has seen the Father; he who is from God is the only one who has seen the Father. I tell you the truth: he who believes has eternal life. I am the bread of life. Your ancestors ate the manna in the desert, but they died. But the bread that comes down from heaven is such that whoever eats it will not die. I am the living bread that came down from heaven. If anyone eats this bread he will live forever. The bread that I will give him is my flesh, which I give so that the world may live."

This started as angry argument among the Jews. "How can this man give us his flesh to eat?" they asked.

Jesus said to them, "I tell you the truth: if you do not eat the flesh of the Son of Man and drink his blood you will not have life in yourselves. Whoever eats my flesh and drinks my blood has eternal life, and I will raise him to life on the last day. For my flesh is the real food, my blood is the real drink. Whoever eats my flesh and drinks my blood lives in me and I live in him. The living Father sent me, and because of him I live also. In the same way, whoever eats me will live because of me. This, then, is the bread that came down from heaven; it is not like the bread that your ancestors ate, but then died. The one who eats this bread will live forever."

Jesus said this as he taught in the synagogue in Capernaum.

Many of his disciples heard this and said, "This teaching is too hard. Who can listen to this?"

Without being told, Jesus knew that his disciples were grumbling about this; so he said to them, "Does this make you want to give up? Suppose, then, that you should see the Son of Man go back up to the place where he was before? What gives life is God's Spirit; man's power is of no use at all. The words I have spoken to you are Spirit and life. Yet some of you do not believe." (Jesus knew from the very beginning who were the ones that would not believe, and which one would betray him.) And he added, "This is the very reason I told you that no one can come to me unless the Father makes it possible for him to do so."

Because of this, many of his followers turned back and would not go with him any more. So Jesus said to the twelve disciples, "And you—would you like to leave also?"

Simon Peter answered him, "Lord, to whom would we go? You have the words that give eternal life. And now we believe and know that you are the Holy One from God."

Jesus answered them, "Did I not choose the twelve of you? Yet one of you is a devil!" He was talking about Judas, the son of Simon Iscariot. For Judas, even though he was one of the twelve disciples, was going to betray him.

Six

COMING EVENTS CAST THEIR SHADOWS

The Teaching of the Ancestors
The Pharisees and some teachers of the Law who had come from Jerusalem gathered around Jesus. They noticed that some of his disciples were eating their food with unclean hands—that is, they had not washed them in the way the Pharisees said people should.

For the Pharisees, as well as the rest of the Jews, follow the teaching they received from their ancestors: they do not eat unless they wash their hands in the proper way, nor do they eat anything that comes from the market unless they wash it first. And they follow many other rules which they have received, such as the proper way to wash cups, pots, copper bowls, and beds.

So the Pharisees and the teachers of the Law asked Jesus, "Why is it that your disciples do not follow the teaching handed down by our ancestors, but instead eat with unclean hands?"

Jesus answered them, "How right Isaiah was when he prophesied about you! You are hypocrites, just as he wrote: 'These people, says God, honor me with their words, but their heart is really far away from me. It is no use for them to worship me, because they teach man-made commandments as though they were God's rules!'

"You put aside the commandment of God and obey the teachings of men."

And Jesus continued, "You have a clever way of rejecting God's law in order to uphold your own teaching. For Moses commanded, 'Honor your father and mother, and, 'Anyone who says bad things about his father or mother must be put to death.' But you teach that if a person has something he could use to help his father or mother, but says, 'This is Corban' (which means, it belongs to God), he is excused from helping his father or mother. In this way you disregard the word of God with the teaching you pass on to others. And there are many other things like this that you do."

The Things That Make a Person Unclean
Then Jesus called the crowd to him once more and said to them, "Listen to me, all of you, and understand. There is nothing that goes into a person from the outside which can make him unclean. Rather, it is what comes out of a person that makes him unclean. [Listen, then, if you have ears to hear with!]"

When he left the crowd and went into the house, his disciples asked him about this parable. "You are no more intelligent than the others," Jesus said to them. "Don't you understand? Nothing that goes into a person from the outside can really make him unclean, because it does not go into his heart but into his stomach and then goes on out of the body." (In saying this Jesus declared that all foods are fit to be eaten.)

And he went on to say, "It is what comes out of a person that makes him unclean. For from the inside, from a man's heart, come the evil ideas which lead him to do immoral things, to rob, kill, commit adultery, be greedy, and do all sorts of evil things; deceit, indecency, jealousy, slander, pride, and folly—all these evil things come from inside a man and make him unclean."

A Woman's Faith
Jesus left that place and went off to the territory near the cities of Tyre and Sidon. A Canaanite woman who lived in that region came to him. "Son of David, sir!" she cried. "Have mercy on me! My daughter has a demon and is in a terrible condition."

But Jesus did not say a word to her. His disciples came to him and begged him, "Send her away! She is following us and making all this noise!"

Then Jesus replied, "I have been sent only to the lost sheep of the people of Israel."

At this the woman came and fell at his feet. "Help me, sir!" she said.

Jesus answered, "It isn't right to take the children's food and throw it to the dogs."

"That is true, sir," she answered; "but even the dogs eat the leftovers that fall from their masters' table."

So Jesus answered her, "You are a woman of great faith! What you want will be done for you." And at that very moment her daughter was healed.

Jesus Heals a Deaf and Dumb Man

Jesus then left the neighborhood of Tyre and went on through Sidon to Lake Galilee, going by way of the territory of the Ten Towns. Some people brought him a man who was deaf and could hardly speak, and begged Jesus to place his hand on him. So Jesus took him off alone, away from the crowd, put his fingers in the man's ears, spat, and touched the man's tongue. Then Jesus looked up to heaven, gave a deep groan, and said to the man, "*Ephphatha,*" which means, "Open up!"

At once the man's ears were opened, his tongue was set loose, and he began to talk without any trouble. Then Jesus ordered them all not to speak of it to anyone; but the more he ordered them, the more they told it. And all who heard were completely amazed. "How well he does everything!" they exclaimed. "He even makes the deaf to hear and the dumb to speak!"

Jesus Feeds the Four Thousand

Not long afterward, another large crowd came together. When they had nothing left to eat, Jesus called the disciples to him and said, "I feel sorry for these people, because they have been with me for three days and now have nothing to eat. If I send them home without feeding them they will faint as they go, because some of them have come a long way."

His disciples asked him, "Where in this desert can anyone find enough food to feed all these people?"

"How much bread do you have?" Jesus asked.

"Seven loaves," they answered.

He ordered the crowd to sit down on the ground. Then he took the seven loaves, gave thanks to God, broke them, and gave them to his disciples to distribute to the crowd; and the disciples did so. They also had a few small fish. Jesus gave thanks for these and told the disciples to distribute them too. Everybody ate and had enough—there were about four thousand people. Then the disciples took up seven baskets full of pieces left over. Jesus sent the people away, and at once got into the boat with his disciples and went to the district of Dalmanutha.

Some Pharisees came to Jesus and started to argue with him. They wanted to trap him, so they asked him to perform a miracle to show God's approval. Jesus gave a deep groan and said, "Why do the people of this day ask for a miracle? No, I tell you! No such proof will be given this people!"

He left them, got back into the boat, and started across to the other side of the lake.

The disciples had forgotten to bring any extra bread, and had only one loaf with them in the boat. "Look out," Jesus warned them, "and be on your guard against the yeast of the Pharisees and the yeast of Herod."

They started discussing among themselves, "He says this because we don't have any bread."

Jesus knew what they were saying, so he asked them, "Why are you discussing about not having any bread? Don't you know or understand yet? Are your minds so dull? You have eyes—can't you see? You have ears—can't you hear? Don't you remember when I broke the five loaves for the five thousand people? How many baskets full of leftover pieces did you take up?"

"Twelve," they answered.

"And when I broke the seven loaves for the four thousand people," asked Jesus, "how many baskets full of leftover pieces did you take up?"

"Seven," they answered.

"And you still don't understand?" he asked them.

Jesus Heals a Blind Man at Bethsaida

They came to Bethsaida, where some people brought a blind man to Jesus and begged him to touch him. Jesus took the blind man by the hand and led him out of the village. After spitting on the man's eyes, Jesus placed his hands on him and asked him, "Can you see anything?"

The man looked up and said, "Yes, I can see people, but they look like trees walking around."

Jesus again placed his hands on the man's eyes. This time the man looked hard, his eyesight came back, and he saw everything clearly. Jesus then sent him home with the order, "Don't go back into the village."

Peter's Declaration About Jesus
Jesus went to the territory near the town of Caesarea Philippi, where he asked his disciples, "Who do men say the Son of Man is?"

"Some say John the Baptist," they answered. "Others say Elijah, while others say Jeremiah or some other prophet."

"What about you?" he asked them. "Who do you say I am?"

Simon Peter answered, "You are the Messiah, the Son of the living God."

"Good for you, Simon, son of John!" answered Jesus. "Because this truth did not come to you from any human being, but it was given to you directly by my Father in heaven. And so I tell you: you are a rock, Peter, and on this rock foundation I will build my church, which not even death will ever be able to overcome. I will give you the keys of the Kingdom of heaven; what you prohibit on earth will be prohibited in heaven; what you permit on earth will be permitted in heaven."

Then Jesus ordered his disciples not to tell anyone that he was the Messiah.

Jesus Speaks About His Suffering and Death
From that time on Jesus began to say plainly to his disciples, "I must go to Jerusalem and suffer much from the elders, the chief priests, and the teachers of the Law. I will be put to death, and on the third day I will be raised to life."

Peter took him aside and began to rebuke him. "God forbid it, Lord!" he said. "This must never happen to you!"

Jesus turned around and said to Peter, "Get away from me, Satan! You are an obstacle in my way, because these thoughts of yours are men's thoughts, not God's!"

Then Jesus said to his disciples, "If anyone wants to come with me, he must forget himself, carry his cross, and follow me. For whoever wants to save his own life will lose it; but whoever loses his life for my sake will find it. Will a man gain anything if he wins the whole world but loses his life? Of course not! There is nothing a man can give to regain his life. For the Son of Man is about to come in the glory of his Father with his angels, and then he will repay everyone according to his deeds. Remember this! There are some here who will not die until they have seen the Son of Man come as King."

The Transfiguration

Six days later Jesus took Peter, James, and John with him, and led them up a high mountain by themselves. As they looked on, a change came over him, and his clothes became shining white, whiter than anyone in the world could wash them. Then the three disciples saw Elijah and Moses, who were talking with Jesus. Peter spoke up and said to Jesus, "Teacher, it is a good thing that we are here. We will make three tents, one for you, one for Moses, and one for Elijah." He and the others were so frightened that he did not know what to say.

A cloud appeared and covered them with its shadow, and a voice came from the cloud, "This is my own dear Son—listen to him!" They took a quick look around but did not see anyone else; only Jesus was with them.

As they came down the mountain Jesus ordered them, "Don't tell anyone what you have seen, until the Son of Man has risen from death."

They obeyed his order, but among themselves they started discussing the matter, "What does this 'rising from death' mean?" And they asked Jesus, "Why do the teachers of the Law say that Elijah has to come first?"

His answer was, "Elijah does indeed come first to get everything ready. Yet why do the Scriptures say that the Son of Man will suffer much and be rejected? I tell you, however, that Elijah has already come, and that people did to him what they wanted to, just as the Scriptures say abut him."

Jesus Heals a Boy with an Evil Spirit

When they joined the rest of the disciples, they saw a large crowd there. Some teachers of the Law were arguing with the disciples. As soon as the people saw Jesus, they were greatly surprised and ran to him and greeted him. Jesus asked his disciples, "What are you arguing with them about?"

A man in the crowd answered, "Teacher, I brought my son to you, because he has an evil spirit in him and cannot talk. Whenever the spirit attacks him, it throws him to the ground, and he foams at the mouth, grits his teeth, and becomes stiff all over. I asked your disciples to drive the spirit out, but they could not."

Jesus said to them, "How unbelieving you people are! How long must I stay with you? How long do I have to put up with you? Bring the boy to me!" They brought him to Jesus.

As soon as the spirit saw Jesus, it threw the boy into a fit, so that he fell on the ground and rolled around, foaming at the mouth. "How long has he been like this?" Jesus asked the father.

"Ever since he was a child," he replied. "Many times it has tried to kill him by throwing him in the fire and in the water. Have pity on us and help us, if you possibly can!"

"Yes," said Jesus, "if *you* can! Everything is possible for the person who has faith."

The father at once cried out, "I do have faith, but not enough. Help me have more!"

Jesus noticed that the crowd was closing in on them, so he gave a command to the evil spirit. "Deaf and dumb spirit," he said, "I order you to come out of the boy and never go into him again!"

Jesus commanded the demon and it went out, so that the boy was healed at that very moment.

Then the disciples came to Jesus in private and asked him, "Why couldn't we drive the demon out?"

"It was because you do not have enough faith," answered Jesus. "Remember this! If you have faith as big as a mustard seed, you can say to this hill, 'Go from here to there!' and it will go. You could do anything! [But only prayer and fasting can drive this kind out; nothing else can.]"

They left that place and went on through Galilee. Jesus did not want anyone to know where he was, because he was teaching his disciples, "The Son of Man will be handed over to men who will kill him; three days later, however, he will rise to life."

They did not understand what his teaching meant, but they were afraid to ask him.

Who is the Greatest?

They came to Capernaum, and after going indoors Jesus asked his disciples, "What were you arguing about on the road?"

But they would not answer him, because on the road they had been arguing among themselves about who was the greatest. Jesus sat down, called the twelve disciples, and said to them, "Whoever wants to be first must place himself last of all and be the servant of all."

Jesus knew what they were thinking, so he took a child, stood him by his side, and said to them, "Whoever in my name welcomes this child, welcomes me; and whoever welcomes me, also welcomes the one who sent me. For he who is least among you all is the greatest."

Payment of the Temple Tax

When Jesus and his disciples came to Capernaum, the collectors of the temple tax came to Peter and asked, "Does your teacher pay the temple tax?"

"Of course," Peter answered.

When Peter went into the house, Jesus spoke up first, "Simon, what is your opinion? Who pays duties or taxes to the kings of this world? The citizens of the country or the foreigners?"

"The foreigners," answered Peter.

"Well, then," replied Jesus, "that means that the citizens don't have to pay. But we don't want to offend these people. So go to the lake and drop in a line; pull up the first fish you hook, and in its mouth you will find a coin worth enough for my temple tax and yours; take it and pay them our taxes."

Who Is Not Against Us Is for Us
John said to him, "Teacher, we saw a man who was driving out demons in your name, and we told him to stop, because he doesn't belong to our group."

"Do not try to stop him," Jesus told them, "because no one who performs a miracle in my name will be able soon after to say bad things about me. For whoever is not against us is for us. Remember this! Anyone who gives you a drink of water because you belong to Christ will certainly receive his reward."

Temptations to Sin
"If anyone should cause one of these little ones to turn away from his faith in me, it would be better for that man to have a large millstone tied around his neck and be thrown into the sea. So if your hand makes you turn away, cut it off! It is better for you to enter life without a hand than to keep both hands and go off to hell, to the fire that never goes out. [There 'their worms never die, and the fire is never put out.'] And if your foot makes you turn away, cut it off! It is better for you to enter life without a foot than to keep both feet and be thrown into hell. [There 'their worms never die, and the fire is never put out.'] And if your eye makes you turn away, take it out! It is better for you to enter the Kingdom of God with only one eye, than to keep both eyes and be thrown into hell. There 'their worms never die, and the fire is never put out.'

"For everyone will be salted with fire. Salt is good; but if it loses its saltness, how can you make it salty again? Have salt in yourselves, and be at peace with one another."

Be Merciful
"What do you think? What will a man do who has one hundred sheep and one of them gets lost? He will leave the other ninety-nine grazing on the hillside and go to look for the lost sheep. When he finds it, I tell you, he feels far happier over this one sheep than over the

ninety-nine that did not get lost. In just the same way your Father in heaven does not want any of these little ones to be lost.

"If your brother sins against you, go to him and show him his fault. But do it privately, just between yourselves. If he listens to you, you have won your brother back. But if he will not listen to you, take one or two other persons with you, so that 'every accusation may be upheld by the testimony of two or three witnesses,' as the scripture says. But if he will not listen to them, then tell the whole thing to the church. And then, if he will not listen to the church, treat him as though he were a foreigner or a tax collector.

"And I tell you more: whenever two of you on earth will be prohibited in heaven; what you permit on earth will be permitted in heaven.

"And I tell you more: whenever two of you on earth agree about anything you pray for, it will be done for you by my Father in heaven. For where two or three come together in my name, I am there with them."

Then Peter came to Jesus and asked, "Lord, how many times can my brother sin against me and I have to forgive him? Seven times?"

"No, not seven times," answered Jesus, "but seventy times seven. Because the Kingdom of heaven is like a king who decided to check on his servants' accounts. He had just begun to do so when one of them was brought in who owed him millions of dollars. The servant did not have enough to pay his debt, so his master ordered him to be sold as a slave, with his wife and his children and all that he had, in order to pay the debt. The servant fell on his knees before his master. 'Be patient with me,' he begged, 'and I will pay you everything!' The master felt sorry for him, so he forgave him the debt and let him go.

"The man went out and met one of his fellow servants who owed him a few dollars. He grabbed him and started choking him. 'Pay back what you owe me!' he said. His fellow servant fell down and begged him, 'Be patient with me and I will pay you back!' But he would not; instead, he had him thrown into jail until he should pay the debt. When the other servants saw what had happened, they were very upset, and went to their master and told him everything. So the master called the servant in. 'You worthless slave!' he said. 'I forgave you the whole amount you owed me, just because you asked me to. You should have had mercy on your fellow servant, just as I had mercy on you.' The master was very angry, and he sent the servant to jail to be punished until he should pay back the whole amount."

And Jesus concluded, "That is how my Father in heaven will treat you if you do not forgive your brother, every one of you, from your heart."

Jesus and His Brothers

After this, Jesus traveled in Galilee; he did not want to travel in Judea, because the Jewish authorities there were wanting to kill him. The Jewish Feast of Tabernacles was near, so Jesus' brothers said to him, "Leave this place and go to Judea, so that your disciples will see the works you are doing. No one hides what he is doing if he wants to be well known. Since you are doing these things, let the whole world know about you!" (Not even his brothers believed in him.)

Jesus said to them, "The right time for me has not yet come. Any time is right for you. The world cannot hate you, but it hates me, because I keep telling it that its ways are bad. You go on to the feast. I am not going to this feast, because the right time has not come for me." He said this, and then stayed on in Galilee.

Jesus at the Feast of Tabernacles

After his brothers went to the feast, Jesus also went; however, he did not go openly, but went secretly. The Jewish authorities were looking for him at the feast. "Where is he?" they asked.

There was much whispering about him in the crowd. "He is a good man," some people said. "No," others said, "he fools the people." But no one talked about him openly, because they were afraid of the Jewish authorities.

The feast was nearly half over when Jesus went to the temple and began teaching. The Jewish authorities, greatly surprised, said, "How does this man know so much when he has never been to school?"

Jesus answered, "What I teach is not my teaching, but comes from God, who sent me. Whoever is willing to do what God wants will know whether what I teach comes from God or whether I speak on my own authority. A person who speaks on his own is trying to gain glory for himself. He who wants glory for the one who sent him, however, is honest and there is nothing false in him. Moses gave you the Law, did he not? But not one of you obeys the Law. Why are you trying to kill me?"

The crowd answered, "You have a demon in you! Who is trying to kill you?"

Jesus answered, "I did one great work and you were all surprised. Because Moses ordered you to circumcise your sons (although it was not Moses but your ancestors who started it), you will circumcise a boy on the Sabbath. If a boy is circumcised on the Sabbath so that Moses' Law will not be broken, why are you angry with me because I made a man completely well on the Sabbath? Stop judging by external standards, and judge by true standards."

Is He the Messiah?
Some of the people of Jerusalem said, "Isn't this the man they are trying to kill? Look! He is talking in public, and nobody says anything against him! Can it be that the authorities really know that he is the Messiah? But when the Messiah comes, no one will know where he is from. And we all know where this man comes from."

As Jesus taught in the temple he said in a loud voice, "Do you really know me, and know where I am from? But I have not come on my own. He who sent me, however, is true. You do not know him, but I know him, because I come from him and he sent me."

Then they tried to arrest him, but no one laid a hand on him, because his hour had not yet come. But many in the crowd believed in him, and said, "When the Messiah comes, will he do more mighty works than this man has done?"

The Pharisees heard the crowd whispering these things about him, so they and the chief priests sent some guards to arrest Jesus. Jesus said, "I shall be with you a little while longer, and then I shall go away to him who sent me. You will look for me, but you will not find me, because where I shall be you cannot go."

The Jewish authorities said among themselves, "Where is he about to go so that we shall not find him? Will he go to the Greek cities where the Jews live, and teach the Greeks? He says, 'You will look for me but you will not find me,' and, 'You cannot go where I shall be.' What does he mean?"

Streams of Living Water
The last day of the feast was the most important. On that day Jesus stood up and said in a loud voice, "Whoever is thirsty should come to me and drink. As the scripture says, 'Whoever believes in me, streams of living water will pour out from his heart.'" Jesus said this about the Spirit, which those who believed in him were going to receive. At that time the Spirit had not yet been given, because Jesus had not been raised to glory.

Many of the people in the crowd heard him say this and said, "This man is really the Prophet!"

Others said, "He is the Messiah!"

But others said, "The Messiah will not come from Galilee! The scripture says that the Messiah will be a descendant of David, and will be born in Bethlehem, the town where David lived." So there was a division in the crowd because of him. Some wanted to arrest him, but no one laid a hand on him.

[Then everyone went home, but Jesus went to the Mount of Olives.]

The Woman Caught in Adultery
[Early the next morning he went back to the temple. The whole crowd gathered around him, and he sat down and began to teach them. The teachers of the Law and the Pharisees brought in a woman who had been caught committing adultery, and made her stand before them all. "Teacher," they said to Jesus, "this

woman was caught in the very act of committing adultery. In our Law Moses gave a commandment that such a woman must be stoned to death. Now, what do you say?" They said this to trap him, so they could accuse him. But Jesus bent over and wrote on the ground with his finger. As they stood there asking him questions, he straightened up and said to them, "Whichever one of you has committed no sin may throw the first stone at her." Then he bent over again and wrote on the ground. When they heard this they all left, one by one, the older ones first. Jesus was left alone, with the woman still standing there. He straightened up and said to her, "Where are they, woman? Is there no one left to condemn you?"

"No one, sir," she answered.

"Well, then," Jesus said, "I do not condemn you either. Go, but do not sin again."]

Jesus the Light of the World
Jesus spoke to them again, "I am the light of the world. Whoever follows me will have the light of life and will never walk in the darkness."

The Pharisees said to him, "Now you are testifying on your own behalf; what you say proves nothing."

"No," Jesus answered, "even if I do testify on my own behalf, what I say is true, because I know where I came from and where I am going. You do not know where I came from or where I am going. You make judgments in a purely human way; I pass judgment on no one. But if I were to pass judgment, my judging would be true, because I am not alone in this; the Father who sent me is with me. It is written in your Law that when two witnesses agree, what they say is true. I testify on my own behalf, and the Father who sent me also testifies on my behalf."

"Where is your father?" they asked him.

"You know neither me nor my Father," Jesus answered. "If you knew me you would know my Father also."

Jesus said all this as he taught in the temple, in the room where the offering boxes were placed. And no one arrested him, because his hour had not come.

Jesus said to them again, "I will go away; you will look for me, but you will die in your sins. You cannot go where I am going."

So the Jewish authorities said, "He says, 'You cannot go where I am going.' Does this mean that he will kill himself?"

Jesus answered, "You come from here below, but I come from above. You come from this world, but I do not come from this world. That is why I told you that you will die in your sins. And you will die in your sins if you do not believe that 'I Am Who I Am'."

"Who are you?" they asked him.

Jesus answered, "What I have told you from the very beginning. There are many things I have to say and judge about you. The one who sent me, however, is true, and I tell the world only what I have heard from him."

They did not understand that he was talking to them about the Father. So Jesus said to them, "When you lift up the Son of Man you will know that 'I Am Who I Am'; then you will know that I do nothing on my own, but say only what the Father has taught me. And he who sent me is with me; he has not left me alone, because I always do what pleases him."

Many who heard Jesus say these things believed in him.

So Jesus said to the Jews who believed in him, "If you obey my teaching you are really my disciples; you will know the truth, and the truth will make you free."

"We are the descendants of Abraham," they answered, "and we have never been anybody's slaves. What do you mean, then, by saying, 'You will be free'?"

Jesus said to them, "I tell you the truth: everyone who sins is a slave of sin. A slave does not belong to the family always, but a son belongs there forever. If the son makes you free, then you will be really free. I know you are Abraham's descendants. Yet you are trying to kill me, because you will not accept my teaching. I talk about what my Father has shown me, but you do what your father has told you."

They answered him, "Our father is Abraham."

"If you really were Abraham's children," Jesus replied, "you would do the same works that he did. All I have ever done is to tell you the truth I heard from God. Yet you are trying to kill me. Abraham did nothing like this! You are doing what your father did."

"God himself is the only Father we have," they answered. "We are his true sons."

Jesus said to them, "If God really were your father, you would love me, because I came from God and now I am here. I did not come on my own, but he sent me. Why do you not understand what I say? It is because you cannot bear to listen to my message. You are the children of your father, the Devil, and you want to follow your father's desires. From the very beginning he was a murderer. He has never been on the side of truth, because there is no truth in him. When he tells a lie he is only doing what is natural to him, because he is a liar and the father of all lies. I tell the truth, and that is why you do not believe me. Which one of you can prove that I am guilty of sin? If I tell the truth, then why do you not believe me? He who comes from God listens to God's words. You, however, are not from God, and this is why you will not listen."

The Jews replied to Jesus, "Were we not right in saying that you are a Samaritan and have a demon in you?"

"I have no demon," Jesus answered. "I honor my Father, but you dishonor me. I am not seeking honor for myself. There is one who is seeking it and who judges in my favor. I tell you the truth: whoever obeys my message will never die."

The Jews said to him, "Now we know for sure that you have a demon! Abraham died, and the prophets died, yet you say, 'Whoever obeys my message will never die.' Our father Abraham died; you do not claim to be greater than Abraham, do you? And the prophets also died. Who do you think you are?"

Jesus answered, "If I were to honor myself, my own honor would be worth nothing. The one who honors me is my Father—the very one you say is your God. You have never known him, but I know him. If I were to say that I do not know him, I would be a liar, like you. But I do know him, and I obey his word. Your father Abraham rejoiced that he was to see my day; he saw it and was glad."

The Jews said to him, "You are not even fifty years old—and you have seen Abraham?"

"I tell you the truth," Jesus replied. "Before Abraham was born, 'I Am'."

They picked up stones to throw at him; but Jesus hid himself and left the temple.

Jesus Heals a Man Born Blind

As Jesus walked along he saw a man who had been born blind. His disciples asked him, "Teacher, whose sin was it that caused him to be born blind? His own or his parents' sin?"

Jesus answered, "His blindness has nothing to do with his sins or his parents' sins. He is blind so that God's power might be seen at work in him. We must keep on doing the works of him who sent me, as long as it is day; the night is coming, when no one can work. While I am in the world I am the light for the world."

After he said this, Jesus spat on the ground and made some mud with the spittle; he rubbed the mud on the man's eyes, and told him, "Go wash your face in the Pool of Siloam." (This name means "Sent.") So the man went, washed his face, and came back seeing.

His neighbors, then, and the people who had seen him begging before this, asked, "Isn't this the man who used to sit and beg?"

Some said, "He is the one," but others said, "No he isn't, he just looks like him."

So the man himself said, "I am the man."

"How were your eyes opened?" they asked him.

He answered, "The man named Jesus made some mud, rubbed it on my eyes, and told me, 'Go to Siloam and wash your face.' So I went, and as soon as I washed I could see."

"Where is he?" they asked.

"I do not know," he answered.

Then they took the man who had been blind to the Pharisees. The day that Jesus made the mud and opened the man's eyes was a Sabbath. The Pharisees, then, asked the man again how he had received his sight. He told them, "He put some mud on my eyes, I washed my face, and now I can see."

Some of the Pharisees said, "The man who did this cannot be from God, because he does not obey the Sabbath law."

Others, however, said, "How could a man who is a sinner do such mighty works as these?" And there was a division among them.

So the Pharisees asked the man once more, "You say he opened your eyes—well, what do you say about him?"

"He is a prophet," he answered.

The Jewish authorities, however, were not willing to believe that he had been blind and could now see, until they called the man's parents and asked them, "Is this your son? You say that he was born blind; well, how is it that he can see now?"

His parents answered, "We know that he is our son, and we know that he was born blind. But we do not know how it is that he is now able to see, nor do we know who opened his eyes. Ask him; he is old enough, and he can answer for himself!" His parents said this because they were afraid of the Jewish authorities, who had already agreed that anyone who professed that Jesus was the Messiah would be put out of the synagogue. That is why his parents said, "He is old enough; ask him!"

A second time they called back the man who had been born blind and said to him, "Promise before God that you will tell the truth! We know that this man is a sinner."

"I do not know if he is a sinner or not," the man replied. "One thing I do know: I was blind, and now I see."

"What did he do to you?" they asked. "How did he open your eyes?"

"I have already told you," he answered, "and you would not listen. Why do you want to hear it again? Maybe you, too, would like to be his disciples?"

They insulted him and said, "You are that fellow's disciple; we are Moses' disciples. We know that God spoke to Moses; as for that fellow, we do not even know where he comes from!"

The man answered, "What a strange thing this is! You do not know where he comes from, but he opened my eyes! We know that God does not listen to sinners; he does listen to people who respect him and do what he wants them to do. Since the beginning of the world it has never been heard of that someone opened the eyes of a man born blind; unless this man came from God, he would not be able to do a thing."

They answered back, "You were born and raised in sin—and you are trying to teach us?" And they threw him out of the synagogue.

Jesus heard that they had thrown him out. He found him and said, "Do you believe in the Son of Man?"

The man answered, "Tell me who he is, sir, so I can believe in him!"

Jesus said to him, "You have already seen him, and he is the one who is talking with you now."

"I believe, Lord!" the man said, and knelt down before Jesus.

Jesus said, "I came to this world to judge, so that the blind should see, and those who see should become blind."

Some Pharisees, who were there with him, heard him say this and asked him, "You don't mean that we are blind, too?"

Jesus answered, "If you were blind, then you would not be guilty; but since you say, 'We can see,' this means that you are still guilty."

Jesus the Good Shepherd
"I tell you the truth: the man who does not enter the sheepfold by the door, but climbs in some other way, is a thief and a robber. The man who goes in by the door is the shepherd of the sheep. The gatekeeper opens the gate for him; the sheep hear his voice as he calls his own sheep by name, and he leads them out. When he has brought them out, he goes ahead of them, and the sheep follow him, because they know his voice. They will not follow someone else; instead, they will run away from him, because they do not know his voice."

Jesus told them this parable, but they did not understand what he was telling them.

So Jesus said again, "I tell you the truth: I am the door for the sheep. All others who came before me are thieves and robbers; but the sheep did not listen to them. I am the door. Whoever comes in by me will be saved; he will come in and go out, and find pasture. The thief comes only in order to steal, kill, and destroy. I have come in order that they might have life, life in all its fulness.

"I am the good shepherd. The good shepherd is willing to die for the sheep. The hired man, who is not a shepherd and does not own the sheep, leaves them and runs away when he sees a wolf coming; so the wolf snatches the sheep and scatters them. The hired man runs away because he is only a hired man and does not care for the sheep. I am the good shepherd. As the Father knows me and I know the Father, in the same way I know my sheep and they know me. And I am willing to die for them. There are other sheep that belong to me that are not in this sheepfold. I must bring them, too; they will listen to my voice, and they will become one flock with one shepherd.

"The Father loves me because I am willing to give up my life, in order that I may receive it back again. No one takes my life away from me. I give it up of my own free will. I have the right to give it, and I have the right to take it back. This is what my Father has commanded me to do."

Again there was a division among the Jews because of these words. Many of them were saying, "He has a demon! He is crazy! Why do you listen to him?"

But others were saying, "A man with a demon could not talk like this! How could a demon open the eyes of blind men?"

Jesus Rejected by the Jews

The time came to celebrate the Feast of Dedication in Jerusalem; it was winter. Jesus was walking in Solomon's Porch in the temple, when the Jews gathered around him and said, "How long are you going to keep us in suspense? Tell us the plain truth: are you the Messiah?"

Jesus answered, "I have already told you, but you would not believe me. The works I do by my Father's authority speak on my behalf; but you will not believe because you are not my sheep. My sheep listen to my voice; I know them, and they follow me. I give them eternal life, and they shall never die; and no one can snatch them away from me. What my Father has given me is greater than all, and no one can snatch them away from the Father's care. The Father and I are one."

Then the Jews once more picked up stones to throw at him. Jesus said to them, "I have done many good works before you which the Father gave me to do; for which one of these do you want to stone me?"

The Jews answered back, "We do not want to stone you because of any good works, but because of the way in which you insult God! You are only a man, but you are trying to make yourself God!"

Jesus answered, "It is written in your own Law that God said, 'You are gods.' We know that what the scripture says is true forever; and God called them gods, those people to whom his message was given. As for me, the Father chose me and sent me into the world. How, then, can you say that I insult God because I said that I am the Son of God? Do not believe me, then, if I am not doing my Father's works. But if I do them, even though you do not believe me, you should at least believe my works, in order that you may know once and for all that the Father is in me, and I am in the Father."

Once more they tried to arrest him, but he slipped out of their hands.

Jesus went back again across the Jordan River to the place where John had been baptizing, and stayed there. Many people came to him. "John did no mighty works," they said, "but everything he said about this man was true." And many people there believed in him.

Seven

"TO SEARCH OUT AND TO SAVE WHAT WAS LOST"

The Would-Be Followers of Jesus
As the days drew near when Jesus would be taken up to heaven, he made up his mind and set out on his way to Jerusalem. He sent messengers ahead of him, who left and went into a Samaritan village to get everything ready for him. But the people there would not receive him, because it was plain that he was going to Jerusalem. When the disciples James and John saw this, they said, "Lord, do you want us to call fire down from heaven and destroy them?"

Jesus turned and rebuked them; and they went on to another village.

As they went on their way, a certain man said to Jesus, "I will follow you wherever you go."

Jesus said to him, "Foxes have holes, and birds have nests, but the Son of Man has no place to lie down and rest." He said to another man, "Follow me."

But that man said, "Sir, first let me go back and bury my father."

Jesus answered, "Let the dead bury their own dead. You go and preach the Kingdom of God."

Another man said, "I will follow you, sir; but first let me go and say good-bye to my family."

Jesus said to him, "Anyone who starts to plow and then keeps looking back is of no use for the Kingdom of God."

"TO SEARCH OUT AND TO SAVE WHAT WAS LOST"

Jesus Sends Out the Seventy-two

After this the Lord chose another seventy-two men and sent them out, two by two, to go ahead of him to every town and place where he himself was about to go. He said to them, "There is a large harvest, but few workers to gather it in. Pray to the owner of the harvest that he will send out workers to gather in his harvest. Go! I am sending you like lambs among wolves. Don't take a purse, or a beggar's bag, or shoes; don't stop to greet anyone on the road. Whenever you go into a house, first say, 'Peace be with this house.' If a peace-loving man lives there, let your greeting of peace remain on him; if not, take back your greeting of peace. Stay in that same house, eating and drinking what they offer you, because a worker should be given his pay. Don't move around from one house to another. Whenever you go into a town and are made welcome, eat what is set before you, heal the sick in that town, and say to the people there, 'The Kingdom of God has come near you.' But whenever you go into a town and are not welcomed there, go out in the streets and say, 'Even the dust from your town that sticks to our feet we wipe off against you; but remember this, the Kingdom of God has come near you!' I tell you that on the Judgment Day God will show more mercy to Sodom than to that town!

"How terrible it will be for you, Chorazin! How terrible for you too, Bethsaida! If the miracles which were performed in you had been performed in Tyre and Sidon, long ago the people there would have sat down, put on sackcloth, and sprinkled ashes on themselves to show that they had turned from their sins! God will show more mercy on the Judgment Day to Tyre and Sidon than to you. And as for you, Capernaum! You wanted to lift yourself up to heaven? You will be thrown down to hell!"

Jesus said to his disciples, "Whoever listens to you, listens to me; whoever rejects you, rejects me; and whoever rejects me, rejects the one who sent me."

The Return of the Seventy-two

The seventy-two men came back in great joy. "Lord," they said, "even the demons obeyed us when we commanded them in your name!"

Jesus answered them, "I saw Satan fall like lightning from heaven. Listen! I have given you authority, so that you can walk on snakes and scorpions, and over all the power of the Enemy, and nothing will hurt you. But don't be glad because the evil spirits obey you; rather be glad because your names are written in heaven."

At that time Jesus was filled with joy by the Holy Spirit, and said, "Father, Lord of heaven and earth! I thank you because you have shown to the unlearned what you have hidden from the wise and learned. Yes, Father, this was done by your own choice and pleasure.

"My Father has given me all things. No one knows who the Son is except the Father, and no one knows who the Father is except the Son and those to whom the Son wants to reveal him."

Then Jesus turned to the disciples and said to them privately, "How fortunate you are, to see the things you see! Many prophets and kings, I tell you, wanted to see what you see, but they could not, and to hear what you hear, but they did not."

The Parable of the Good Samaritan

A certain teacher of the Law came up and tried to trap Jesus. "Teacher," he asked, "what must I do to receive eternal life?"

Jesus answered him, "What do the Scriptures say? How do you interpret them?"

The man answered, " 'You must love the Lord your God with all your heart, with all your soul, with all your strength, and with all your mind'; and, 'You must love your fellow-man as yourself.' "

"Your answer is correct," replied Jesus; "do this and you will live."

But the teacher of the Law wanted to put himself in the right, so he asked Jesus, "Who is my fellow-man?"

Jesus answered, "There was a man who was going down from Jerusalem to Jericho, when robbers attacked him, stripped him, and beat him up, leaving him half dead. It so happened that a priest was going down that road; when he saw the man he walked on by, on the other side. In the same way a Levite also came there, went over and looked at the man, and then walked on by, on the other side. But a certain Samaritan who was traveling that way came upon him, and when he saw the man his heart was filled with pity. He went over to him, poured oil and wine on his wounds and bandaged them; then he put the man on his own animal and took him to an inn, where he took care of him. The next day he took out two silver coins and gave them to the innkeeper. 'Take care of him,' he told the innkeeper, 'and when I come back this way I will pay you back whatever you spend on him.' "

And Jesus concluded, "In your opinion, which one of these three acted like a fellow-man toward the man attacked by the robbers?"

The teacher of the Law answered, "The one who was kind to him."

Jesus replied, "You go, then, and do the same."

Jesus' Teaching on Prayer

One time Jesus was praying in a certain place. When he finished, one of his disciples said to him, "Lord, teach us to pray, just as John taught his disciples."

Jesus said to them, "This is what you should pray: 'Father: May your holy name be honored; may your Kingdom come. Give us day by day the food we need. Forgive us our sins, because we forgive everyone who does us wrong. And do not bring us to hard testing.' "

And Jesus said to his disciples, "Suppose one of you should go to a friend's house at midnight and tell him, 'Friend, let me borrow three loaves of bread. A friend of mine who is on a trip has just come to my house and I don't have any food for him!' And suppose your friend should answer from inside, 'Don't bother me! The door is already locked, and my children and I are in bed. I can't get up to give you anything.' Well, what then? I tell you, even if he will not get up and give you the bread because he is your friend, yet he will get up and give you everything you need because you are not ashamed to keep on asking. And so I say to you: Ask, and you will receive; seek, and you will find; knock, and the door will be opened to you. For everyone who asks will receive, and he who seeks will find, and the door will be opened to him who knocks. Would any of you who are fathers give your son a snake when he asks for fish? Or would you give him a scorpion when he asks for an egg? As bad as you are, you know how to give good things to your children. How much more, then, the Father in heaven will give the Holy Spirit to those who ask him!"

True Happiness
When Jesus had said this, a woman spoke up from the crowd and said to him, "How happy is the woman who bore you and nursed you!"

But Jesus answered, "Rather, how happy are those who hear the word of God and obey it!"

As the people crowded around Jesus he went on to say, "How evil are the people of this day! They ask for a miracle, but none will be given them except the miracle of Jonah. In the same way that the prophet Jonah was a sign for the people of Nineveh, so the Son of Man will be a sign for the people of this day. On the Judgment Day the Queen from the South will stand up and accuse the people of today, because she traveled halfway around the world to listen to Solomon's wise teaching; and there is something here, I tell you, greater than Solomon. On the Judgment Day the people of Nineveh will stand up and accuse you, because they turned from their sins when they heard Jonah preach; and there is something here, I tell you, greater than Jonah!

"No one lights a lamp and then hides it or puts it under a bowl; instead, he puts it on the lampstand, so that people may see the light as they come in. Your eyes are like a lamp for the body. When your eyes are clear your whole body is full of light; but when your eyes are bad your whole body will be in darkness. Be careful, then, that the light in you is not darkness. If, then, your whole body is full of light, with no part of it in darkness, it will be bright all over, as when a lamp shines on you with its brightness."

When Jesus finished speaking, a Pharisee invited him to eat with him; so he went in and sat down to eat. The Pharisee was surprised when he noticed that Jesus had not washed before eating. So the Lord said to him, "Now, then, you Pharisees clean the cup and plate on the outside, but inside you are full of violence and evil. Fools! Did not God, who made the outside, also make the inside? But give what is in your cups and plates to the poor, and everything will be clean for you.

"How terrible for you, Pharisees! You give to God one tenth of the seasoning herbs, such as mint and rue and all the other herbs, but you neglect justice and love for God. These you should practice, without neglecting the others.

"How terrible for you, Pharisees! You love the reserved seats in the synagogues, and to be greeted with respect in the market places. How terrible for you! You are like unmarked graves which people walk on without knowing it."

One of the teachers of the Law said to him, "Teacher, when you say this you insult us too!"

Jesus answered, "How terrible for you, too, teachers of the Law! You put loads on men's backs which are hard to carry, but you yourselves will not stretch out a finger to help them carry those loads. How terrible for you! You make fine tombs for the prophets—the very prophets your ancestors murdered. You yourselves admit, then, that you approve of what your ancestors did; because they murdered the prophets, and you build their tombs. For this reason the Wisdom of God said, 'I will send them prophets and messengers; they will kill some of them and persecute others.' So the people of this time will be punished for the murder of all the prophets killed since the creation of the world, from the murder of Abel to the murder of Zechariah, who was killed between the altar and the holy place. Yes, I tell you, the people of this time will be punished for them all!

"How terrible for you, teachers of the Law! You have kept the key that opens the door to the house of knowledge; you yourselves will not go in, and you stop those who are trying to go in!"

When Jesus left that place the teachers of the Law and the Pharisees began to criticize him bitterly and ask him questions about many things, trying to lay traps for him and catch him in something wrong he might say.

Trust in God's Providence

As thousands of people crowded together, so that they were stepping on each other, Jesus said first to his disciples, "Be on guard against the yeast of the Pharisees—I mean their hypocrisy. Whatever is covered up will be uncovered, and every secret will be made known. So then, whatever you have said in the dark will be heard in broad daylight, and whatever you have whispered in men's ears in a closed room will be shouted from the housetops.

"I tell you, my friends, do not be afraid of those who kill the body but cannot afterward do anything worse. I will show you whom to fear: fear God who, after killing, has the authority to throw into hell. Yes, I tell you, be afraid of him!

"Aren't five sparrows sold for two pennies? Yet not a single one of them is forgotten by God. Even the hairs of your head have all been numbered. So do not be afraid; you are worth much more than many sparrows!

"I tell you: whoever declares publicly that he belongs to me, the Son of Man will do the same for him before the angels of God; but whoever denies publicly that he belongs to me, the Son of Man will also deny him before the angels of God.

"Anyone who says a word against the Son of Man can be forgiven; but the one who says evil things against the Holy Spirit will not be forgiven.

"When they bring you to be tried in the synagogues, or before governors or rulers, do not be worried about how you will defend yourself or what you will say. For the Holy Spirit will teach you at that time what you should say."

A man in the crowd said to him, "Teacher, tell my brother to divide with me the property our father left us."

Jesus answered him, "Man, who gave me the right to judge, or to divide the property between you two?" And he went on to say to them all, "Watch out, and guard yourselves from all kinds of greed; because a man's true life is not made up of the things he owns, no matter how rich he may be."

Then Jesus told them this parable, "A rich man had land which bore good crops. He began to think to himself, 'I don't have a place to keep all my crops. What can I do? This is what I will do,' he told himself; 'I will tear my barns down and build bigger ones, where I will store the grain and all my other goods. Then I will say to myself, Lucky man! You have all the good things you need for many years. Take life easy, eat, drink, and enjoy yourself!' But God said to him, 'You fool! This very night you will have to give up your life; then who will get all these things you have kept for yourself?'"

And Jesus concluded, "This is how it is with those who pile up riches for themselves but are not rich in God's sight."

Then Jesus said to the disciples, "This is why I tell you: do not be worried about the food you need to stay alive, or about the clothes you need for your body. Life is much more important than food, and body much more important than clothes. Look at the crows: they don't plant seeds or gather a harvest; they don't have storage rooms or barns; God feeds them! You are worth so much more than birds! Which one of you can live a few more years by worrying about it? If you can't manage even such a small thing, why worry about the other things? Look how the wild flowers grow: they don't work or make clothes for themselves. But I tell you that not even Solomon, as rich as he was, had clothes as beautiful as one of these flowers. It is God who clothes the wild grass—grass that is here today, gone tomorrow, burned up in the oven. Won't he be all the more sure to clothe you? How little faith you have! So don't be all upset, always concerned about what you will eat and drink. (For the heathen of this world are always concerned about all these things.) Your Father knows that you need these things. Instead, be concerned with his Kingdom, and he will provide you with these things.

"Do not be afraid, little flock; because your Father is

pleased to give you the Kingdom. Sell all your belongings and give the money to the poor. Provide for yourselves purses that don't wear out, and save your riches in heaven, where they will never decrease, because no thief can get to them, no moth can destroy them. For your heart will always be where your riches are.

"Be ready for whatever comes, with your clothes fastened tight at the waist and your lamps lit, like servants who are waiting for their master to come back from a wedding feast. When he comes and knocks, they will open the door for him at once. How happy are those servants whose master finds them awake and ready when he returns! I tell you, he will fasten his belt, have them sit down, and wait on them. How happy are they if he finds them ready, even if he should come as late as midnight or even later! And remember this! If the man of the house knew the time when the thief would come, he would not let the thief break into his house. And you, too, be ready, because the Son of Man will come at an hour when you are not expecting him."

The Faithful or the Unfaithful Servant.

Peter said, "Lord, are you telling this parable to us, or do you mean it for everyone?"

The Lord answered, "Who, then, is the faithful and wise servant? He is the one whom his master will put in charge, to run the household and give the other servants their share of the food at the proper time. How happy is that servant if his master finds him doing this when he comes home! Indeed, I tell you, the master will put that servant in charge of all his property. But if that servant says to himself, 'My master is taking a long time to come back,' and begins to beat the other servants, both the men and the women, and eats and drinks and gets drunk, then the master will come back some day when the servant does not expect him and at a time he does not know. The master will cut him to pieces, and make him share the fate of the disobedient.

"The servant who knows what his master wants him to do, but does not get himself ready and do what his master wants, will be punished with a heavy whipping; but the servant who does not know what his master wants, and does something for which he deserves a whipping, will be punished with a light whipping. The man to whom much is given, of him much is required; the man to whom more is given, of him much more is required.

"I came to set the earth on fire; how I wish it were already kindled! I have a baptism to receive; how distressed I am until it is over! Do you suppose that I came to bring peace to the world? Not peace, I tell you, but division. From now on a family of five will be divided, three against two, two against three. Fathers will be against their sons, and sons against their fathers; mothers will be against their daughters, and daughters against their mothers; mothers-in-law will be against their daughters-in-law, and daughters-in-law against their mothers-in-law."

Jesus said also to the people, "When you see a cloud coming up in the west, at once you say, 'It is going to rain,' and it does. And when you feel the south wind blowing, you say, 'It is going to get hot,' and it does. Hypocrites! You can look at the earth and the sky and tell what it means; why, then, don't you know the meaning of this present time?

"Why do you not judge for yourselves the right thing to do? If a man brings a lawsuit against you and takes you to court, do your best to settle the matter with him while you are on the way, so that he won't drag you before the judge, and the judge hand you over to the police, and the police put you in jail. You will not come out of there, I tell you, until you pay the last penny of your fine."

Turn from Your Sins or Die
At that time some people were there who told Jesus about the Galileans whom Pilate had killed while they were offering sacrifices to God. Jesus answered them, "Because these Galileans were killed in that way, do you think it proves that they were worse sinners than all the other Galileans? No! I tell you that if you do not turn from your sins, you will all die as they did. What about those eighteen in Siloam who were killed when the tower fell on them? Do you suppose this proves that

they were worse than all the other people living in Jerusalem, No! I tell you that if you do not turn from your sins, you will all die as they did."

Then Jesus told them this parable, "A man had a fig tree growing in his vineyard. He went looking for figs on it but found one. So he said to his gardener, "Look, for three years I have been coming here looking for figs on this fig tree and I haven't found any. Cut it down! Why should it go on using up the soil?' But the gardener answered, 'Leave it alone, sir, just this one year; I will dig a trench around it and fill it up with fertilizer. Then if the tree bears figs next year, so much the better; if not, then you will have it cut down.' "

Jesus Heals a Crippled Woman on the Sabbath
One Sabbath day Jesus was teaching in a synagogue. A woman was there who had an evil spirit in her that had kept her sick for eighteen years; she was bent over and could not straighten up at all. When Jesus saw her he called out to her, "Woman, you are free from your sickness!" He placed his hands on her and at once she straightened herself up and praised God.

The official of the synagogue was angry that Jesus had healed on the Sabbath; so he spoke up and said to the people, "There are six days in which we should work; so come during those days and be healed, but not on the Sabbath!"

The Lord answered him by saying, "You hypocrites! Any one of you would untie his ox or his donkey from the stall and take it out to give it water on the Sabbath. Now here is this descendant of Abraham whom Satan has kept in bonds for eighteen years; should she not be freed from her bonds on the Sabbath?" His answer made all his enemies ashamed of themselves, while all the people rejoiced over every wonderful thing that he did.

The Narrow Door
Jesus went through towns and villages, teaching and making his way toward Jerusalem. Someone asked him, "Sir, will just a few people be saved?"

Jesus answered them, "Do your best to go in through

the narrow door; because many people, I tell you, will try to go in but will not be able. The master of the house will get up and close the door; then when you stand outside and begin to knock on the door and say, 'Open the door for us, sir!' he will answer you, 'I don't know where you come from!' Then you will answer back, 'We ate and drank with you; you taught in our town!' He will say again, 'I don't know where you come from. Get away from me, all you evildoers!' What crying and gnashing of teeth there will be when you see Abraham, Isaac, and Jacob and all the prophets in the Kingdom of God, while you are thrown out! People will come from the east and the west, from the north and the south, and sit at the table in the Kingdom of God. Then those who are now last will be first, and those who are now first will be last."

Jesus' Love for Jerusalem

At that same time some Pharisees came to Jesus and said to him, "You must get out of here and go somewhere else, because Herod wants to kill you."

Jesus answered them, "Go tell that fox: 'I am driving out demons and performing cures today and tomorrow, and on the third day I shall finish my work.' Yet I must be on my way today, tomorrow, and the next day; it is not right for a prophet to be killed anywhere except in Jerusalem.

"Jerusalem, Jerusalem! You kill the prophets, you stone the messengers God has sent you! How many times I wanted to put my arms around all your people, just as a hen gathers her chicks under her wings, but you would not let me! Now your home will be completely forsaken. You will not see me, I tell you, until the time comes when you say, 'God bless him who comes in the name of the Lord.' "

Jesus Visits Martha and Mary

As Jesus and his disciples went on their way, he came to a certain village where a woman named Martha welcomed him in her home. She had a sister named Mary, who sat down at the feet of the Lord and listened to his teaching. Martha was upset over all the work she had to do; so she came and said, "Lord, don't you care that my sister has left me to do all the work by myself? Tell her to come and help me!"

The Lord answered her, "Martha, Martha! You are worried and troubled over so many things, but just one is needed. Mary has chosen the right thing, and it will not be taken away from her."

Jesus Heals a Sick Man

One Sabbath day Jesus went to eat a meal at the home of one of the leading Pharisees; and people were watching Jesus closely. A man whose legs and arms were swollen came to Jesus, and Jesus spoke up and asked the teachers of the Law and the Pharisees, "Does our Law allow healing on the Sabbath, or not?"

But they would not say a thing. Jesus took the man, healed him, and sent him away. Then he said to them, "If any one of you had a son or an ox that happened to fall in a well on a Sabbath, would you not pull him out at once on the Sabbath itself?"

But they were not able to answer him about this.

Humility and Hospitality

Jesus noticed how some of the guests were choosing the best places, so he told this parable to all of them, "When someone invites you to a wedding feast, do not sit down in the best place. It could happen that someone more important than you had been invited, and your host, who invited both of you, would come and say to you, 'Let him have this place.' Then you would be ashamed and have to sit in the lowest place. Instead, when you are invited, go and sit in the lowest place, so that your host will come to you and say, 'Come on up, my friend, to a better place.' This will bring you honor in the presence of all the other guests. Because everyone who makes himself great will be humbled, and everyone who humbles himself will be made great."

Then Jesus said to his host, "When you give a lunch or a dinner, do not invite your friends, or your brothers, or your relatives, or your rich neighbors—because they will invite you back and in this way you will be paid for what you did. When you give a feast, invite the poor, the crippled, the lame, and the blind, and you will be blessed; because they are not able to pay you back. You will be paid by God when the good people rise from death."

The Parable of the Great Feast

One of the men sitting at the table heard this and said to Jesus, "How happy are those who will sit at the table in the Kingdom of God!"

Jesus said to him, "There was a man who was giving a great feast, to which he invited many people. At the time for the feast he sent his servant to tell his guests, 'Come, everything is ready!' But they all began, one after another, to make excuses. The first one told the servant, 'I bought a field, and have to go and look at it; please accept my apologies.' Another one said, 'I bought five pairs of oxen and am on my way to try them out; please accept my apologies.' Another one said, 'I have just gotten married, and for this reason I cannot come.' The servant went back and told all this to his master. The master of the house was furious and said to his servant, 'Hurry out to the streets and alleys of the town, and bring back the poor, the crippled, the blind, and the lame.' Soon the servant said, 'Your order has been carried out, sir, but there is room for more.' So the master said to the servant, 'Go out to the country roads and lanes, and make people come in, so that my house will be full. I tell you all that none of those men who were invited will taste my dinner!' "

The Cost of Being a Disciple

Great crowds of people were going along with Jesus. He turned and said to them, "Whoever comes to me cannot be my disciple unless he hates his father and his mother, his wife and his children, his brothers and his sisters, and himself as well. Whoever does not carry his own cross and come after me cannot be my disciple. If one of you is planning to build a tower, he sits down first and figures out what it will cost, to see if he has enough money to finish the job. If he doesn't, he will not be able to finish the tower after laying the foundation; and all who see what happened will make fun of him. 'This man began to build but can't finish the job!' they will say. If a king goes out with ten thousand men to fight another king, who comes against him with twenty thousand men, he will sit down first and decide if he is strong enough to face that other king. If he isn't, he will send messengers to meet the other king, while he is still a long way off, to ask for terms of peace. In the same way," concluded Jesus, "none of you can be my disciple unless he gives up everything he has."

The Lost Son
Jesus went on to say, "There was a man who had two sons. The younger one said to him, 'Father, give me now my share of the property.' So the man divided the property between his two sons. After a few days the younger son sold his part of the property and left home with the money. He went to a country far away, where he wasted his money in reckless living. He spent everything he had. Then a severe famine spread over that country, and he was left without a thing. So he went to work for one of the citizens of that country, who sent him out to his farm to take care of the pigs. He wished he could fill himself with the bean pods the pigs ate, but no one gave him anything to eat. At last he came to his senses and said, 'All my father's hired workers have more than they can eat, and here I am, about to starve! I will get up and go to my father and say, "Father, I have sinned against God and against you. I am no longer fit to be called your son; treat me as one of your hired workers."' So he got up and started back to his father.

"He was still a long way from home when his father saw him; his heart was filled with pity and he ran, threw his arms around his son, and kissed him. 'Father,' the son said, 'I have sinned against God and against you. I am no longer fit to be called your son.' But the father called his servants: 'Hurry!' he said. 'Bring the best robe and put it on him. Put a ring on his finger and shoes on his feet. Then go get the prize calf and kill it, and let us celebrate with a feast! Because this son of mine was dead, but now he is alive; he was lost, but now he has been found.' And so the feasting began.

"The older son, in the meantime, was out in the field.

On his way back, when he came close to the house, he heard the music and dancing. He called one of the servants and asked him. 'What's going on?' 'Your brother came back home,' the servant answered, 'and your father killed the prize calf, because he got him back safe and sound.' The older brother was so angry that he would not go into the house; so his father came out and begged him to come in. 'Look,' he answered back to his father, 'all these years I have worked like a slave for you, and I never disobeyed your orders. What have you given me? Not even a goat for me to have a feast with my friends! But this son of yours wasted all your property on prostitutes, and when he comes back home you kill the prize calf for him!' 'My son,' the father answered, 'you are always here with me and everything I have is yours. But we had to have a feast and be happy, because your brother was dead, but now he is alive; he was lost, but now he has been found.' "

The Shrewd Manager
Jesus said to his disciples, "There was a rich man who had a manager, and he was told that the manager was wasting his master's money. He called him in and said, 'What is this I hear about you? Turn in a complete account of your handling of my property, because you cannot be my manager any longer.' 'My master is going to dismiss me from my job,' the man said to himself. 'What shall I do? I am not strong enough to dig ditches, and I am ashamed to beg. Now I know what I will do! Then when my job is gone I shall have friends who will welcome me in their homes.' So he called in all the people who were in debt to his master. He said to the first one, 'How much do you owe my master?' 'One hundred barrels of olive oil,' he answered. 'Here is your account,' the manager told him; 'sit down and write fifty.' He said to another one, 'And you—how much do you owe?' 'A thousand bushels of wheat,' he answered. 'Here is your account,' the manager told him; 'write eight hundred.' The master of this dishonest manager praised him for doing such a shrewd thing; because the people of this world are much more shrewd in handling their affairs than the people who belong to the light."

And Jesus went on to say, "And so I tell you: make friends for yourselves with worldly wealth, so that when it gives out you will be welcomed in the eternal home. Whoever is faithful in small matters will be faithful in large ones; whoever is dishonest in small matters will be dishonest in large ones. If, then, you have not been faithful in handling worldly wealth, how can you be trusted with true wealth? And if you have not been faithful with what belongs to someone else, who will give you what belongs to you?

"No servant can be the slave of two masters; he will hate one and love the other; he will be loyal to one and despise the other. You cannot serve both God and money."

Some Sayings of Jesus

The Pharisees heard all this, and they made fun of Jesus, because they loved money. Jesus said to them, "You are the ones who make yourselves look right in men's sight, but God knows your hearts. For what men think is of great value is worth nothing in God's sight.

"The Law of Moses and the writings of the prophets were in effect up to the time of John the Baptist; since then the Good News about the Kingdom of God is being told, and everyone forces his way in. But it is easier for heaven and earth to disappear than for the smallest detail of the Law to be done away with.

"Any man who divorces his wife and marries another woman commits adultery; and the man who marries a divorced woman commits adultery.

"There was once a rich man who dressed in the most expensive clothes and lived in great luxury every day. There was also a poor man, named Lazarus, full of sores, who used to be brought to the rich man's door, hoping to fill himself with the bits of food that fell from the rich man's table. Even the dogs would come and lick his sores. The poor man died and was carried by the angels to Abraham's side, at the feast in heaven; the rich man died and was buried. He was in great pain in Hades; and he looked up and saw Abraham, far away, with Lazarus at his side. So he called out, 'Father Abraham! Take pity on me, and send Lazarus to dip his finger in some water and cool off my tongue, because I am in great pain in this fire!' But Abraham said, 'Remember, my son, that in your lifetime you were given all the good things, while Lazarus got all the bad things; but now he is enjoying himself here, while you are in pain. Besides all that, there is a deep pit lying between us, so that those who want to cross over from here to you cannot do it, nor can anyone cross over to us from where you are.' The rich man said, 'Well, father, I beg you, send Lazarus to my father's house, where I have five brothers; let him go and warn them so that they, at least, will not come to this place of pain.' Abraham said, 'Your brothers have Moses and the prophets to warn them; let your brothers listen to what they say.' The rich man answered, 'That is not enough, father Abraham! But if someone were to rise from death and go to them, then they would turn from their sins.' But Abraham said, 'If they will not listen to Moses and the prophets, they will not be convinced even if someone were to rise from death.'"

Sin

Jesus said to his disciples, "Things that make people fall into sin are bound to happen; but how terrible for the one who makes them happen! It would be better for him if a large millstone were tied around his neck and he were thrown into the sea, than for him to cause one of these little ones to sin. Be on your guard!

"If your brother sins, rebuke him, and if he repents, forgive him. If he sins against you seven times in one day, and each time he comes to you, saying, 'I repent,' you must forgive him."

The apostles said to the Lord, "Make our faith greater."

The Lord answered, "If you had faith as big as a mustard seed, you could say to this mulberry tree, 'Pull yourself up by the roots and plant yourself in the sea!' and it would obey you.

"Suppose one of you has a servant who is plowing or looking after the sheep. When he comes in from the field, do you say to him, 'Hurry along and eat your meal'? Of course not! Instead, you say to him, 'Get my supper ready, then put on your apron and wait on me while I eat and drink; after that you may eat and drink.' The servant does not deserve thanks for obeying orders, does he? It is the same with you; when you have done all you have been told to do, say, 'We are ordinary servants; we have only done our duty.'"

The Death of Lazarus

A man named Lazarus, who lived in Bethany, became sick. Bethany was the town where Mary and her sister Martha lived. (This Mary was the one who poured the perfume on the Lord's feet and wiped them with her hair; it was her brother Lazarus who was sick.) The sisters sent Jesus a message, "Lord, your dear friend is sick."

When Jesus heard it he said, "The final result of this sickness will not be the death of Lazarus; this has happened to bring glory to God, and will be the means by which the Son of God will receive glory."

Jesus loved Martha and her sister, and Lazarus. When he received the news that Lazarus was sick, he stayed where he was for two more days. Then he said to his disciples, "Let us go back to Judea."

"Teacher," the disciples answered, "just a short time ago the Jews wanted to stone you; and you plan to go back there?"

Jesus said, "A day has twelve hours, has it not? So if a man walks in broad daylight he does not stumble, because he sees the light of this world. But if he walks during the night he stumbles, because there is no light in him." Jesus said this, then added, "Our friend Lazarus has fallen asleep, but I will go wake him up."

The disciples answered, "If he is asleep, Lord, he will get well."

But Jesus meant that Lazarus had died; they thought he meant natural sleep. So Jesus told them plainly, "Lazarus is dead; but for your sake I am glad that I was not with him, so you will believe. Let us go to him."

Thomas (called the Twin) said to his fellow disciples, "Let us all go along with the Teacher, so that we may die with him!"

Jesus the Resurrection and the Life

When Jesus arrived, he found that Lazarus had been buried four days before. Bethany was less than two miles from Jerusalem, and many Jews had come to see Martha and Mary to comfort them about their brother's death.

When Martha heard that Jesus was coming, she went out to meet him; but Mary stayed at home. Martha said to Jesus, "If you had been here, Lord, my brother would not have died! But I know that even now God will give you whatever you ask of him."

"Your brother will rise to life," Jesus told her.

"I know," she replied, "that he will rise to life on the last day."

Jesus said to her, "I am the resurrection and the life. Whoever believes in me will live, even though he dies; and whoever lives and believes in me will never die. Do you believe this?"

"Yes, Lord!" she answered. "I do believe that you are the Messiah, the Son of God, who was to come into the world."

After Martha said this she went back and called her sister Mary privately. "The Teacher is here," she told her, "and is asking for you." When Mary heard this she got up and hurried out to meet him. (Jesus had not arrived in the village yet, but was still in the place where Martha had met him.) The Jews who were in the house with Mary comforting her followed her when they saw her get up and hurry out. They thought that she was going to the grave, to weep there.

When Mary arrived where Jesus was and saw him, she fell at his feet. "Lord," she said, "if you had been here, my brother would not have died!"

Jesus saw her weeping, and the Jews who had come with her weeping also; his heart was touched, and he was deeply moved. "Where have you buried him?" he asked them.

"Come and see, Lord," they answered.

Jesus wept. So the Jews said, "See how much he loved him!"

But some of them said, "He opened the blind man's eyes, didn't he? Could he not have kept Lazarus from dying?"

Lazarus Brought to Life

Deeply moved once more, Jesus went to the tomb, which was a cave with a stone placed at the entrance. "Take the stone away!" Jesus ordered.

Martha, the dead man's sister, answered, "There will be a bad smell, Lord. He has been buried four days!"

Jesus said to her, "Didn't I tell you that you would see God's glory if you believed?" They took the stone away. Jesus looked up and said, "I thank you, Father, that you listen to me. I know that you always listen to me, but I say this because of the people here, so they will believe that you sent me." After he had said this he called out in a loud voice, "Lazarus, come out!" The dead man came out, his hands and feet wrapped in grave cloths, and a cloth around his face. "Untie him," Jesus told them, "and let him go."

The Plot Against Jesus

Many of the Jews who had come to visit Mary saw what Jesus did, and believed in him. But some of them returned to the Pharisees and told them what Jesus had done. So the Pharisees and the chief priests met with the Council and said, "What shall we do? All the mighty works this man is doing! If we let him go on in this way everyone will believe in him, and the Roman authorities will take action and destroy the temple and our whole nation!"

One of them, named Caiaphas, who was High Priest that year, said, "You do not know a thing! Don't you realize that it is better for you to have one man die for the people, instead of the whole nation being destroyed?" Actually, he did not say this of his own accord; rather, as he was High Priest that year, he was prophesying that Jesus was going to die for the Jewish people, and not only for them, but also to bring together into one body all the scattered children of God.

From that day on the Jewish authorities made plans to kill Jesus. So Jesus did not travel openly in Judea, but left and went to a place near the desert, to a town named Ephraim, where he stayed with the disciples.

Jesus Makes Ten Lepers Clean
As Jesus made his way to Jerusalem he went between Samaria and Galilee. He was going into a village when he was met by ten lepers. They stood at a distance and shouted, "Jesus! Master! Have pity on us!"

Jesus saw them and said to them, "Go and let the priests examine you."

On the way they were made clean. One of them, when he saw that he was healed, came back, praising God in a loud voice. He threw himself to the ground at Jesus' feet, thanking him. The man was a Samaritan. Jesus spoke up, "There were ten men made clean; where are the other nine? Why is this foreigner the only one who came back to give thanks to God?" And Jesus said to him, "Get up and go; your faith has made you well."

The Coming of the Kingdom
Some Pharisees asked Jesus when the Kingdom of God would come. His answer was, "The Kingdom of God does not come in such a way as to be seen. No one will say, 'Look, here it is!' or, 'There it is'; because the Kingdom of God is within you."

Then he said to the disciples, "The time will come when you will wish you could see one of the days of the Son of Man, but you will not see it. There will be those who will say to you, 'Look, over there!' or 'Look, over here!' But don't go out looking for it. As the lightning flashes across the sky and lights it up from one side to the other, so will the Son of Man be in his day. But first he must suffer much and be rejected by the people of this day. As it was in the time of Noah, so shall it be in the days of the Son of Man. Everybody kept on eating and drinking, men and women married, up to the very day Noah went into the ark and the Flood came and killed them all. It will be as it was in the time of Lot. Everybody kept on eating and drinking, buying and selling, planting and building. On the day Lot left Sodom, fire and sulphur rained down from heaven and killed them all. That is how it will be on the day the Son of Man is revealed.

"The man who is on the roof of his house on that day must not go down into the house to get his belongings that are there; in the same way, the man who is out in the field must not go back to the house. Remember Lot's wife! Whoever tries to save his own life will lose it; whoever loses his life will save it. On that night, I tell you, there will be two men sleeping in one bed: one will be taken away, the other left behind. Two women will be grinding meal together: one will be taken away, the other left behind. [Two men will be in the field: one will be taken away, the other left behind.]"

The disciples asked him, "Where, Lord?"

Jesus answered, "Where there is a dead body the vultures will gather."

The Parable of the Widow and the Judge
Then Jesus told them this parable, to teach them that they should always pray and never become discouraged. "There was a judge in a certain town who neither feared God nor respected men. And there was a widow in that same town who kept coming to him and pleading for her rights: 'Help me against my opponent!' For a long time the judge was not willing, but at last he said to himself, 'Even though I don't fear God or respect men, yet because of all the trouble this widow is giving me I will see to it that she gets her rights; or else she will keep on coming and finally wear me out!'"

And the Lord continued, "Listen to what that corrupt judge said. Now, will God not judge in favor of his own people who cry to him for help day and night? Will he be slow to help them? I tell you, he will judge in their favor, and do it quickly. But will the Son of Man find faith on earth when he comes?"

The Parable of the Pharisee and the Tax Collector
Jesus also told this parable to people who were sure of their own goodness and despised everybody else. "Two men went up to the temple to pray; one was a Pharisee, the other a tax collector. The Pharisee stood apart by himself and prayed, 'I thank you, God, that I am not

greedy, dishonest, or immoral, like everybody else; I thank you that I am not like that tax collector. I fast two days every week, and I give you one tenth of all my income.' But the tax collector stood at a distance and would not even raise his face to heaven, but beat on his breast and said, 'God, have pity on me, a sinner!' I tell you," said Jesus, "this man, and not the other, was in the right with God when he went home. Because everyone who makes himself great will be humbled, and everyone who humbles himself will be made great."

Jesus Blesses Little Children

Some people brought children to Jesus for him to touch them, but the disciples scolded those people. When Jesus noticed it, he was angry and said to his disciples, "Let the children come to me, and do not stop them, because the Kingdom of God belongs to such as these. Remember this! Whoever does not receive the Kingdom of God like a child will never enter it." Then he took the children in his arms, placed his hands on each of them, and blessed them.

The Rich Man

As Jesus was starting again on his way, a man ran up, knelt before him, and asked him, "Good Teacher, what must I do to receive eternal life?"

"Why do you call me good?" Jesus asked him. "No one is good except God alone. You know the commandments: 'Do not murder; do not commit adultery; do not steal; do not lie; do not cheat; honor your father and mother.'"

"Teacher," the man said, "ever since I was young I have obeyed all these commandments."

Jesus looked straight at him with love and said, "You need only one thing. Go and sell all you have and give the money to the poor, and you will have riches in heaven; then come and follow me." When the man heard this, gloom spread over his face and he went away sad, because he was very rich.

Jesus then said to his disciples, "It will be very hard, I tell you, for a rich man to enter the Kingdom of heaven. I tell you something else: it is much harder for a rich man to enter the Kingdom of God than for a camel to go through the eye of a needle."

When the disciples heard this they were completely amazed. "Who can be saved, then?" they asked.

Jesus looked straight at them and answered, "This is impossible for men; but for God everything is possible."

Then Peter spoke up. "Look," he said, "we have left everything and followed you. What will we have?"

Jesus said to them, "I tell you this: when the Son of Man sits on his glorious throne in the New Age, then you twelve followers of mine will also sit on thrones, to judge the twelve tribes of Israel. And every one who has left houses or brothers or sisters or father or mother or children or fields for my sake, will receive a hundred times more, and will be given eternal life. But many who now are first will be last, and many who now are last will be first."

The Workers in the Vineyard

"The Kingdom of heaven is like the owner of a vineyard who went out early in the morning to hire some men to work in his vineyard. He agreed to pay them the regular wage, a silver coin a day, and sent them to work in his vineyard. He went out again to the market place at nine o'clock and saw some men standing there doing nothing, so he told them, 'You also go to work in the vineyard, and I will pay you a fair wage.' So they went. Then at twelve o'clock and again at three o'clock he did the same thing. It was nearly five o'clock when he went to the market place and saw some other men still standing there. 'Why are you wasting the whole day here doing nothing?' he asked them. 'It is because no one hired us,' they answered. 'Well, then, you also go to work in the vineyard,' he told them.

"When evening came, the owner told his foreman. 'Call the workers and pay them their wages, starting with those who were hired last, and ending with those who were hired first.' The men who had begun to work at five o'clock were paid a silver coin each. So when the men who were the first to be hired came to be paid, they thought they would get more; but they too were given a silver coin each. They took their money and started grumbling against the employer. 'These men who were hired last worked only one hour,' they said, 'while we put up with a whole day's work in the hot sun—yet you paid them the same as you paid us!' 'Listen, friend,' the owner answered one of them. 'I have not cheated you. After all, you agreed to do a day's work for a silver coin. Now, take your pay and go home. I want to give this man who was hired last as much as I have given you. Don't I have the right to do as I wish with my own money? Or are you jealous because I am generous?' "

And Jesus concluded, "So those who are last will be first, and those who are first will be last."

Jesus Teaches About Divorce

When Jesus finished saying these things, he left Galilee and went to the territory of Judea, on the other side of the Jordan River. Large crowds followed him, and he healed them there.

Some Pharisees came to him and tried to trap him by asking, "Does our Law allow man to divorce his wife for any reason he wishes?"

Jesus answered, "Haven't you read this scripture? 'In the beginning the Creator made them male and female, and said, "For this reason a man will leave his father and mother and unite with his wife, and the two will become one," ' So they are no longer two, but one. Man must not separate, then, what God has joined together."

The Pharisees asked him, "Why, then, did Moses give the commandment for a man to give his wife a divorce notice and send her away?"

Jesus answered, "Moses gave you permission to divorce your wives because you are so hard to teach. But it was not this way at the time of creation. I tell you, then, that any man who divorces his wife, and she has not been unfaithful, commits adultery if he marries some other woman."

His disciples said to him, "If this is the way it is between a man and his wife, it is better not to marry."

Jesus answered, "This teaching does not apply to everyone, but only to those to whom God has given it. For there are different reasons why men cannot marry:

some, because they were born that way; others, because men made them that way; and others do not marry because of the Kingdom of heaven. Let him who can do it accept this teaching."

Jesus Speaks a Third Time About His Death

They were now on the road going up to Jerusalem. Jesus was going ahead of the disciples, who were filled with alarm; the people who followed behind were afraid. Once again Jesus took the twelve disciples aside and spoke of the things that were going to happen to him. "Listen," he told them, "we are going up to Jerusalem where the Son of Man will be handed over to the chief priests and the teachers of the Law. They will condemn him to death and then hand him over to the Gentiles. These will make fun of him, spit on him, whip him, and kill him. And after three days he will rise to life."

The Request of James and John

Then James and John, the sons of Zebedee, came to Jesus. "Teacher," they said, "there is something we want you to do for us."

"What do you want me to do for you?" Jesus asked them.

They answered, "When you sit on your throne in the glorious Kingdom, we want you to let us sit with you, one at your right and one at your left."

Jesus said to them, "You don't know what you are asking for. Can you drink the cup that I must drink? Can you be baptized in the way I must be baptized?"

"We can," they answered.

Jesus said to them, "You will indeed drink the cup I must drink and be baptized in the way I must be baptized. But I do not have the right to choose who will sit at my right and my left. It is God who will give these places to those for whom he has prepared them."

When the other ten disciples heard about this they became angry with James and John. So Jesus called them all together to him and said, "You know that the men who are considered rulers have power over the people, and their leaders rule over them. This, however,

"TO SEARCH OUT AND TO SAVE WHAT WAS LOST"

is not the way it is among you. If one of you wants to be great, he must be the servant of the rest; and if one of you wants to be first, he must be the slave of all. For even the Son of Man did not come to be served; he came to serve and to give his life to redeem many people."

Jesus Heals a Blind Begger

Jesus was coming near Jericho, and a certain blind man was sitting by the road, begging. When he heard the crowd passing by he asked, "What is this?"

"Jesus of Nazareth is passing by," they told him.

He cried out, "Jesus! Son of David! Have mercy on me!"

The people in front scolded him and told him to be quiet. But he shouted even more loudly, "Son of David! Have mercy on me!"

So Jesus stopped and ordered that the blind man be brought to him. When he came near, Jesus asked him, "What do you want me to do for you?"

"Sir," he answered, "I want to see again."

Then Jesus said to him, "See! Your faith has made you well."

At once he was able to see, and he followed Jesus, giving thanks to God. When the crowd saw it, they all praised God.

Jesus and Zacchaeus

Jesus went on into Jericho and was passing through. There was a chief tax collector there, named Zacchaeus, who was rich. He was trying to see who Jesus was, but he was a little man and could not see Jesus because of the crowd. So he ran ahead of the crowd and climbed a sycamore tree to see Jesus, who would be going that way. When Jesus came to that place, he looked up and said to Zacchaeus, "Hurry down, Zacchaeus, because I must stay in your house today."

Zacchaeus hurried down and welcomed him with great joy. All the people who saw it started grumbling, "This man has gone as a guest to the home of a sinner!"

Zacchaeus stood up and said to the Lord, "Listen,

sir! I will give half my belongings to the poor; and if I have cheated anyone, I will pay him back four times as much."

Jesus said to him, "Salvation has come to this house today; this man, also, is a descendant of Abraham. For the Son of Man came to seek and to save the lost."

The Parable of the Gold Coins

While the people were listening to this, Jesus continued and told them a parable. He was now almost at Jerusalem, and they supposed that the Kingdom of God was just about to appear. So he said, "There was a nobleman who went to a country far away to be made king and then came back home. Before he left, he called his ten servants and gave them each a gold coin and told them, 'See what you can earn with this while I am gone.' Now, his countrymen hated him, and so they sent messengers after him to say, 'We don't want this man to be our king.'

"The nobleman was made king and came back. At once he ordered his servants, to whom he had given the money, to appear before him in order to find out how much they had earned. The first one came and said, 'Sir, I have earned ten gold coins with the one you gave me.' 'Well done,' he said; 'you are a good servant! Since you were faithful in small matters, I will put you in charge of ten cities.' The second servant came and said, 'Sir, I have earned five gold coins with the one you gave me.' To this one he said, 'You will be in charge of five cities.' Another servant came and said, 'Sir, here is your gold coin; I kept it hidden in a handkerchief. I was afraid of you, because you are a hard man. You take what is not yours, and reap what you did not plant.' He said to him, 'You bad servant! I will use your own words to condemn you! You know that I am a hard man, taking what is not mine and reaping what I have not planted. Well, then, why didn't you put my money in the bank? Then I would have received it back with interest when I returned.' Then he said to those who were standing there, 'Take the gold coin away from him and give it to the servant who has ten coins.' They said to him, 'Sir, he already has ten coins!' 'I tell you,' he replied, 'that to every one who has, even more will be given; but the one who does not have, even the little that he has will be taken away from him. Now, as for these enemies of mine who did not want me to be their king: bring them here and kill them before me!'"

Jesus said this and then went on to Jerusalem ahead of them.

Eight

"AND NOW MY SOUL IS DISTRESSED. WHAT AM I TO SAY?"

The Triumphant Entry into Jerusalem
The Jewish Feast of Passover was near, and many people went up from the country to Jerusalem, to perform the ceremony of purification before the feast. They were looking for Jesus, and as they gathered in the temple they asked one another, "What do you think? Surely he will not come to the feast, will he?" The chief priests and the Pharisees had given orders that if anyone knew where Jesus was he must report it, so they could arrest him.

As they came near Jerusalem, at the towns of Bethphage and Bethany, they came to the Mount of Olives. Jesus sent two of his disciples on ahead with these instructions, "Go to the village there ahead of you. As soon as you get there you will find a colt tied up that has never been ridden. Untie it and bring it here. And if someone asks you, 'Why are you doing that?' tell him, 'The Master needs it and will send it back here at once.'"

So they went and found a colt in the street, tied to the door of a house. As they were untying it, some of the bystanders asked them, "What are you doing, untying that colt?"

They answered just as Jesus had told them, so the men let them go. They brought the colt to Jesus, threw their cloaks over the animal, and Jesus got on. Many people spread their cloaks on the road, while others cut branches in the fields and spread them on the road.

When he came near Jerusalem, at the place where the road went down the Mount of Olives, the large

"AND NOW MY SOUL IS DISTRESSED.

crowd of his disciples began to thank God and praise him in loud voices for all the great things that they had seen: "God bless the king who comes in the name of the Lord! Peace in heaven, and glory to God!"

Then some of the Pharisees spoke up from the crowd to Jesus. "Teacher," they said, "command your disciples to be quiet!"

Jesus answered, "If they keep quiet, I tell you, the stones themselves will shout."

He came closer to the city and when he saw it he wept over it, saying, "If you only knew today what is needed for peace! But now you cannot see it! The days will come upon you when your enemies will surround you with barricades, blockade you, and close in on you from every side. They will completely destroy you and the people within your walls; not a single stone will they leave in its place, because you did not recognize the time when God came to save you!"

When Jesus entered Jerusalem the whole city was thrown in an uproar. "Who is he?" the people asked.

"This is the prophet Jesus, from Nazareth of Galilee," the crowds answered.

The blind and the crippled came to him in the temple and he healed them. The chief priests and the teachers of the Law became angry when they saw the wonderful things he was doing, and the children shouting and crying in the temple, "Praise to David's Son!"

So they said to Jesus, "Do you hear what they are saying?"

"Indeed I do," answered Jesus. "Haven't you ever read this scripture? 'You have trained children and babies to offer perfect praise.' "

Jesus left them and went out of the city to Bethany, where he spent the night.

Jesus Curses the Fig Tree

The next day, as they were coming back from Bethany, Jesus was hungry. He saw in the distance a fig tree covered with leaves, so he went to it to see if he could find any figs on it; but when he came to it he found only leaves, because it was not the right time for figs. Jesus said to the fig tree, "No one shall ever eat figs from you again!"

And his disciples heard him.

Jesus Goes to the Temple
When they arrived in Jerusalem, Jesus went to the temple and began to drive out all those who bought and sold in the temple. He overturned the tables of the moneychangers and the stools of those who sold pigeons, and would not let anyone carry anything through the temple courts. He then taught the people, "It is written in the Scriptures that God said, 'My house will be called a house of prayer for all peoples.' But you have turned it into a hideout for thieves!"

The chief priests and the teachers of the Law heard of this, so they began looking for some way to kill Jesus. They were afraid of him, because the whole crowd was amazed at his teaching.

When evening came, Jesus and his disciples left the city.

The Lesson from the Fig Tree
Early next morning, as they walked along the road, they saw the fig tree. It was dead all the way down to its roots. Peter remembered what had happened and said to Jesus, "Look, Teacher, the fig tree you cursed has died!"

Jesus answered them, "Remember this! If you have faith in God, you can say to this hill, 'Get up and throw yourself in the sea.' If you do not doubt in your heart, but believe that what you say will happen, it will be done for you. For this reason I tell you: When you pray and ask for something, believe that you have received it, and you will be given whatever you ask for. And when you stand praying, forgive anything you may have against anyone, so that your Father in heaven will forgive your sins. [If you do not forgive others, neither will your Father in heaven forgive your sins.]"

The Question About Jesus' Authority
One day, when Jesus was in the temple teaching the people and preaching the Good News, the chief priests

and the teachers of the Law, together with the elders, came and said to him, "Tell us, what right do you have to do these things? Who gave you the right to do them?"

Jesus answered them, "Now let me ask you a question. Tell me, did John's right to baptize come from God or from men?"

They started to argue among themselves, "What shall we say? If we say, 'From God,' he will say, 'Why, then, did you not believe John?' But if we say, 'From men,' this whole crowd here will stone us, because they are convinced that John was a prophet." So they answered, "We don't know where it came from."

And Jesus said to them, "Neither will I tell you, then, by what right I do these things."

The Parable of the Two Sons
"Now, what do you think? There was a man who had two sons. He went to the older one and said, 'Son, go work in the vineyard today.' 'I don't want to,' he answered, but later he changed his mind and went to the vineyard. Then the father went to the other son and said the same thing. 'Yes, sir,' he answered, but he did not go. Which one of the two did what his father wanted?"

"The older one," they answered.

"And I tell you this," Jesus said to them. "The tax collectors and the prostitutes are going into the Kingdom of God ahead of you. For John the Baptist came to you showing you the right path to take, and you would not believe him; but the tax collectors and the prostitutes believed him. Even when you saw this you did not change your minds later on and believe him."

The Parable of the Tenants in the Vineyard
"Listen to another parable," Jesus said. "There was a landowner who planted a vineyard, put a fence around it, dug a hole for the winepress, and built a watchtower. Then he rented the vineyard to tenants and left home on a trip. When the time came to harvest the grapes he sent his slaves to the tenants to receive his share. The tenants grabbed his slaves, beat one, killed another, and stoned another. Again the man sent other slaves, more

than the first time, and the tenants treated them the same way. Last of all he sent them his son. 'Surely they will respect my son,' he said. But when the tenants saw the son they said to themselves, 'This is the owner's son. Come on, let us kill him, and we will get his property!' So they grabbed him, threw him out of the vineyard, and killed him.

"Now, when the owner of the vineyard comes, what will he do to those tenants?" Jesus asked.

"He will certainly kill those evil men," they answered, "and rent the vineyard out to other tenants, who will give him his share of the harvest at the right time."

Jesus said to them, "Haven't you ever read what the Scriptures say? 'The very stone which the builders rejected turned out to be the most important stone. This was done by the Lord; how wonderful it is!'

"And so I tell you," added Jesus, "the Kingdom of God will be taken away from you and be given to a people who will produce the proper fruits. [Whoever falls on this stone will be broken to pieces; and if the stones falls on someone it will crush him to dust.]"

The chief priests and the Pharisees heard Jesus' parables and knew that he was talking about them, so they tried to arrest him. But they were afraid of the crowds, who considered Jesus to be a prophet.

The Pharisees Try to Trap Jesus

The Pharisees went off and made a plan to trap Jesus with questions. So they watched for the right time. They bribed some men to pretend they were sincere, and sent them to trap Jesus with questions, so they could hand him over to the authority and power of the Governor. These spies said to Jesus, "Teacher, we know that what you say and teach is right. We know that you pay no attention to a man's status, but teach the truth about God's will for man. Tell us, is it against our Law for us to pay taxes to the Roman Emperor, or not?"

But Jesus saw through their trick and said to them, "Show me the coin to pay the tax!"

They brought him the coin, and he asked them, "Whose face and names are these?"

"The Emperor's," they answered.

So Jesus said to them, "Well, then, pay to the Emperor what belongs to him, and pay to God what belongs to God."

When they heard this, they were filled with wonder; and they left him and went away.

Some Sadducees came to Jesus. (They are the ones who say that people will not rise from death.) They asked him, "Teacher, Moses wrote this law for us: 'If a man dies and leaves a wife, but no children, that man's brother must marry the widow so they can have children for the dead man.' Once there were seven brothers; the oldest got married, and died without having children. The second one married the woman, and then the third. The same thing happened to all seven—they died without having children. Last of all, the woman died. Now, on the day when the dead rise to life, whose wife will she be? All seven of them had married her."

Jesus answered them, "The men and women of this age marry, but the men and women who are worthy to rise from death and live in the age to come do not marry. They are like angels and cannot die. They are the sons of God, because they have risen from death. And Moses clearly proves that the dead are raised to life. In the passage about the burning bush he speaks of the Lord as 'The God of Abraham, the God of Isaac, and the God of Jacob.' This means that he is the God of the living, not of the dead, because all are alive to him."

A teacher of the Law was there who heard the discussion. He saw that Jesus had given the Sadducees a good answer, so he came to him with a question, "Which commandment is the most important of all?"

"This is the most important one," said Jesus. " 'Listen, Israel! The Lord our God is the only Lord. You must love the Lord your God with all your heart, with all your soul, with all your mind, and with all your strength.' The second most important commandment is this: 'You must love your fellow-man as yourself.' There is no other commandment more important than these two."

The teacher of the Law said to Jesus, "Well done, Teacher! It is true, as you say, that only the Lord is

God, and that there is no other god but he. And man must love God with all his heart, and with all his mind, and with all his strength; and he must love his fellowman as himself. It is more important to obey these two commandments that to offer animals and other sacrifices to God on the altar."

Jesus noticed how wise his answer was, and so he told him, "You are not far from the Kingdom of God."

After this nobody dared to ask Jesus any more questions.

The Question About the Messiah

Jesus said to them, "How can it be said that the Messiah will be the descendant of David? Because David himself says in the book of Psalms, 'The Lord said to my Lord: Sit here at my right side, until I put your enemies as a footstool under your feet.' David, then, called him 'Lord.' How can the Messiah be David's descendant?"

As all the people listened to him, Jesus said to his disciples, "Watch out for the teachers of the Law, who like to walk around in their long robes, and love to be greeted with respect in the market place; who choose the reserved seats in the synagogues and the best places at feasts; who take advantage of widows and rob them of their homes, and then make a show of saying long prayers! Their punishment will be all the worse!"

The Widow's Offering

As Jesus sat near the temple treasury he watched the people as they dropped in their money. Many rich men dropped in much money; then a poor widow came along and dropped in two little copper coins, worth about a penny. He called his disciples together and said to them, "I tell you that this poor widow put more in the offering box than all the others. For the others put in what they had to spare of their riches; but she, poor as she is, put in all she had—she gave all she had to live on."

Jesus Warns Against the Teachers of the Law and the Pharisees

Then Jesus spoke to the crowds and to his disciples.

"The teachers of the Law and the Pharisees," he said, "are the authorized interpreters of Moses' Law. So you must obey and follow everything they tell you to do; do not, however, imitate their actions, because they do not practice what they preach. They fix up heavy loads and tie them on men's backs, yet they aren't willing even to lift a finger to help them carry those loads. They do everything just so people will see them. See how big are the containers with scripture verses on their foreheads and arms, and notice how long are the hems of their cloaks! They love the best places at feasts and the reserved seats in the synagogues; they love to be greeted with respect in the market places and have people call them 'Teacher.' You must not be called 'Teacher,' because you are all brothers of one another and have only one Teacher. And you must not call anyone here on earth 'Father,' because you have only the one Father in heaven. Nor should you be called 'Leader,' because your one and only leader is the Messiah. The greatest one among you must be your servant. Whoever makes himself great will be humbled, and whoever humbles himself will be made great.

"How terrible for you, teachers of the Law and Pharisees! Hypocrites! You lock the door to the Kingdom of heaven in men's faces, but you yourselves will not go in, and neither will you let people in who are trying to go in!

["How terrible for you, teachers of the Law and Pharisees! Hypocrites! You take advantage of widows and rob them of their homes, and then make a show of saying long prayers! Because of this your punishment will be all the worse!]

"How terrible for you, teachers of the Law and Pharisees! Hypocrites! You sail the seas and cross whole countries to win one convert; and when you succeed, you make him twice as deserving of going to hell as you yourselves are!

"How terrible for you, blind guides! You teach, 'If a man swears by the temple he isn't bound by his vow; but if he swears by the gold in the temple, he is bound.' Blind fools! Which is more important, the gold or the temple which makes the gold holy? You also teach, 'If a man swears by the altar he isn't bound by his vow; but if he swears by the gift on the altar, he is bound.' How blind you are! Which is more important, the gift or the altar which makes the gift holy? So then, when a man swears by the altar he is swearing by it and by all the gifts on it; and when a man swears by the temple he is swearing by it and by God, the one who lives there; and when a man swears by heaven he is swearing by God's throne and by him who sits on it.

"How terrible for you, teachers of the Law and Pharisees! Hypocrites! You give to God one tenth even of the seasoning herbs, such as mint, dill, and cummin, but you neglect to obey the really inportant teachings of the Law, such as justice and mercy and honesty. These you should practice, without neglecting the others. Blind guides! You strain a fly out of your drink, but swallow a camel!

"How terrible for you, teachers of the Law and Pharisees! Hypocrites! You clean the outside of your cup and plate, while the inside is full of things you have gotten by violence and selfishness. Blind Pharisee! Clean what is inside the cup first, and then the outside will be clean too!

"How terrible for you, teachers of the Law and Pharisees! Hypocrites! You are like whitewashed tombs, which look fine on the outside, but are full of dead men's bones and rotten stuff on the inside. In the same way, on the outside you appear to everybody as good, but inside you are full of hypocrisy and sins.

"How terrible for you, teachers of the Law and Pharisees! Hypocrites! You make fine tombs for the prophets, and decorate the monuments of those who lived good lives, and you say, 'If we had lived long ago in the time of our ancestors, we would not have done what they did and killed the prophets'. So you actually admit that you are the descendants of those who murdered the prophets! Go on, then, and finish up what your ancestors started! Snakes, and sons of snakes! How do you expect to escape from being condemned to hell? And so I tell you: I will send you prophets and wise men and teachers; you will kill some of them, nail others to the cross, and whip others in your synagogues and chase them from town to town. As a result, the punishment for the murder of all innocent men will fall on you, from the murder of innocent Abel to the murder of Zechariah, Barachiah's son, whom you murdered between the temple and the altar. I tell you indeed: the punishment for all these will fall on the people of this day!"

Jesus Speaks About His Death

Some Greeks were among those who went to Jerusalem to worship during the feast. They came to Philip (he was from Bethsaida, in Galilee) and said, "Sir, we want to see Jesus."

Philip went and told Andrew, and the two of them went and told Jesus. Jesus answered them, "The hour has now come for the Son of Man to be given great glory. I tell you the truth: a grain of wheat remains no more than a single grain unless it is dropped into the ground and dies. If it does die, then it produces many grains. Whoever loves his own life will lose it; whoever hates his own life in this world will keep it for life eternal. Whoever wants to serve me must follow me, so that my servant will be with me where I am. My Father will honor him who serves me.

"Now my heart is troubled—and what shall I say? Shall I say, 'Father, do not let this hour come upon me'? But that is why I came, to go through this hour of suffering. Father, bring glory to your name!"

Then a voice spoke from heaven, "I have brought glory to it, and I will do so again."

The crowd standing there heard the voice and said, "It thundered!"

Others said, "An angel spoke to him!"

But Jesus said to them, "It was not for my sake that this voice spoke, but for yours. Now is the time for the world to be judged; now the ruler of this world will be overthrown. When I am lifted up from the earth, I will draw all men to me." (In saying this he indicated the kind of death he was going to suffer.)

The crowd answered back, "Our Law tell us that the Messiah will live forever. How, then, can you say that the Son of Man must be lifted up? Who is this Son of Man?"

Jesus answered, "The light will be among you a little longer. Continue on your way while you have the light, so the darkness will not come upon you; because the one who walks in the dark, does not know where he is going. Believe in the light, then, while you have it, so that you will be the people of the light."

Even then, many Jewish authorities believed in Jesus; but because of the Pharisees they did not talk about it openly, so as not to be put out of the synagogue. They loved the approval of men rather than the approval of God.

Jesus said in a loud voice, "Whoever believes in me, believes not only in me but also in him who sent me. Whoever sees me, also sees him who sent me. I have come into the world as light, that everyone who believes in me should not remain in the darkness. Whoever hears my message and does not obey it, I will not judge him. I came, not to judge the world, but to save it. Whoever rejects me and does not accept my message, has one who will judge him. The word I have spoken will be his judge on the last day! Yes, because I have not spoken on my own, but the Father who sent me has commanded me what I must say and speak. And I know that his command brings eternal life. What I say, then, is what the Father has told me to say."

Portents of the Destruction of Jerusalem and the Second Coming

As Jesus was leaving the temple, one of his disciples said, "Look, Teacher! What wonderful stones and buildings!"

Jesus answered, "You see these great buildings? Not a single stone here will be left in its place; every one of them will be thrown down."

Jesus was sitting on the Mount of Olives, across from the temple, when Peter, James, John, and Andrew came to him in private. "Tell us when this will be," they said, "and tell us what will happen to show that the time has come for all these things to take place."

Jesus said to them, "Watch out, and don't let anyone fool you. Many men will come in my name, saying, 'I am he!' and fool many people. And don't be troubled when you hear the noise of battles close by and news of battles far away. Such things must happen, but they do not mean that the end has come. Countries will fight each other, kingdoms will attack one another. There will be earthquakes everywhere, and there will be famines. These things are like the first pains of childbirth.

"You yourselves must watch out. You will be arrested and taken to court. You will be beaten in the synagogues; you will stand before rulers and kings for my sake, to tell them the Good News. The gospel must first be preached to all peoples. And when they arrest you and take you to court, do not worry ahead of time about what you are going to say; when the time comes, say whatever is given to you then. For the words you speak will not be yours; they will come from the Holy Spirit. Make up your minds ahead of time not to worry about how you will defend yourselves; because I will give you such words and wisdom that none of your enemies will be able to resist or deny what you say. You will be handed over by your parents, your brothers, your relatives, and your friends; they will put some of you to death. Everyone will hate you because of me. But not a single hair from your heads will be lost. Stand firm, because this is how you will save yourselves.

"Then many false prophets will appear and fool many people. Such will be the spread of evil that many people's love will grow cold. But whoever holds out to the end will be saved. And this Good News about the Kingdom will be preached through all the world, for a witness to all mankind; and then will come the end.

"You will see 'The Awful Horror,' of which the prophet Daniel spoke, standing in the holy place." (Note to the reader: understand what this means!)

"When you see Jerusalem surrounded by armies, then you will know that soon she will be destroyed. Then those who are in Judea must run away to the hills; those who are in the city must leave, and those who are out in the country must not go into the city. The man who is on the roof of his house must not take the time to go down and get his belongings from the house. The man who is in the field must not go back to get his cloak. How terrible it will be in those days for women who are pregnant, and for mothers with little babies! Terrible distress will come upon this land, and God's wrath will be against this people. Pray to God that these things will not happen in wintertime! For the trouble of those days will be far worse than any the world has ever known, from the very beginning when God created the world until the present time. Nor will there ever again be anything like it. But the Lord has reduced the number of those days; if he had not, nobody would survive. For the sake of his chosen people, however, he has reduced those days.

"Then, if anyone says to you, 'Look, here is the Messiah!' or 'There he is!'—do not believe him. For false Messiahs and false prophets will appear; they will perform great signs and wonders for the purpose of deceiving God's chosen people, if possible. Listen! I have told you this ahead of time.

"Or, if people should tell you, 'Look, he is out in the desert!'—don't go there; or if they say, 'Look, he is hiding here!'—don't believe it. For the Son of Man will come like the lightning which flashes across the whole sky from the east to the west.

"Wherever there is a dead body the vultures will gather.

"Soon after the trouble of those days the sun will grow dark, the moon will no longer shine, the stars will fall from heaven, and the powers in space will be driven from their courses. Then the sign of the Son of Man will appear in the sky; then all the tribes of earth will weep, and they will see the Son of Man coming on the clouds of heaven with power and great glory. The great trumpet will sound, and he will send out his angels to the four corners of the earth, and they will gather his chosen people from one end of the world to the other. When these things begin to happen, stand up and raise your heads, because your salvation is near.

"Let the fig tree teach you a lesson. When its branches become green and tender, and it starts putting out leaves, you know that summer is near. In the same way, when you see all these things, you will know that the time is near, ready to begin. Remember this! All these things will happen before the people now living

"AND NOW MY SOUL IS DISTRESSED. 145

have all died. Heaven and earth will pass away; my words will never pass away.

"Watch yourselves! Don't let yourselves become occupied with too much feasting and strong drink, and the worries of this life, or that Day may come on you suddenly. For it will come like a trap upon all men over the whole earth. Be on watch and pray always that you will have the strength to go safely through all these things that will happen, and to stand before the Son of Man.

"No one knows, however, when that day or hour will come—neither the angels in heaven, nor the Son; only the Father knows. Be on watch, be alert, for you do not know when the time will be. The coming of the Son of Man will be like what happened in the time of Noah. Just as in the days before the Flood, people ate and drank, men and women married, up to the very day Noah went into the ark; yet they did not know what was happening until the Flood came and swept them all away. That is how it will be when the Son of Man comes. At that time two men will be working in the field: one will be taken away, the other will be left behind. Two women will be at the mill grinding meal: one will be taken away, the other will be left behind. Watch out, then, because you do not know what day your Lord will come. It will be like a man who goes away from home on a trip and leaves his servants in charge, each one with his own work to do; and he tells the doorkeeper to keep watch. Watch, then, because you do not know when the master of the house is coming—it might be in the evening, or at midnight, or before dawn, or at sunrise. If he comes suddenly, he must not find you asleep. What I say to you, then, I say to all: Watch!

"Remember this: if the man of the house knew the time when the thief would come, he would stay awake and not let the thief break into his house. For this reason, then, you also must be always ready, because the Son of Man will come at an hour when you are not expecting him.

"Who, then, is the faithful and wise servant? He is the one whom his master has placed in charge of the other servants, to give them their food at the proper time. How happy is that servant if his master finds him doing this when he comes home! Indeed, I tell you, the master will put that servant in charge of all his property. But if he is a bad servant, he will tell himself, 'My master will not come back for a long time,' and he will begin to beat his fellow servants, and eat and drink with drunkards. Then that servant's master will come back some day when he does not expect him and at a time he does not know. The master will cut him to pieces, and make him share the fate of the hypocrites. There he will cry and gnash his teeth.

"On that day the Kingdom of heaven will be like ten girls who took their oil lamps and went out to meet the bridegroom. Five of them were foolish, and the other five were wise. The foolish ones took their lamps but did not take any extra oil with them, while the wise ones took containers full of oil with their lamps. The bridegroom was late in coming, so the girls began to nod and fall asleep.

"It was already midnight when the cry rang out, 'Here is the bridegroom! Come and meet him!' The ten girls woke up and trimmed their lamps. Then the foolish ones said to the wise ones, 'Let us have some of your oil, because our lamps are going out.' 'No, indeed,' the wise ones answered back, 'there is not enough for you and us. Go to the store and buy some for yourselves.' So the foolish girls went off to buy some oil, and while they were gone the bridegroom arrived. The five girls who were ready went in with him to the wedding feast, and the door was closed.

"Later the other girls arrived. 'Sir, sir! Let us in!' they cried. 'But I really don't know you,' the bridegroom answered."

And Jesus concluded, "Watch out, then, because you do not know the day or hour.

"It will be like a man who was about to leave home on a trip; he called his servants and put them in charge of his property. He gave to each one according to his ability: to one he gave five thousand dollars, to the other two thousand dollars, and to the other one thousand dollars. Then he left on his trip. The servant who had received five thousand dollars went at once and invested his money and earned another five thousand dollars. In the same way the servant who received two thousand dollars earned another two thousand dollars. But the servant who received one thousand dollars went off, dug a hole in the ground, and hid his master's money.

"After a long time the master of those servants came back and settled accounts with them. The servant who had received five thousand dollars came in and handed over the other five thousand dollars. 'You gave me five thousand dollars, sir,' he said. 'Look! Here are another five thousand dollars that I have earned.' 'Well done, good and faithful servant!' said his master. 'You have been faithful in managing small amounts, so I will put you in charge of large amounts. Come on in and share my happiness!' Then the servant who had been given two thousand dollars came in and said, 'You gave me two thousand dollars, sir. Look! Here are another two thousand dollars that I have earned.' 'Well done, good and faithful servant!' said his master. 'You have been faithful in managing small amounts, so I will put you in charge of large amounts. Come on in and share my happiness!' Then the servant who had received one thousand dollars came in and said, "Sir, I know you are a hard man: you reap harvests where you did not plant, and gather crops where you did not scatter seed. I was afraid, so I went off and hid your money in the ground. Look! Here is what belongs to you.' 'You bad and lazy servant!' his master said. 'You knew, did you, that I reap harvests where I did not plant, and gather crops where I did not scatter seed? Well, then, you should have deposited my money in the bank, and I would have received it all back with interest when I returned. Now, take the money away from him and give it to the one who has ten thousand dollars. For to every one who has, even more will be given, and he will have more than enough; but the one who has nothing, even the little he has will be taken away from him. As for this useless servant—throw him outside in the darkness; there he will cry and gnash his teeth.'

"When the Son of Man comes as King, and all the angels with him, he will sit on his royal throne, and all the earth's people will be gathered before him. Then he will divide them into two groups, just as a shepherd separates the sheep from the goats: he will put the sheep at his right and the goats at his left. Then the King will say to the people on his right, 'You that are blessed by my Father: come! Come and receive the kingdom which has been prepared for you ever since the creation of the world. I was hungry and you fed me, thirsty and you gave me drink; I was a stranger and you received me in your homes, naked and you clothed me; I was sick and you took care of me, in prison and you visited me.' The righteous will then answer him, 'When, Lord, did we ever see you hungry and feed you, or thirsty and give you drink? When did we ever see you a stranger and welcome you in our homes, or naked and clothe you? When did we ever see you sick or in prison, and visit you?' The King will answer back, 'I tell you, indeed, whenever you did this for one of the least important of these brothers of mine, you did it for me!'

"Then he will say to those on his left, 'Away from me, you that are under God's curse! Away to the eternal fire which has been prepared for the Devil and his angels! I was hungry but you would not feed me, thirsty but you would not give me drink; I was a stranger but you would not welcome me in your homes, naked but you would not clothe me; I was sick and in prison but you would not take care of me.' Then they will answer him, 'When, Lord, did we ever see you hungry, or thirsty, or a stranger, or naked, or sick, or in prison, and we would not help you?' The King will answer them back, 'I tell you, indeed, whenever you refused to help one of these least important ones, you refused to help me.' These, then, will be sent off to eternal punishment; the righteous will go to eternal life."

Nine

FINAL PREACHING OF JESUS; HIS BETRAYAL AND ARREST

Jesus Anointed at Bethany
Six days before the Passover, Jesus went to Bethany, where Lazarus lived, the man Jesus had raised from death. They prepared a dinner for him there, and Martha helped serve it, while Lazarus sat at the table with Jesus. Then Mary took a whole pint of a very expensive perfume made of pure nard, poured it on Jesus' feet, and wiped them with her hair. The sweet smell of the perfume filled the whole house. One of Jesus' disciples, Judas Iscariot—the one who was going to betray him—said, "Why wasn't this perfume sold for three hundred dollars and the money given to the poor?" He said this, not because he cared for the poor, but because he was a thief; he carried the money bag and would help himself from it.

But Jesus said, "Leave her alone! Why are you bothering her? She has done a fine and beautiful thing for me. You will always have poor people with you, and any time you want to you can help them. But I shall not be with you always. She did what she could; she poured perfume on my body to prepare it ahead of time for burial. Now, remember this! Wherever the gospel is preached, all over the world, what she has done will be told in memory of her."

A large crowd of the Jews heard that Jesus was in Bethany, so they went there; they went, not only because of Jesus, but also to see Lazarus, whom Jesus had raised from death. So the chief priests made plans to kill

Lazarus too; because on his account many Jews were leaving their leaders and believing in Jesus.

The time was near for the Feast of Unleavened Bread, which is called the Passover.

Judas Agrees to Betray Jesus

It was now two days before the Feast of Passover and Unleavened Bread. The chief priests and the teachers of the Law were looking for a way to arrest Jesus secretly and put him to death. "We must not do it during the feast," they said, "or the people might riot."

Then Satan went into Judas, called Iscariot, who was one of the twelve disciples. So Judas went off and spoke with the chief priests and the officers of the temple guard about how he could hand Jesus over to them. They were pleased and offered to pay him money. Judas agreed to it and started looking for a good chance to betray Jesus to them without the people knowing about it.

Jesus Prepares to Eat the Passover Meal

The day came during the Feast of Unleavened Bread when the lambs for the Passover meal had to be killed. Jesus sent Peter and John with these instructions. "Go and get our Passover meal ready for us to eat."

"Where do you want us to get it ready?" they asked him.

He said, "Listen! As you go into the city a man carrying a jar of water will meet you. Follow him into the house that he enters, and say to the owner of the house: 'The Teacher says to you, Where is the room where my disciples and I will eat the Passover meal?' He will show you a large furnished room upstairs, where you will get everything ready."

They went off and found everything just as Jesus had told them, and prepared the Passover meal.

The Lord's Supper

When the hour came, Jesus took his place at the table with the apostles. He said to them, "I have wanted so much to eat this Passover meal with you before I suffer! For I tell you, I will never eat it until it is given its full meaning in the Kingdom of God."

Then Jesus took the cup, gave thanks to God, and said, "Take this and share it among yourselves; for I tell you that I will not drink this wine from now on until the Kingdom of God comes." So Jesus rose from the table, took off his outer garment, and tied a towel around his waist. Then he poured some water into a washbasin and began to wash the disciples' feet and dry them with the towel around his waist. He came to Simon Peter, who said to him, "Are you going to wash my feet, Lord?"

Jesus answered him, "You do not know now what I am doing, but you will know later."

Peter declared, "You will never, at any time, wash my feet!"

"If I do not wash your feet," Jesus answered, "you will no longer be my disciple."

Simon Peter answered, "Lord, do not wash only my feet, then! Wash my hands and head, too!"

Jesus said, "Whoever has taken a bath is completely clean and does not have to wash himself, except for his feet. All of you are clean—all except one." (Jesus already knew who was going to betray him; that is why he said, "All of you, except one, are clean.")

After he had washed their feet, Jesus put his outer garment back on and returned to his place at the table. "Do you understand what I have just done to you?" he asked. "You call me Teacher and Lord, and it is right that you do so, because I am. I am your Lord and Teacher, and I have just washed your feet. You, then, should wash each other's feet. I have set an example for you, so that you will do just what I have done for you. I tell you the truth: no slave is greater than his master; no messenger is greater than the one who sent him. Now you know this truth; how happy will you be if you put it into practice!"

Then he took the bread, gave thanks to God, broke it, and gave it to them, saying, "This is my body [which is given for you. Do this in memory of me."]

Then he took the cup, gave thanks to God, and gave it to them. "Drink it, all of you," he said; "this is my blood, which seals God's covenant, my blood poured out for many for the forgiveness of sins. I tell you, I will never again drink this wine until the day I drink the new wine with you in my Father's Kingdom."

Jesus Predicts His Betrayal

While they were at the table eating, Jesus said, "I tell you this: one of you will betray me. But look! The one who betrays me is here at the table with me! Because the Son of Man will die as God has decided it; but how terrible for that man who betrays him!

"I am not talking about all of you; I know those I have chosen. But the scripture must come true that says, 'The man who ate my food turned against me.' I tell you this now before it happens, so that when it does happen you will believe that 'I Am Who I Am'. I tell you the truth: whoever receives anyone I send, receives me also; and whoever receives me, receives him who sent me."

After Jesus said this, he was deeply troubled, and declared openly, "I tell you the truth: one of you is going to betray me."

The disciples looked at one another, completely puzzled about whom he meant. The disciples were upset and began to ask him, one after the other, "Surely you don't mean me, do you?"

Jesus answered, "It will be one of you twelve, one who dips his bread in the dish with me. The Son of Man will die as the Scriptures say he will; but how terrible for that man who will betray the Son of Man! It would have been better for that man if he had never been born!"

One of the disciples, whom Jesus loved, was sitting next to Jesus. Simon Peter motioned to him and said, "Ask him who it is that he is talking about."

So that disciple moved closer to Jesus' side and asked, "Who is it, Lord?"

Jesus answered, "I will dip the bread in the sauce and give it to him; he is the man." So he took a piece of bread, dipped it, and gave it to Judas, the son of Simon Iscariot. As soon as Judas took the bread, Satan went into him. Jesus said to him, "Hurry and do what you must!" None of those at the table understood why Jesus said this to him. Since Judas was in charge of the money bag, some of the disciples thought that Jesus had told him to go and buy what they needed for the feast, or else that he had told him to give something to the poor.

Judas accepted the bread and went out at once. It was night.

The New Commandment

After Judas had left, Jesus said, "Now the Son of Man's glory is revealed; now God's glory is revealed through him. And if God's glory is revealed through him, then God will reveal the glory of the Son of Man in himself, and he will do so at once. My children, I shall not be with you very much longer. You will look for me; but I tell you now what I told the Jews, 'You cannot go where I am going.' A new commandment I give you: love one another. As I have loved you, so you must love one another. If you have love for one another, then all will know that you are my disciples."

Jesus Predicts Peter's Denial

"Where are you going, Lord?" Simon Peter asked him.

"You cannot follow me now where I am going," answered Jesus; "but later you will follow me."

"Lord, why can't I follow you now?" asked Peter. "I am ready to die for you!"

Jesus answered, "Are you really ready to die for me? I tell you the truth: before the rooster crows you will say three times that you do not know me. Simon, Simon! Listen! Satan has received permission to test all of you, as a farmer separates the wheat from the chaff. But I have prayed for you, Simon, that your faith will not fail. And when you turn back to me, you must strengthen your brothers."

Peter answered, "Lord, I am ready to go to prison with you and to die with you!"

"I tell you, Peter," Jesus answered, "the rooster will not crow today until you have said three times that you do not know me."

The Argument About Greatness

An argument came up among the disciples as to which one of them should be thought of as the greatest. Jesus said to them, "The kings of this world have power over their people, and the rulers are called 'Friends of the People.' But this is not the way it is with you; rather, the greatest one among you must be like the youngest, and the leader must be like the servant. Who is greater, the one who sits down to eat or the one who serves him? The one who sits down, of course. But I am among you as one who serves.

"You have stayed with me all through my trials; and just as my Father has given me the right to rule, so I will make the same agreement with you. You will eat and drink at my table in my Kingdom, and you will sit on thrones to judge the twelve tribes of Israel."

Purse, Bag, and Sword

Then Jesus said to them, "When I sent you out that time without purse, bag, or shoes, did you lack anything?"

"Not a thing," they answered.

"But now," Jesus said, "whoever has a purse or a bag must take it; and whoever does not have a sword must sell his coat and buy one. For I tell you this: the scripture that says, 'He was included with criminals,' must come true about me. Because that which was written about me is coming true."

The disciples said, "Look! Here are two swords, Lord!"

"That is enough!" he answered.

Final Discourses to His Apostles

"Do not be worried and upset," Jesus told them. "Believe in God, and believe also in me. There are many rooms in my Father's house, and I am going to prepare a place for you. I would not tell you this if it were not so. And after I go and prepare a place for you, I will come back and take you to myself, so that you will be where I am. You know how to get to the place where I am going."

Thomas said to him, "Lord, we do not know where you are going; how can we know the way to get there?"

Jesus answered him, "I am the way, the truth, and the life; no one goes to the Father except by me. Now that you have known me," he said to them, "you will know my Father also; and from now on you do know him, and you have seen him."

Philip said to him, "Lord, show us the Father; that is all we need."

Jesus answered, "For a long time I have been with you all; yet you do not know me, Philip? Whoever has seen me has seen the Father. Why, then, do you say, 'Show us the Father'? Do you not believe, Philip, that I am in the Father and the Father is in me? The words that I have spoken to you," Jesus said to his disciples, "do not come from me. The Father, who remains in me, does his own works. Believe me that I am in the Father and the Father is in me. If not, believe because of these works. I tell you the truth: whoever believes in me will do the works I do—yes, he will do even greater ones, because I am going to the Father. And I will do whatever you ask for in my name, so that the Father's glory will be shown through the Son. If you ask me for anything in my name, I will do it.

"If you love me, you will obey my commandments. I will ask the Father, and he will give you another Helper, the Spirit of truth, to stay with you forever. The world cannot receive him, because it cannot see him or know him. But you know him, because he remains with you and lives in you.

"I will not leave you alone; I will come back to you. In a little while the world will see me no more, but you will see me; and because I live, you also will live. When that day comes, you will know that I am in my Father, and that you are in me, just as I am in you.

"Whoever accepts my commandments and obeys them, he is the one who loves me. My Father will love him who loves me; I too will love him and reveal myself to him."

Judas (not Judas Iscariot) said, "Lord, how can it be that you will reveal yourself to us and not to the world?"

Jesus answered him, "Whoever loves me will obey my message. My Father will love him, and my Father and I will come to him and live with him. Whoever does not love me does not obey my words. The message you have heard is not mine, but comes from the Father, who sent me.

"I have told you this while I am still with you. The Helper, the Holy Spirit whom the Father will send in my name, will teach you everything, and make you remember all that I have told you.

"Peace I leave with you; my own peace I give you. I do not give it to you as the world does. Do not be worried and upset; do not be afraid. You heard me say to you, 'I am leaving, but I will come back to you.' If you loved me, you would be glad that I am going to the Father, because he is greater than I. I have told you this now, before it all happens, so that when it does happen you will believe. I cannot talk with you much longer, because the ruler of this world is coming. He has no power over me, but the world must know that I love the Father; that is why I do everything as he commands me.

"Come, let us go from this place.

"I am the real vine, and my Father is the gardener. He breaks off every branch in me that does not bear fruit, and prunes every branch that does bear fruit, so that it will be clean and bear more fruit. You have been made clean already by the message I have spoken to you. Remain united to me, and I will remain united to you. A branch cannot bear fruit by itself; it can do so only if it remains in the vine. In the same way you cannot bear fruit unless you remain in me.

"I am the vine, you are the branches. Whoever remains in me, and I in him, will bear much fruit; for you can do nothing without me. Whoever does not remain in me is thrown out, like a branch, and dries up; such branches are gathered up and thrown into the fire, where they are burned. If you remain in me, and my words remain in you, then you will ask for anything you wish, and you shall have it. This is how my Father's glory is shown: by your bearing much fruit; and in this way you become my disciples. I love you just as the Father loves me; remain in my love. If you obey my commands, you will remain in my love, just as I have obeyed my Father's commands and remain in his love.

"I have told you this so that my joy may be in you, and that your joy may be complete. My commandment is this: love one another, just as I love you. The greatest love a man can have for his friends is to give his life for them. And you are my friends, if you do what I command you. I do not call you servants any longer, because a servant does not know what his master is doing. Instead, I call you friends, because I have told you everything I heard from my Father. You did not choose me; I chose you, and appointed you to go and bear much fruit, the kind of fruit that endures. And so the Father will give you whatever you ask of him in my name. This, then, is what I command you: love one another.

"If the world hates you, you must remember that it has hated me first. If you belonged to the world, then the world would love you as its own. But I chose you from this world, and you do not belong to it; that is why the world hates you. Remember what I told you: 'No slave is greater than his master.' If they persecuted me, they will persecute you too; if they obeyed my message, they will obey yours too. But they will do all this to you because you are mine; for they do not know him who sent me. They would not have been guilty of sin if I had not come and spoken to them; as it is, they no longer have any excuse for their sin. Whoever hates me hates my Father also. They would not have been guilty of sin if I had not done the works among them that no one else ever did; as it is, they have seen what I did and they hate both me and my Father. This must be, however, so that what is written in their Law may come true, 'They hated me for no reason at all.'

"The Helper will come—the Spirit of truth, who comes from the Father. I will send him to you from the Father, and he will speak about me. And you, too, will speak about me, because you have been with me from the very beginning.

"I have told you this so that you will not fall away. They will put you out of their synagogues. And the time will come when anyone who kills you will think that by doing this he is serving God. They will do these things to you because they have not known either the Father or me. But I have told you this, so that when the time comes for them to do these things, you will remember that I told you.

"I did not tell you these things at the beginning, because I was with you. But now I am going to him who sent me; yet none of you asks me, 'Where are you going?' And now that I have told you, sadness has filled your hearts. But I tell you the truth: it is better for you that I go away, because if I do not go, the Helper will not come to you. But if I do go away, then I will send him to you. And when he comes he will prove to the people of the world that they are wrong about sin, and about what is right, and about God's judgment. They are wrong about sin, because they do not believe in me; about what is right, because I am going to the Father and you will not see me any more; about judgment, because the ruler of this world has already been judged.

"I have much more to tell you, but now it would be too much for you to bear. But when the Spirit of truth comes, he will lead you into all the truth. He will not speak on his own, but he will speak of what he hears and tell you of things to come. He will give me glory, because he will take what I have to say and tell it to you. All that my Father has is mine; that is why I said that the Spirit will take what I give him and tell it to you.

"In a little while you will not see me any more; and then a little while later you will see me."

Some of his disciples said to the others, "What does this mean? He tells us, 'In a little while you will not see me, and then a little while later you will see me'; and he also says, 'It is because I am going to the Father.' What does this 'a little while' mean?" they asked. "We do not know what he is talking about!"

Jesus knew that they wanted to ask him, so he said to them, "I said, 'In a little while you will not see me, and then a little while later you will see me.' Is this what you are asking about among yourselves? I tell you the truth: you will cry and weep, but the world will be glad; you will be sad, but your sadness will turn into gladness.

When a woman is about to give birth to a child she is sad, because her hour of suffering has come; but when the child is born she forgets her suffering, because she is happy that a baby has been born into the world. That is the way it is with you: now you are sad, but I will see you again, and your hearts will be filled with gladness, the kind of gladness that no one can take away from you.

"When that day comes you will not ask me for anything. I tell you the truth: the Father will give you whatever you ask of him in my name. Until now you have not asked for anything in my name; ask and you will receive, so that your happiness may be complete.

"I have told you these things by means of parables. But the time will come when I will use parables no more, but I will speak to you in plain words abut the Father. When that day comes you will ask him in my name; and I do not say that I will ask him on your behalf, because the Father himself loves you. He loves you because you love me and have believed that I came from God. I did come from the Father and I came into the world; and now I am leaving the world and going to the Father."

Then his disciples said to him, "Look, you are speaking very plainly now, without using parables. We know now that you know everything; you do not need someone to ask you questions. This makes us believe that you came from God."

Jesus answered them, "Do you believe now? The time is coming, and is already here, when all of you will be scattered, each one to his own home, and I will be left all alone. But I am not really alone, because the Father is with me. I have told you this so that you will have peace by being united to me. The world will make you suffer. But be brave! I have defeated the world!"

Jesus Prays for His Disciples
After Jesus finished saying this, he looked up to heaven and said, "Father, the hour has come. Give glory to your Son, that the Son may give glory to you. For you gave him authority over all men, so that he might give eternal life to all those you gave him. And this is eternal

life: for men to know you, the only true God, and to know Jesus Christ, whom you sent. I showed your glory on earth; I finished the work you gave me to do. Father! Give me glory in your presence now, the same glory I had with you before the world was made.

"I have made you known to the men you gave me out of the world. They belonged to you, and you gave them to me. They have obeyed your word, and now they know that everything you gave me comes from you. I gave them the message that you gave me, and they received it; they know that it is true that I came from you, and they believe that you sent me.

"I pray for them. I do not pray for the world, but for the men you gave me, because they belong to you. All I have is yours, and all you have is mine; and my glory is shown through them. And now I am coming to you; I am no longer in the world, but they are in the world. Holy Father! Keep them safe by the power of your name, the name you gave me, so they may be one just as you and I are one. While I was with them I kept them safe by the power of your name, the name you gave me. I protected them, and not one of them was lost, except the man who was bound to be lost—that the scripture might come true. And now I am coming to you, and I say these things in the world so that they might have my joy in their hearts, in all its fulness. I gave them your message and the world hated them, because they do not belong to the world, just as I do not belong to the world. I do not ask you to take them out of the world, but I do ask you to keep them safe from the Evil One. Just as I do not belong to the world, they do not belong to the world. Dedicate them to yourself, by means of the truth; your word is truth. I sent them into the world just as you sent me into the world. And for their sake I dedicate myself to you, in order that they, too, may be truly dedicated to you.

"I do not pray only for them, but also for those who believe in me because of their message. I pray that they may all be one. Father! May they be in us, just as you are in me and I am in you. May they be one, so that the world will believe that you sent me. I gave them the same glory you gave me, so that they may be one, just as you and I are one: I in them and you in me, so that they may be completely one, in order that the world may know that you sent me and that you love them as you love me.

"Father! You have given them to me, and I want them to be with me where I am, so that they may see my glory, the glory you gave me; because you loved me before the world was made. Righteous Father! The world does not know you, but I know you, and these know that you sent me. I made you known to them and I will continue to do so, in order that the love you have for me may be in them, and I also may be in them."

The Agony in the Garden

Then they sang a hymn and went out to the Mount of Olives.

Then Jesus said to them, "This very night all of you will run away and leave me, because the scripture says, 'God will kill the shepherd and the sheep of the flock will be scattered.' But after I am raised to life I will go to Galilee ahead of you."

Peter spoke up and said to Jesus, "I will never leave you, even though all the rest do!"

"Remember this!" Jesus said to Peter, "Before the rooster crows tonight you will say three times that you do not know me."

Peter answered, "I will never say I do not know you, even if I have to die with you!"

And all the disciples said the same thing.

They came to a place called Gethsemane, and Jesus said to his disciples, "Sit here while I pray."

Then he took Peter, James, and John with him. When he came to the place he said to them, "Pray that you will not fall into temptation."

Then he went off from them, about the distance of a stone's throw, and knelt down and prayed. Grief and anguish came over him, and he said to them, "The sorrow in my heart is so great that it almost crushes me. Stay here and watch with me."

He went a little farther on, threw himself face down to the ground, and prayed, "My Father, if it is possible, take this cup away from me! But not what I want, but what you want."

[An angel from heaven appeared to him and strengthened him. In great anguish he prayed even more fervently; his sweat was like drops of blood, falling to the ground.]

Then he returned to the three disciples and found them asleep; and he said to Peter, "How is it that you three were not able to watch with me for one hour? Keep watch, and pray so that you will not fall into temptation. The spirit is willing, but the flesh is weak."

Again a second time Jesus went away and prayed, "My Father, if this cup cannot be taken away unless I drink it, your will be done."

Rising from his prayer, he went back to the disciples and found them asleep, worn out by their grief. And he said to them, "Why are you sleeping? Get up, and pray that you will not fall into temptation."

Again Jesus left them, went away, and prayed the third time, saying the same words. "Father!" he prayed, "my Father! All things are possible for you. Take this cup away from me. But not what I want, but what you want."

The Betrayal and Arrest
Then he came back to the disciples and found them asleep; they could not keep their eyes open. And they did not know what to say to him.

When he came back the third time, he said to them, "Are you still sleeping and resting? Enough! The hour has come! Look, the Son of Man is now handed over to the power of sinful men. Get up, let us go. Look, here is the man who is betraying me!"

Jesus was still speaking when Judas, one of the twelve disciples, arrived. With him was a crowd carrying swords and clubs, sent by the chief priests, the teachers of the Law, and the elders. Jesus knew everything that was going to happen to him; so he stepped forward and said to them,

"Who is it you are looking for?"

"Jesus of Nazareth," they answered.

"I am he," he said.

Judas, the traitor, was standing there with them. When Jesus said to them, "I am he," they moved back and fell to the ground. Jesus asked them again, "Who is it you are looking for?"

"Jesus of Nazareth," they said.

"I have already told you that I am he," Jesus said. "If, then, you are looking for me, let these others go." (He said this so that what he had said might come true, "Father, I have not lost even one of those you gave me.")

The traitor had given the crowd a signal: "The man I kiss is the one you want. Arrest him!"

When Judas arrived he went straight to Jesus and said, "Peace be with you, Teacher," and kissed him.

But Jesus said, "Is it with a kiss, Judas, that you betray the Son of Man?"

So they arrested Jesus and held him tight. When the disciples who were with Jesus saw what was going to happen, they said, "Shall we strike with our swords, Lord?"

Simon Peter had a sword; he drew it and struck the High Priest's slave, cutting off his right ear. The name of the slave was Malchus. But Jesus said, "Enough of this!" He touched the man's ear and healed him.

Jesus said to Peter, "Put your sword back in its place, because all who take the sword will die by the sword. Don't you know that I could call on my Father for help and at once he would send me more than twelve armies of angels? But in that case, how could the Scriptures come true that say it must happen in this way?"

Then Jesus spoke to the crowd, "Did you have to come with swords and clubs to capture me, as though I were an outlaw? Every day I sat down and taught in the temple, and you did not arrest me. But all this has happened to make come true what the prophets wrote in the Scriptures."

Then all the disciples left him and ran away.

Ten

THE TRIAL OF JESUS;
HIS CRUCIFIXION, DEATH, AND TRIUMPH

Jesus Before Annas
The group of soldiers with their commanding officer and the Jewish guards arrested Jesus, tied him up, and took him first to Annas. He was the father-in-law of Caiaphas, who was High Priest that year. It was Caiaphas who had advised the Jews that it was better that one man die for all the people.

The High Priest Questions Jesus
The High Priest questioned Jesus about his disciples and about his teaching. Jesus answered, "I have always spoken publicly to everyone; all my teaching was done in the synagogues and in the temple, where all the Jews come together. I have never said anything in secret. Why, then, do you question me? Question the people who heard me. Ask them what I told them—they know what I said."

When Jesus said this, one of the guards there slapped him and said, "How dare you talk like this to the High Priest!"

Jesus answered him, "If I have said something wrong, tell everyone here what it was. But if I am right in what I have said, why do you hit me?"

So Annas sent him, still tied up, to Caiaphas the High Priest.

Jesus Before the Council
Those who had arrested Jesus took him to the house of Caiaphas, the High Priest, where the teachers of the

Law and the elders had gathered together. Peter followed him from a distance, as far as the courtyard of the High Priest's house. He went into the courtyard and sat down with the guards, to see how it would all come out. The chief priests and the whole Council tried to find some false evidence against Jesus, to put him to death; but they could not find any, even though many came up and told lies about him. Finally two men stepped forward and said, "This man said, 'I am able to tear down God's temple and three days later build it back up.'"

The High Priest stood up and said to Jesus, "Have you no answer to give to this accusation against you?" But Jesus kept quiet. Again the High Priest spoke to him, "In the name of the living God, I now put you on oath: tell us if you are the Messiah, the Son of God."

Jesus answered him, "So you say. But I tell all of you: from this time on you will see the Son of Man sitting at the right side of the Almighty, and coming on the clouds of heaven!"

At this the High Priest tore his clothes and said, "Blasphemy! We don't need any more witnesses! Right here you have heard his wicked words! What do you think?"

They answered, "He is guilty, and must die."

Then they spat in his face and beat him; and those who slapped him said, "Prophesy for us, Messiah! Guess who hit you!"

Peter Denies Jesus

Peter was sitting outside in the courtyard, when one of the High Priest's servant girls came to him and said, "You, too, were with Jesus of Galilee."

But he denied it in front of them all. "I don't know what you are talking about," he answered, and went on out to the entrance of the courtyard. Another servant girl saw him and said to the men there, "He was with Jesus of Nazareth."

Again Peter denied it, and answered, "I swear that I don't know that man!"

After a little while the men standing there came to Peter. "Of course you are one of them," they said. "After all, the way you speak gives you away!"

Then Peter made a vow: "May God punish me if I am not telling the truth! I do not know that man!"

Just then a rooster crowed, and Peter remembered what Jesus had told him, "Before the rooster crows, you will say three times that you do not know me." He went out and wept bitterly.

Jesus Before the Council

When day came, the elders of the Jews, the chief priests, and the teachers of the Law met together, and Jesus was brought to their Council. "Tell us," they said, "are you the Messiah?"

He answered, "If I tell you, you will not believe me, and if I ask you a question you will not answer. But from now on the Son of Man will be seated at the right side of the Almighty God."

They all said, "Are you, then, the Son of God?"

He answered them, "You say that I am."

And they said, "We don't need any witnesses! We ourselves have heard his very own words!"

The Death of Judas

Early in the morning all the chief priests and the Jewish elders made their plan against Jesus to put him to death. They put him in chains, took him, and handed him over to Pilate, the Roman governor.

When Judas, the traitor, saw that Jesus had been condemned, he repented and took back the thirty silver coins to the chief priests and the elders. "I have sinned by betraying an innocent man to death!" he said.

"What do we care about that?" they answered. "That is your business!"

Judas threw the money into the sanctuary and left them; then he went off and hanged himself.

The chief priests picked up the money and said, "This is blood money, and it is against our Law to put it in the temple treasury." After reaching an agreement about it, they used the money to buy Potter's Field, as a cemetery for foreigners. That is why that field is called "Field of Blood" to this very day.

Then what the prophet Jeremiah had said came true, "They took the thirty silver coins, the amount the people of Israel had agreed to pay for him, and used them to buy the potter's field, as the Lord commanded me."

Jesus Before Pilate

They took Jesus from Caiaphas' house to the governor's palace. It was early in the morning. The Jews did not go inside the palace because they wanted to keep themselves ritually clean, in order to be able to eat the passover meal. So Pilate went outside to them and asked, "What do you accuse this man of?"

Their answer was, "We would not have brought him to you if he had not committed a crime."

Pilate said to them, "You yourselves take him and try him according to your own law."

The Jews replied, "We are not allowed to put anyone to death." (This happened to make come true what Jesus had said when he indicated the kind of death he would die.)

Pilate went back into the palace and called Jesus. "Are you the king of the Jews?" he asked him.

Jesus answered, "Does this question come from you or have others told you about me?"

Pilate replied, "Do you think I am a Jew? It was your own people and their chief priests who handed you over to me. What have you done?"

Jesus said, "My kingdom does not belong to this world; if my Kingdom belonged to this world, my followers would fight to keep me from being handed over to the Jews. No, my kingdom does not belong here!"

So Pilate asked him, "Are you a king, then?"

Jesus answered, "You say that I am a king. I was born and came into the world for this one purpose, to speak about the truth. Whoever belongs to the truth listens to me."

"And what is truth?" Pilate asked.

Then Pilate went back outside to the Jews and said to them, "I cannot find any reason to condemn him. But according to the custom you have, I always set free a prisoner for you during the Passover. Do you want me to set the king of the Jews free for you?"

They answered him with a shout, "No, not him! We want Barabbas!" (Barabbas was a bandit.)

When the chief priests and the guards saw him they shouted, "Nail him to the cross! Nail him to the cross!"

Pilate said to them, "You take him, then, and nail him to the cross. I find no reason to condemn him."

The Jews answered back, "We have a law that says he ought to die, because he claimed to be the Son of God."

When Pilate heard them say this, he was even more afraid. He went back into the palace and asked Jesus, "Where do you come from?"

But Jesus did not answer. Pilate said to him, "You will not speak to me? Remember, I have the authority to set you free, and also to have you nailed to the cross."

Jesus answered, "You have authority over me only because it was given to you by God. So the man who handed me over to you is guilty of a worse sin."

When Pilate heard this he tried to find a way to set Jesus free. But the Jews shouted back, "If you set him free that means you are not the Emperor's friend! Anyone who claims to be a king is the Emperor's enemy!"

Pilate asked him, "Are you the king of the Jews?"

"You say it," answered Jesus. He said nothing, however, to the accusations of the chief priests and elders.

So Pilate said to him, "Don't you hear all these things they accuse you of?"

But Jesus refused to answer a single word, so that the Governor was greatly surprised.

Then Pilate said to the chief priests and the crowds, "I find no reason to condemn this man."

But they insisted even more strongly, "He is starting a riot among the people all through Judea with his teaching. He began in Galilee, and now has come here."

When Pilate heard this he asked, "Is this man a Galilean?" When he learned that Jesus was from the region ruled by Herod, he sent him to Herod, who was also in Jerusalem at that time. Herod was very pleased when he saw Jesus, because he had heard about him and had been wanting to see him for a long time. He was hoping to see Jesus perform some miracle. So Herod asked Jesus many questions, but Jesus did not answer a word. The chief priests and the teachers of the Law stepped forward and made strong accusations against Jesus. Herod and his soldiers made fun of Jesus and treated him with contempt. They put a fine robe on him and sent him back to Pilate. On that very day Herod and Pilate became friends; they had been enemies before this.

Pilate called together the chief priests, the leaders, and the people, and said to them, "You brought this man to me and said that he was misleading the people. Now, I have examined him here in your presence, and I have not found him guilty of any of the crimes you accuse him of. Nor did Herod find him guilty, because he sent him back to us. There is nothing this man has done to deserve death. I will have him whipped, then, and let him go."

Jesus Sentenced to Death

At every Passover Feast the Governor was in the habit of setting free any prisoner the crowd asked for. At that time there was a well-known prisoner named Jesus Barabbas. So when the crowd gathered, Pilate asked them, "Which one do you want me to set free for you? Jesus Barabbas or Jesus called the Christ?" He knew very well that they had handed Jesus over to him because they were jealous.

When Pilate was sitting in the judgment hall, his wife sent him a message: "Have nothing to do with that innocent man, because in a dream last night I suffered much on account of him."

The chief priests and the elders persuaded the crowds to ask Pilate to set Barabbas free and have Jesus put to death. But the Governor asked them, "Which one of these two do you want me to set free for you?"

"Barabbas!" they answered.

"What, then, shall I do with Jesus called the Christ?" Pilate asked them.

"Nail him to the cross!" they all answered.

But Pilate asked, "What crime has he committed?"

Then they started shouting at the top of their voices, "Nail him to the cross!"

When Pilate saw it was no use to go on, but that a riot might break out, he took some water, washed his hands in front of the crowd, and said, "I am not responsible for the death of this man! This is your doing!"

The whole crowd answered back, "Let the punishment for his death fall on us and on our children!"

Then Pilate set Barabbas free for them; he had Jesus whipped and handed him over to be nailed to the cross.

The Soliders Make Fun of Jesus
Then Pilate's soliders took Jesus into the governor's palace, and the whole company gathered around him. They stripped off his clothes and put a scarlet robe on him. Then they made a crown out of thorny branches and placed it on his head, and put a stick in his right hand; then they knelt before him and made fun of him. "Long live the King of the Jews!" they said. They spat on him, and took the stick and hit him over the head. When they had finished making fun of him, they took the robe off and put his own clothes back on him. Then they led him out to nail him to the cross.

Jesus Nailed to the Cross
A large crowd of people followed him; among them were some women who were weeping and wailing for him. Jesus turned to them and said, "Women of Jerusalem! Don't cry for me, but for yourselves and your children. For the days are coming when people will say, 'How lucky are the women who never had children, who never bore babies, who never nursed them!' That will be the time people will say to the mountains, 'Fall on us!' and to the hills, 'Hide us!' For if such things as these are done when the wood is green, what will it be like when it is dry?"

On the way they met a man named Simon, who was coming into the city from the country, and they forced him to carry Jesus' cross. (This was Simon from Cyrene, the father of Alexander and Rufus.) They brought Jesus to a place called Golgotha, which means "The Place of the Skull."

The Crucifixion and Death on the Cross
There they offered him wine to drink, mixed with gall; after tasting it, however, he would not drink it.

THE TRIAL OF JESUS; HIS CRUCIFIXION, DEATH,

They took two others also, both of them criminals, to be put to death with Jesus. When they came to the place called "The Skull," they nailed Jesus to the cross there, and the two criminals, one on his right and one on his left. Jesus said, "Forgive them, Father! They don't know what they are doing."

Pilate wrote a notice and had it put on the cross. "Jesus of Nazareth, the King of the Jews," is what he wrote. Many Jews read this, because the place where Jesus was nailed to the cross was not far from the city. The notice was written in Hebrew, Latin, and Greek. The Jewish chief priests said to Pilate, "Do not write 'The King of the Jews,' but rather, 'This man said, I am the King of the Jews.' "

Pilate answered, "What I have written stays written."

After the soliders had nailed Jesus to the cross, they took his clothes and divided them into four parts, one part for each solider. They also took the robe, which was made of one piece of woven cloth, without any seams in it. The soldiers said to each other, "Let us not tear it; let us throw dice to see who will get it." This happened to make the scripture come true, "They divided my clothes among themselves, and gambled for my robe." So the soldiers did this.

People passing by shook their heads and hurled insults at Jesus: "Aha! You were going to tear down the temple and build it up in three days! Now come down from the cross and save yourself!"

The soldiers also made fun of him; they came up to him and offered him cheap wine, and said, "Save yourself, if you are the king of the Jews!"

In the same way the chief priests and the teachers of the Law made fun of Jesus, saying to each other, "He saved others, but he cannot save himself!"

One of the criminals hanging there hurled insults at him, "Aren't you the Messiah? Save yourself and us!"

The other one, however, rebuked him, saying, "Don't you fear God? We are all under the same sentence. Ours, however, is only right, because we are getting what we deserve for what we did; but he has done no wrong." And he said to Jesus, "Remember me, Jesus, when you come as King!"

Jesus said to him, "I tell you this: today you will be in Paradise with me."

Standing close to Jesus' cross were his mother, his mother's sister, Mary the wife of Clopas, and Mary Magdalene. Jesus saw his mother and the disciple he loved standing there; so he said to his mother, "Woman, here is your son."

Then he said to the disciple, "Here is your mother." From that time the disciple took her to live in his home.

At noon the whole country was covered with darkness, which lasted for three hours. At three o'clock Jesus cried out with a loud shout, *"Eloi, Eloi, lema sabachthani?"* which means, "My God, my God, why did you abandon me?"

Jesus knew that by now everything had been completed; and in order to make the scripture come true he said, "I am thirsty."

A bowl was there, full of cheap wine; they soaked a sponge in the wine, put it on a branch of hyssop, and lifted it up to his lips. Jesus took the wine and said, "It is finished!"

Jesus cried out in a loud voice, "Father! In your hands I place my spirit!" He said this and died.

Jesus' Side Pierced

Then the Jews asked Pilate to allow them to break the legs of the men who had been put to death, and take them down from the crosses. They did this because it was Friday, and they did not want the bodies to stay on the crosses on the Sabbath day, since the coming Sabbath was especially holy. So the soldiers went and broke the legs of the first man and then of the other man who had been put to death with Jesus. But when they came to Jesus they saw that he was already dead, so they did not break his legs. One of the soldiers, however, plunged his spear into Jesus' side, and at once blood and water poured out. (The one who saw this happen has spoken of it, so that you also may believe. What he said is true, and he knows that he speaks the truth.) This was done to make the scripture come true, "Not one of his bones will be broken." And there is another scripture that says, "People will look at him whom they pierced."

The Burial of Jesus

Then the curtain hanging in the temple was torn in two, from top to bottom. The earth shook, the rocks split apart, the graves broke open, and many of God's people who had died were raised to life. They left the graves; and after Jesus rose from death they went into the Holy City, where many people saw them.

When the army officer and the soldiers with him who were watching Jesus saw the earthquake and everything else that happened, they were terrified and said, "He really was the Son of God!"

There were many women there, looking on from a distance, who had followed Jesus from Galilee and helped him. Among them were Mary Magdalene, Mary the mother of James and Joseph, and the mother of Zebedee's sons.

When it was evening, a rich man from Arimathea arrived; his name was Joseph, and he also was a disciple of Jesus. He went into the presence of Pilate and asked for the body of Jesus. Pilate gave orders for the body to be given to Joseph. So Joseph took it, wrapped it in a new linen sheet, and placed it in his own grave, which he had just recently dug out of the rock. Then he rolled a large stone across the entrance to the grave and went away. Mary Magdalene and the other Mary were sitting there, facing the grave.

On the next day—that is, the day following Friday—the chief priests and the Pharisees met with Pilate and said, "Sir, we remember that while that liar was still alive he said, 'I will be raised to life after three days.' Give orders, then, for the grave to be safely guarded until the third day, so that his disciples will not be able to go and steal him, and then tell the people, 'He was raised from death.' This last lie would be even worse than the first one."

"Take a guard," Pilate told them; "go and guard the grave as best you can."

So they left, and made the grave secrue by putting a seal on the stone and leaving the guard on watch.

The Resurrection

Very early on Sunday morning the women went to the grave carrying the spices they had prepared. They found the stone rolled away from the entrance to the grave, so they went in; but they did not find the body of the Lord Jesus. They stood there puzzled about this, when suddenly two men in bright shining clothes stood by them. Full of fear, the women bowed down to the ground, as the men said to them, "Why are you looking among the dead for one who is alive? He is not here; he has been raised. Remember what he said to you while he was in Galilee: 'The Son of Man must be handed over to sinful men, be nailed to the cross, and rise to life on the third day.'"

Jesus Appears to Mary Magdalene

Mary stood crying outside the tomb. Still crying, she bent over and looked in the tomb, and saw two angels there, dressed in white, sitting where the body of Jesus had been, one at the head, the other at the feet. "Woman, why are you crying?" they asked her.

She answered, "They have taken my Lord away, and I do not know where they have put him!"

When she had said this, she turned around and saw Jesus standing there; but she did not know that it was Jesus. "Woman, why are you crying?" Jesus asked her. "Who is it that you are looking for?"

She thought he was the gardener, so she said to him, "If you took him away, sir, tell me where you have put him, and I will go and get him."

Jesus said to her, "Mary!"

She turned toward him and said in Hebrew, "Rabboni!" (This means "Teacher.")

"Do not hold on to me," Jesus told her, "because I have not yet gone back up to the Father. But go to my brothers and tell them for me, 'I go back up to him who is my Father and your Father, my God and your God.'"

So Mary Magdalene went and told the disciples that she had seen the Lord, and that he had told her this. And when they heard her say that Jesus was alive and that she had seen him, they did not believe her. But

Peter got up and ran to the grave; he bent down and saw the grave cloths and nothing else. Then he went back home wondering at what had happened.

The Walk to Emmaus

On that same day two of them were going to a village named Emmaus, about seven miles from Jerusalem, and they were talking to each other about all the things that had happened. As they talked and discussed, Jesus himself drew near and walked along with them; they saw him, but somehow did not recognize him. Jesus said to them, "What are you talking about, back and forth, as you walk along?"

They stood still, with sad faces. One of them, named Cleopas, asked him, "Are you the only man living in Jerusalem who does not know what has been happening there these last few days?"

"What things?" he asked.

"The things that happened to Jesus of Nazareth," they answered. "This man was a prophet, and was considered by God and by all the people to be mighty in words and deeds. Our chief priests and rulers handed him over to be sentenced to death, and he was nailed to the cross. And we had hoped that he would be the one who was going to redeem Israel! Besides all that, this is now the third day since it happened. Some of the women of our group surprised us; they went at dawn to the grave, but could not find his body. They came back saying they had seen a vision of angels who told them that he is alive. Some of our group went to the grave and found it exactly as the women had said; but they did not see him."

Then Jesus said to them, "How foolish you are, how slow you are to believe everything the prophets said! Was it not necessary for the Messiah to suffer these things and enter his glory?" And Jesus explained to them what was said about him in all the Scriptures, beginning with the books of Moses and the writings of all the prophets.

They came near the village to which they were going, and Jesus acted as if he were going farther; but they held him back, saying, "Stay with us; the day is almost over and it is getting dark." So he went in to stay with them. He sat at table with them, took the bread, and said the blessing; then he broke the bread and gave it to them. Their eyes were opened and they recognized him; but he disappeared from their sight. They said to each other, "Wasn't it like a fire burning in us when he talked to us on the road and explained the Scriptures to us?"

They got up at once and went back to Jerusalem, where they found the eleven disciples gathered together with the others and saying, "The Lord is risen indeed! He has appeared to Simon!"

The two then explained to them what had happened on the road, and how they had recognized the Lord when he broke the bread.

Jesus Appears to His Disciples

While they were telling them this, suddenly the Lord himself stood among them and said to them, "Peace be with you."

Full of fear and terror, they thought that they were seeing a ghost. But he said to them, "Why are you troubled? Why are these doubts coming up in your minds? Look at my hands and my feet and see that it is I, myself. Feel me, and you will see, because a ghost doesn't have flesh and bones, as you can see I have."

He said this and showed them his hands and his feet. They still could not believe, they were so full of joy and wonder; so he asked them, "Do you have anything to eat here?" They gave him a piece of cooked fish, which he took and ate before them.

Then Jesus said to them again, "Peace be with you. As the Father sent me, so I send you." He said this, and then he breathed on them and said, "Receive the Holy Spirit. If you forgive men's sins, they are forgiven; if you do not forgive them, they are not forgiven."

Jesus and Thomas

One of the twelve disciples, Thomas (called the Twin), was not with them when Jesus came. So the other disciples told him, "We saw the Lord!"

Thomas said to them, "If I do not see the scars of the

nails in his hands, and put my finger on those scars, and my hand in his side, I will not believe."

A week later the disciples were together indoors again, and Thomas was with them. The doors were locked, but Jesus came and stood among them and said, "Peace be with you." Then he said to Thomas, "Put your finger here, and look at my hands; then stretch out your hands and put it in my side. Stop your doubting, and believe!"

Thomas answered him, "My Lord and my God!"

Jesus said to him, "Do you believe because you see me? How happy are those who believe without seeing me!"

Jesus Appears to Seven Disciples

After this, Jesus showed himself once more to his disciples at Lake Tiberias. This is how he did it. Simon Peter, Thomas (called the Twin), Nathanael (the one from Cana in Galilee), the sons of Zebedee, and two other disciples of Jesus were all together. Simon Peter said to the others, "I am going fishing."

"We will come with you," they told him. So they went and got into the boat; but all that night they did not catch a thing. As the sun was rising, Jesus stood at the water's edge, but the disciples did not know that it was Jesus. Then he said to them, "Young men, haven't you caught anything?"

"Not a thing," they answered.

He said to them, "Throw your net out on the right side of the boat, and you will find some." So they threw the net out, and could not pull it back in, because they had caught so many fish.

The disciple whom Jesus loved said to Peter, "It is the Lord!" When Simon Peter heard that it was the Lord, he wrapped his outer garment around him (for he had taken his clothes off) and jumped into the water. The other disciples came to shore in the boat, pulling the net full of fish. They were not very far from land, about a hundred yards away. When they stepped ashore they saw a charcoal fire there with fish on it, and some bread. Then Jesus said to them, "Bring some of the fish you have just caught."

Simon Peter went aboard and dragged the net ashore, full of big fish, a hundred and fifty-three in all; even though there were so many, still the net did not tear. Jesus said to them, "Come and eat." None of the disciples dared to ask him, "Who are you?" because they knew it was the Lord. So Jesus went over, took the bread, and gave it to them; he did the same with the fish.

This, then, was the third time Jesus showed himself to the disciples after he was raised from death.

Jesus and Peter
After they had eaten, Jesus said to Simon Peter, "Simon, son of John, do you love me more than these?"

"Yes, Lord," he answered, "you know that I love you."

Jesus said to him, "Take care of my lambs." A second time Jesus said to him, "Simon, son of John, do you love me?"

"Yes, Lord," he answered, "you know that I love you."

Jesus said to him, "Take care of my sheep." A third time Jesus said, "Simon, son of John, do you love me?"

Peter became sad because Jesus asked him the third time, "Do you love me?" and said to him, "Lord, you know everything; you know that I love you!"

Jesus said to him, "Take care of my sheep. I tell you the truth: when you were young you used to fasten your belt and go anywhere you wanted to; but when you are old you will stretch out your hands and someone else will tie them and take you where you don't want to go." (In saying this Jesus was indicating the way in which Peter would die and bring glory to God.) Then Jesus said to him, "Follow me!"

Jesus and the Other Disciple
Peter turned around and saw behind him that other disciple, whom Jesus loved—the one who had leaned close to Jesus at the meal and asked, "Lord, who is going to betray you?" When Peter saw him, he said to Jesus, "Lord, what about this man?"

Jesus answered him, "If I want him to live until I come, what is that to you? Follow me!"

So a report spread among the followers of Jesus that this disciple would not die. But Jesus did not say that he would not die; he said, "If I want him to live until I come, what is that to you?"

Jesus Appears to the Eleven

The eleven disciples went to the hill in Galilee where Jesus had told them to go. When they saw him they worshiped him, even though some of them doubted. He said to them, "Go to the whole world and preach the gospel to all mankind. Whoever believes and is baptized will be saved; whoever does not believe will be condemned. Believers will be given these signs of power: they will drive out demons in my name; they will speak in strange tongues; if they pick up snakes or drink any poison, they will not be harmed; they will place their hands on the sick, who will get well."

Jesus drew near and said to them, "I have been given all authority in heaven and on earth. Go, then, to all peoples everywhere and make them my disciples: baptize them in the name of the Father, the Son, and the Holy Spirit, and teach them to obey everything I have commanded you. And remember! I will be with you always, to the end of the age."

Then he said to them, "These are the very things I told you while I was still with you: everything written about me in the Law of Moses, the writings of the prophets, and the Psalms had to come true."

Then he opened their minds to understand the Scriptures, and said to them, "This is what is written: that the Messiah must suffer, and rise from death on the third day, and that in his name the message about repentance and the forgiveness of sins must be preached to all nations, beginning in Jerusalem. You are witnesses of these things. And I myself will send upon you what my Father has promised. But you must wait in the city until the power from above comes down upon you."

Jesus Is Taken Up to Heaven

Then he led them out of the city as far as Bethany, where he raised his hands and blessed them.

When the apostles met together with Jesus they asked him, "Lord, will you at this time give the Kingdom back to Israel?"

Jesus said to them, "The times and occasions are set by my Father's own authority, and it is not for you to know when they will be. But you will be filled with power when the Holy Spirit comes on you, and you will be witnesses for me in Jerusalem, in all of Judea and Samaria, and to the ends of the earth." After saying this, he was taken up to heaven as they watched him; and a cloud hid him from their sight.

They still had their eyes fixed on the sky as he went away, when two men dressed in white suddenly stood beside them. "Men of Galilee," they said, "why do you stand there looking up at the sky? This Jesus, who was taken up from you into heaven, will come back in the same way that you saw him go to heaven."

EPILOGUE

The Purpose of This Book
Jesus did many other mighty works in his disciples' presence which are not written down in this book. These have been written that you may believe that Jesus is the Messiah, the Son of God, and that through this faith you may have life in his name.

Now, there are many other things that Jesus did. If they were all written down one by one, I suppose that the whole world could not hold the books that would be written.

PART 2

The Rest of the Narrative

Eleven

THE PLIGHT AND STRUGGLE OF THE BELIEVERS

Judas' Successor
Then the apostles went back to Jerusalem from the Mount of Olives, which is about half a mile away from the city. They entered Jerusalem and went up to the room where they were staying: Peter, John, James and Andrew, Philip and Thomas, Bartholomew and Matthew, James, the son of Alphaeus, Simon the Patriot, and Judas, the son of James. They gathered frequently to pray as a group, together with the women, and with Mary the mother of Jesus, and his brothers.

A few days later there was a meeting of the believers, about one hundred and twenty in all, and Peter stood up to speak. "My brothers," he said, "the scripture had to come true in which the Holy Spirit, speaking through David, predicted about Judas, who was the guide of those who arrested Jesus. Judas was a member of our group, because he had been chosen to have a part in our work."

(With the money that Judas got for his evil act he bought a field, where he fell to his death; he burst open and all his insides spilled out. All the people living in Jerusalem heard about it, and so in their own language they call that field Akeldama, which means "Field of Blood.")

"For it is written in the book of Psalms, 'May his house become empty; let no one live in it.' It is also written, 'May someone else take his place of service.'

"So then, someone must join us as a witness to the resurrection of the Lord Jesus. He must be one of those who were in our group during the whole time that the Lord Jesus traveled about with us, beginning from the time John preached his baptism until the day Jesus was taken up from us to heaven."

So they proposed two men: Joseph, who was called Barsabbas (he was also called Justus), and Matthias. Then they prayed, "Lord, you know the hearts of all men. And so, Lord, show us which one of these two you have chosen to take this place of service as an apostle which Judas left to go to the place where he belongs." Then they drew lots to choose between the two names. The name chosen was that of Matthias, and he was added to the group of the eleven apostles.

The Coming of the Holy Spirit

When the day of Pentecost arrived, all the believers were gathered together in one place. Suddenly there was a noise from the sky which sounded like a strong wind blowing, and it filled the whole house where they were sitting. Then they saw what looked like tongues of fire spreading out; and each person there was touched by a tongue. They were all filled with the Holy Spirit and began to talk in other languages, as the Spirit enabled them to speak.

There were Jews living in Jerusalem, religious men who had come from every country in the world. When they heard this noise, a large crowd gathered. They were all excited, because each one of them heard the believers talking in his own language. In amazement and wonder they exclaimed, "These men who are talking like this—they are all Galileans! How is it, then, that all of us hear them speaking in our own native language? We are from Parthia, Media, and Elam; from Mesopotamia, Judea, and Cappadocia; from Pontus and Asia, from Phrygia and Pamphylia, from Egypt and the regions of Libya near Cyrene; some of us are from Rome, both Jews and Gentiles converted to Judaism; and some of us are from Crete and Arabia—yet all of us hear them speaking in our own languages of the great things that God has done!" Amazed and confused they all kept asking each other, "What does this mean?"

But others made fun of the believers, saying, "These men are drunk!"

Peter's Message

Then Peter stood up with the other eleven apostles, and in a loud voice began to speak to the crowd, "Fellow Jews, and all of you who live in Jerusalem, listen to me and let me tell you what this means. These men are not drunk, as you suppose; it is only nine o'clock in the morning. Rather, this is what the prophet Joel spoke about, 'This is what I will do in the last days, God says: I will pour out my Spirit upon all men. Your sons and your daughters will prophesy; your young men will see visions, and your old men will dream dreams. Yes, even on my slaves, both men and women, I will pour out my Spirit in those days, and they will prophesy. I will perform miracles in the sky above, and marvels on the earth below. There will be blood, and fire, and thick smoke; the sun will become dark, and the moon red as blood, before the great and glorious Day of the Lord arrives. And then, whoever calls on the name of the Lord will be saved.'

"Listen to these words, men of Israel! Jesus of Nazareth was a man whose divine mission was clearly shown to you by the miracles, wonders, and signs which God did through him; you yourselves know this, for it took place here among you. God, in his own will and knowledge, had already decided that Jesus would be handed over to you; and you killed him, by letting sinful men nail him to the cross. But God raised him from the dead; he set him free from the pains of death, because it was impossible that death should hold him prisoner. For David said about him, 'I saw the Lord before me at all times; he is by my right side, so that I will not be troubled. Because of this my heart is glad and my words are full of joy; and I, mortal though I am, will rest assured in hope, because you will not abandon my soul in the world of the dead; you will not allow your devoted servant to suffer decay. You have shown me the paths that lead to life, and by your presence you will fill me with joy.'

"Brothers: I must speak to you quite plainly about

our patriarch David. He died and was buried, and his grave is here with us to this very day. He was a prophet, and he knew God's promise to him: God made a vow that he would make one of David's descendants a king, just as David was. David saw what God was going to do, and so he spoke about the resurrection of the Messiah when he said, 'He was not abandoned in the world of the dead; his flesh did not decay.'

"God has raised this very Jesus from the dead, and we are all witnesses to this fact. He has been raised to the right side of God and received from him the Holy Spirit, as his Father had promised; and what you now see and hear is his gift that he has poured out on us. For David himself did not go up into heaven; rather he said, 'The Lord said to my Lord: Sit here at my right side, until I put your enemies as a footstool under your feet.'

"All the people of Israel, then, are to know for sure that it is this Jesus, whom you nailed to the cross, that God has made Lord and Messiah!"

When the people heard this, they were deeply troubled, and said to Peter and the other apostles, "What shall we do, brothers?"

Peter said to them, "Turn away from your sins, each one of you, and be baptized in the name of Jesus Christ, so that your sins will be forgiven; and you will receive God's gift, the Holy Spirit. For God's promise was made to you and your children, and to all who are far away—all whom the Lord our God calls to himself."

Peter made his appeal to them and with many other words he urged them, saying, "Save yourselves from the punishment coming to this wicked people!" Many of them believed his message and were baptized; about three thousand people were added to the group that day. They spent their time in learning from the apostles, taking part in the fellowship, and sharing in the fellowship meals and the prayers.

Life Among the Believers
Many miracles and wonders were done through the apostles, and this caused everyone to be filled with awe. All the believers continued together in close fellowship

THE PLIGHT AND STRUGGLE OF THE BELIEVERS 189

and shared their belongings with one another. They would sell their property and possessions and distribute the money among all, according to what each one needed. Every day they continued to meet as a group in the temple, and they had their meals together in their homes, eating the food with glad and humble hearts, praising God, and enjoying the good will of all the people. And every day the Lord added to their group those who were being saved.

The Lame Man Healed
One day Peter and John went to the temple at three o'clock in the afternoon, the hour for prayers. There, at the "Beautiful Gate," as it was called, was a man who had been lame all his life. Every day he was carried to this gate to beg for money from the people who were going into the temple. When he saw Peter and John going in, he begged them to give him something. They looked straight at him and Peter said, "Look at us!" So he looked at them, expecting to get something from them. Peter said to him, "I have no money at all, but I will give you what I have: in the name of Jesus Christ of Nazareth I order you to walk!" Then he took him by his right hand and helped him up. At once the man's feet and ankles became strong; he jumped up, stood on his feet, and started walking around. Then he went into the temple with them, walking and jumping and praising God. The whole crowd saw him walking and praising God; and when they recognized him as the beggar who sat at the temple's "Beautiful Gate," they were all filled with surprise and amazement at what had happened to him.

Peter's Message in the Temple
As the man held on to Peter and John, all the people were amazed and ran to them in "Solomon's Porch," as it was called. When Peter saw the people, he said to them, "Men of Israel, why are you surprised at this, and why do you stare at us? Do you think that it was by means of our own power or godliness that we made this man walk? The God of Abraham, Isaac, and Jacob, the God of our ancestors, has given divine glory to his Serv-

ant Jesus. You handed him over to the authorities, and you rejected him in Pilate's presence, even after Pilate had decided to set him free. He was holy and good, but you rejected him and instead you asked Pilate to do you the favor of turning loose a murderer. And so you killed the one who leads men to life. But God raised him from the dead—and we are witnesses to this. It was the power of his name that gave strength to this lame man. What you see and know was done by faith in his name; it was faith in Jesus that made him well like this before you all.

"And now, my brothers, I know that what you and your leaders did to Jesus was done because of your ignorance. God long ago announced by means of all the prophets that his Messiah had to suffer; and he made it come true in this way. Repent, then, and turn to God, so that he will wipe away your sins."

Peter and John Before the Council

Peter and John were still speaking to the people when the priests, the officer in charge of the temple guards, and the Sadducees came to them. They were annoyed because the two apostles were teaching the people that Jesus had risen from death, which proved that the dead will rise to life. So they arrested them and put them in jail until the next day, since it was already late. But many who heard the message believed; and the number of men came to about five thousand.

The next day the Jewish leaders, the elders, and the teachers of the Law gathered in Jerusalem. They met with the High Priest Annas, and Caiaphas, and John, and Alexander, and the others who belonged to the High Priest's family. They made the apostles stand before them and asked them, "How did you do this? What power do you have, or whose name did you use?"

Peter, full of the Holy Spirit, answered them, "Leaders of the people and elders: if we are being questioned today about the good deed done to the lame man and how he was made well, then you should all know, and all the people of Israel should know, that this man stands here before you completely well by the power of the name of Jesus Christ of Nazareth—whom you crucified and God raised from death. Jesus is the one of whom the scripture says, 'The stone that you the builders despised turned out to be the most important stone.' Salvation is to be found through him alone; for there is no one else in all the world, whose name God has given to men, by whom we can be saved."

The members of the Council were amazed to see how bold Peter and John were, and to learn that they were ordinary men of no education. They realized then that they had been companions of Jesus. But there was nothing that they could say, because they saw the man who had been made well standing there with Peter and John. So they told them to leave the Council room, and started discussing among themselves. "What shall we do with these men?" they asked. "Everyone living in Jerusalem knows that this extraordinary miracle has been performed by them, and we cannot deny it. But to keep this matter from spreading any further among the people, let us warn these men never again to speak to anyone in the name of Jesus."

So they called them back in and told them that under no condition were they to speak or to teach in the name of Jesus. But Peter and John answered them, "You yourselves judge which is right in God's sight, to obey you or to obey God. For we cannot stop speaking of what we ourselves have seen and heard." The Council warned them even more strongly, and then set them free. They could find no reason for punishing them, because the people were all praising God for what had happened. The man on whom this miracle of healing had been performed was over forty years old.

The Believers Pray for Boldness

As soon as they were set free, Peter and John returned to their group and told them what the chief priests and the elders had said. When they heard it, they all joined together in prayer to God: "Master and Creator of heaven, earth, and sea, and all that is in them! By means of the Holy Spirit you spoke through our ancestor David, your servant, when he said, 'Why were the Gentiles furious; why did the peoples plot in vain? The kings of the earth prepared themselves, and the rulers met together against the Lord and his Messiah.' For indeed Herod and Pontius Pilate met together in this city with the Gentiles and the people of Israel against Jesus, your holy Servant, whom you made Messiah. They gathered to do everything that you, by your power and will, had already decided would take place. And now, Lord, take notice of the threats they made and allow us, your servants, to speak your message with all boldness. Stretch out your hand to heal, and grant that wonders and miracles may be performed through the name of your holy Servant Jesus."

When they finished praying, the place where they were meeting was shaken. They were all filled with the Holy Spirit and began to speak God's message with boldness.

All Things Together
The group of believers was one in mind and heart. No one said that any of his belongings was his own, but they all shared with one another everything they had. With great power the apostles gave witness of the resurrection of the Lord Jesus, and God poured rich blessings on them all. There was no one in the group who was in need. Those who owned fields or houses would sell them, bring the money received from the sale and turn it over to the apostles; and the money was distributed to each one according to his need.

And so it was that Joseph, a Levite born in Cyprus, whom the apostles called Barnabas (which means "One who Encourages"), sold a field he owned, brought the money, and turned it over to the apostles.

Miracles and Wonders
But more and more people were added to the group—a crowd of men and women who believed in the Lord. As a result of what the apostles were doing, the sick people were carried out in the streets and placed on beds and mats so that, when Peter walked by, at least his shadow might fall on some of them. And crowds of people came in from the towns around Jerusalem, bringing their sick and those who had evil spirits in them; and they were all healed.

The Seven Helpers

Some time later, as the number of disciples kept growing, there was a quarrel between the Greek-speaking Jews and the native Jews. The Greek-speaking Jews said that their widows were being neglected in the daily distribution of funds. So the twelve apostles called the whole group of disciples together and said, "It is not right for us to neglect the preaching of God's word in order to handle finances. So then, brothers, choose seven men among you who are known to be full of the Holy Spirit and wisdom, and we will put them in charge of this matter. We ourselves, then, will give our full time to prayers and the work of preaching."

The whole group was pleased with the apostles' proposal; so they chose Stephen, a man full of faith and the Holy Spirit, and Philip, Prochorus, Nicanor, Timon, Parmenas, and Nicolaus, a Gentile from Antioch who had been converted to Judaism. The group presented them to the apostles, who prayed and placed their hands on them.

And so the word of God continued to spread. The number of disciples in Jerusalem grew larger and larger, and a great number of priests accepted the faith.

The Arrest of Stephen

Stephen, a man richly blessed by God and full of power, performed great miracles and wonders among the people. But some men opposed him; they were members of the synagogue of the Free Men (as it was called), which had Jews from Cyrenia and Alexandria. They and other Jews from Cilicia and Asia started arguing with Stephen. But the Spirit gave Stephen such wisdom that when he spoke they could not resist him. So they bribed some men to say, "We heard him speaking against Moses and against God!" In this way they stirred up the people, the elders, and the teachers of the Law. They came to Stephen, seized him, and took him before the Council. Then they brought in some men to tell lies about him. "This man," they said, "is always talking against our sacred temple and the Law of Moses. We heard him say that this Jesus of Nazareth will tear down the temple and change all the customs which have come down to us from Moses!" All those sitting in the Council fixed their eyes on Stephen and saw that his face looked like the face of an angel.

Stephen's Speech
The High Priest asked Stephen, "Is this really so?" Stephen answered, "Brothers and fathers! Listen to me! The God of glory appeared to our ancestor Abraham while he was living in Mesopotamia, before he had gone to live in Haran. Our ancestors had the tent of God's presence with them in the desert. It had been made as God had told Moses to make it, according to the pattern that Moses had been shown. Later on, our ancestors who received the tent from their fathers carried it with them when they went with Joshua and took over the land from the nations that God drove out before them. And it stayed there until the time of David. He won God's favor, and asked God to allow him to provide a house for the God of Jacob. But it was Solomon who built him a house.

"But the Most High God does not live in houses built by men; as the prophet says, 'Heaven is my throne, says the Lord, and earth is my footstool. What kind of house would you build for me? Where is the place for me to rest? Did not I myself make all these things?'

"How stubborn you are! How heathen your hearts, how deaf you are to God's message! You are just like your ancestors: you too have always resisted the Holy Spirit! Was there any prophet that your ancestors did not persecute? They killed God's messengers, who long ago announced the coming of his righteous Servant. And now you have betrayed and murdered him. You are the ones who received God's law, that was handed down by angels—yet you have not obeyed it!"

The Stoning of Stephen
As the members of the Council listened to Stephen they became furious and ground their teeth at him in anger. But Stephen, full of the Holy Spirit, looked up to heaven and saw God's glory, and Jesus standing at the right side of God. "Look!" he said. "I see heaven

opened and the Son of Man standing at the right side of God!"

With a loud cry they covered their ears with their hands. Then they all rushed together at him at once, threw him out of the city and stoned him. The witnesses left their cloaks in charge of a young man named Saul. They kept on stoning Stephen as he called on the Lord, "Lord Jesus, receive my spirit!" He knelt down and cried out in a loud voice, "Lord! Do not remember this sin against them!" He said this and died.

And Saul approved of his murder.

Saul Persecutes the Church

That very day the church in Jerusalem began to suffer cruel persecution. All the believers, except the apostles, were scattered throughout the provinces of Judea and Samaria. Some devout men buried Stephen, mourning for him with loud cries.

But Saul tried to destroy the church; going from house to house, he dragged out the believers, both men and women, and threw them into jail.

The Gospel Preached in Samaria

The believers who were scattered went everywhere, preaching the message. Philip went to the city of Samaria and preached the Messiah to the people there. The crowds paid close attention to what Philip said. They all listened to him and saw the miracles that he performed. So there was great joy in Samaria.

In that city lived a man named Simon, who for some time had astounded the Samaritans with his magic. He claimed that he was someone great, and everyone in the city, from all classes of society, paid close attention to him. "He is that power of God known as 'The Great Power,' " they said. He had astounded them with his magic for such a long time that they paid close attention to him. But when they believed Philip's message about the Good News of the Kingdom of God and the name of Jesus Christ, they were baptized, both men and women. Simon himself also believed; and after being baptized he stayed close to Philip, and was astounded when he saw the great wonders and miracles that were being performed.

The apostles in Jerusalem heard that the people of Samaria had received the word of God; so they sent Peter and John to them. When they arrived, they prayed for the believers that they might receive the Holy Spirit. For the Holy Spirit had not yet come down on any of them; they had only been baptized in the name of the Lord Jesus. Then Peter and John placed their hands on them, and they received the Holy Spirit.

Simon saw that the Spirit had been given to them when the apostles placed their hands on them. So he offered money to Peter and John, and said, "Give this power to me too, so that anyone I place my hands on will receive the Holy Spirit."

But Peter answered him, "May you and your money go to hell, for thinking that you can buy God's gift with money! You have no part or share in our work, because your heart is not right in God's sight. Repent, then, from this evil plan of yours, and pray to the Lord that he will forgive you for thinking such a thing as this."

The Conversion of Saul

In the meantime Saul kept up his violent threats of murder against the disciples of the Lord. He went to the High Priest and asked for letters of introduction to the Jewish synagogues in Damascus, so that if he should find any followers of the Way of the Lord there, he would be able to arrest them, both men and women, and take them back to Jerusalem.

On his way to Damascus, as he came near the city, suddenly a light from the sky flashed around him. He fell to the ground and heard a voice saying to him, "Saul, Saul! Why do you persecute me?"

"Who are you, Lord?" he asked.

"I am Jesus, whom you persecute," the voice said. "But get up and go into the city, where you will be told what you must do."

The men who were traveling with Saul had stopped, not saying a word; they heard the voice but could not see anyone. Saul got up from the ground and opened his eyes, but could not see a thing. So they took him by the hand and led him into Damascus. For three days he was not able to see, and during that time he did not eat or drink anything.

There was a disciple in Damascus named Ananias. He had a vision, in which the Lord said to him, "Ananias!"

"Here I am, Lord," he answered.

The Lord said to him, "Get ready and go to Straight Street, and at the house of Judas ask for a man from Tarsus named Saul. He is praying, and in a vision he saw a man named Ananias come in and place his hands on him so that he might see again."

Ananias answered, "Lord, many people have told me about this man, about all the terrible things he has done to your people in Jerusalem. And he has come to Damascus with authority from the chief priests to arrest all who call on your name."

The Lord said to him, "Go, because I have chosen him to serve me, to make my name known to Gentiles and kings, and to the people of Israel. And I myself will show him all that he must suffer for my sake."

So Ananias went, entered the house, and placed his hands on Saul. "Brother Saul," he said, "the Lord has sent me—Jesus himself, who appeared to you on the road as you were coming here. He sent me so that you might see again and be filled with the Holy Spirit." At once something like fish scales fell from Saul's eyes and he was able to see again. He stood up and was baptized; and after he had eaten, his strength came back.

Saul stayed for a few days with the disciples in Damascus.

Saul Preaches in Damascus

He went straight to the synagogues and began to preach about Jesus. "He is the Son of God," he said.

All who heard him were amazed, and asked, "Isn't this the man who in Jerusalem was killing those who call on this name? And didn't he come here for the very purpose of arresting them and taking them back to the chief priests?"

But Saul's preaching became even more powerful,

and his proofs that Jesus was the Messiah were so convincing that the Jews who lived in Damascus could not answer him.

After many days had gone by, the Jews gathered and made plans to kill Saul; but he was told of what they planned to do. Day and night they watched the city gates in order to kill him. But one night Saul's followers took him and let him down through an opening in the wall, lowering him in a basket.

Saul in Jerusalem

Saul went to Jerusalem and tried to join the disciples. They would not believe, however, that he was a disciple, and they were all afraid of him. Then Barnabas came to his help and took him to the apostles. He explained to them how Saul had seen the Lord on the road, and that the Lord had spoken to him. He also told them how boldly Saul had preached in the name of Jesus in Damascus. And so Saul stayed with them and went all over Jerusalem, preaching boldly in the name of the Lord. He also talked and disputed with the Greek-speaking Jews, but they tried to kill him. When the brothers found out about this, they took Saul down to Caesarea and sent him away to Tarsus.

Peter Set Free from Prison

About that time some prophets went down from Jerusalem to Antioch. One of them, named Agabus, stood up and by the power of the Spirit predicted that a great famine was about to come over all the earth. (It came when Claudius was Emperor.) The disciples decided that each of them would send as much as he could to help their brothers who lived in Judea. They did this, then, and sent the money to the church elders by Barnabas and Saul.

About this time King Herod began to persecute some members of the church. He had James, the brother of John, put to death by the sword. When he saw that this pleased the Jews, he went ahead and had Peter arrested. (This happened during the time of the Feast of Unleavened Bread.) After his arrest Peter was put in jail, where he was handed over to be guarded by four groups of four soldiers each. Herod planned to put him on trial in public after Passover. So Peter was kept in jail, but the people of the church were praying earnestly to God for him.

The night before Herod was going to bring him out to the people, Peter was sleeping between two guards. He was tied with two chains, and there were guards on duty at the prison gate. Suddenly an angel of the Lord stood there, and a light shone in the cell. The angel shook Peter by the shoulder, woke him up, and said, "Hurry! Get up!" At once the chains fell off Peter's hands. Then the angel said, "Tighten your belt and tie on your sandals." Peter did so, and the angel said, "Put your cloak around you and come with me." Peter followed him out of prison. He did not know, however, if what the angel was doing was real; he thought he was seeing a vision. They passed by the first guard station, and then the second, and came at last to the iron gate that opens into the city. The gate opened for them by itself, and they went out. They walked down a street, and suddenly the angel left Peter.

Then Peter realized what had happened to him, and said, "Now I know that it is really true! The Lord sent his angel, and he rescued me from Herod's power and from all the things the Jewish people expected to do."

Aware of his situation, he went to the home of Mary, the mother of John Mark. Many people had gathered there and were praying. Peter knocked at the outside door, and a servant girl named Rhoda came to answer it. She recognized Peter's voice and was so happy that she ran back in without opening the door, and announced that Peter was standing outside. "You are crazy!" they told her. But she insisted that it was true. So they answered, "It is his angel."

Meanwhile, Peter kept on knocking. They opened the door at last and when they saw him they were amazed. He motioned with his hand for them to be quiet, and explained to them how the Lord had brought him out of prison. "Tell this to James and the rest of the brothers," he said; then he left and went somewhere else.

When morning came, there was a tremendous confusion among the guards; what had happened to Peter?

Herod gave orders to search for him, but they could not find him. So he had the guards questioned and ordered them to be put to death.

After this Herod went down from Judea and spent some time in Caesarea.

The Death of Herod
Herod was very angry with the people of Tyre and Sidon; so they went in a group to see Herod. First they won Blastus over to their side; he was in charge of the palace. Then they went to Herod and asked him for peace, because their country got its food supplies from the king's country.

On a chosen day Herod put on his royal robes, sat on his throne, and made a speech to the people. "It isn't a man speaking, but a god!" they shouted. At once the angel of the Lord struck Herod down, because he did not give honor to God. He was eaten by worms and died.

The word of God continued to spread and grow.

Barnabas and Saul finished their mission and returned from Jerusalem, taking John Mark with them.

Barnabas and Saul Chosen and Sent
In the church at Antioch there were some prophets and teachers: Barnabas, Simeon (called the Black), Lucius (from Cyrene), Manaen (who had been brought up with Governor Herod), and Saul. While they were serving the Lord and fasting, the Holy Spirit said to them, "Set apart for me Barnabas and Saul, to do the work to which I have called them."

They fasted and prayed, placed their hands on them, and sent them off.

Barnabas and Saul, then, having been sent by the Holy Spirit, went down to Seleucia and sailed from there to the island of Cyprus. When they arrived at Salamis, they preached the word of God in the Jewish synagogues. They had John Mark with them to help in the work.

They went all the way across the island to Paphos, where they met a certain magician named Bar-Jesus, a Jew who claimed to be a prophet. He was a friend of the Governor of the island, Sergius Paulus, who was an intelligent man. The Governor called Barnabas and Saul before him because he wanted to hear the word of God. But they were opposed by the magician Elymas (this is his name in Greek); he tried to turn the Governor away from the faith. Then Saul—also known as Paul—was filled with the Holy Spirit; he looked straight at the magician and said, "You son of the Devil! You are the enemy of everything that is good; you are full of all kinds of evil tricks, and you always keep trying to turn the Lord's truths into lies! The Lord's hand will come down on you now; you will be blind, and will not see the light of day for a time."

At once Elymas felt a black mist cover his eyes, and he walked around trying to find someone to lead him by the hand. The Governor believed when he saw what had happened; he was greatly amazed at the teaching about the Lord.

Paul and his companions sailed from Paphos and came to Perga, in Pamphylia; but John Mark left them there and went back to Jerusalem. They went on from Perga and came to Antioch of Pisidia; and on the Sabbath day they went into the synagogue and sat down. After the reading from the Law of Moses and the writings of the prophets, the officials of the synagogue sent them a message: "Brothers, we want you to speak to the people if you have a message of encouragement for them." Paul stood up, motioned with his hand, and began to speak:

"Fellow Israelites and all Gentiles here who worship God: hear me! The God of this people of Israel chose our ancestors, and made the people a great nation during the time they lived as foreigners in the land of Egypt. God brought them out of Egypt by his great power. And we are here to bring the Good News to you: what God promised our ancestors he would do, he has now done for us, who are their descendants, by raising Jesus to life. As it is written in the second Psalm, 'You are my Son; today I have become your Father.' And this is what God said about raising him from the dead, never again to return to decay, 'I will give you the sacred and sure blessings that I promised to David.' As indeed he says in another passage, 'You will not allow your devoted servant to suffer decay.' For David served God's purposes in his own time; and then he died, was buried beside his ancestors, and suffered decay. But the one whom God raised from the dead did not suffer decay. All of you, my brothers, are to know for sure that it is through Jesus that the message about forgiveness of sins is preached to you; you are to know that everyone who believes in him is set free from all the sins from which the Law of Moses could not set you free."

The next Sabbath day nearly everyone in the town came to hear the word of the Lord. When the Jews saw the crowds, they were filled with jealousy; they spoke against what Paul was saying and insulted him. But Paul and Barnabas spoke out even more boldly, "It was necessary that the word of God should be spoken first to you. But since you reject it, and do not consider yourselves worthy of eternal life, we will leave you and go to the Gentiles. For this is the commandment that the Lord has given us, 'I have set you to be a light for the Gentiles, to be the way of salvation for the whole world.'"

When the Gentiles heard this they were glad and praised the Lord's message; and those who had been chosen for eternal life became believers.

The word of the Lord spread everywhere in that region. But the Jews stirred up the leading men of the city and the Gentile women of high social standing who worshiped God. They started a persecution against Paul and Barnabas, and threw them out of their region. The apostles shook the dust off their feet against them and went on to Iconium. The disciples in Antioch were full of joy and the Holy Spirit.

In Iconium

The same thing happened in Iconium: Paul and Barnabas went to the Jewish synagogue and spoke in such a way that a great number of Jews and Gentiles became believers. But the Jews who would not believe stirred up the Gentiles and turned their feelings against the brothers. The apostles stayed there for a long time. They spoke boldly about the Lord, who proved that their message about his grace was true by giving them the power to perform miracles and wonders. The crowd in the city was divided: some were for the Jews, others for the apostles.

Then the Gentiles and the Jews, together with their leaders, decided to mistreat the apostles and stone them. When the apostles learned about it they fled to Lystra and Derbe, cities in Lycaonia, and to the surrounding territory. There they preached the Good News.

The Return to Antioch in Syria

Some Jews came from Antioch of Pisidia and from Iconium; they won the crowds to their side, stoned Paul and dragged him out of town, thinking that he was dead. But when the believers gathered around him, he got up and went back into the town. The next day he and Barnabas went to Derbe.

Paul and Barnabas preached the Good News in Derbe, and won many disciples. Then they went back to Lystra, then to Iconium, and then to Antioch of Pisidia. They strengthened the believers and encouraged them to remain true to the faith. "We must pass through many troubles to enter the Kingdom of God," they taught. In each church they appointed elders for them; and with prayers and fasting they commended them to the Lord, in whom they had put their trust.

After going through the territory of Pisidia, they came to Pamphylia. They preached the message in Perga and then went down to Attalia, and from there they sailed back to Antioch, the place where they had been commended to the care of God's grace for the work they had now completed.

When they arrived in Antioch they gathered the people of the church together and told them of all that God had done with them, and how he had opened the way for the Gentiles to believe. They stayed a long time there with the believers.

The Meeting at Jerusalem

Some men came from Judea to Antioch and started teaching the brothers, "You cannot be saved unless you are circumcised as the Law of Moses requires." Paul and Barnabas had a fierce argument and dispute with them about this; so it was decided that Paul and Barnabas and some of the others in Antioch should go to Jerusalem and see the apostles and elders about this matter.

After a long debate Peter stood up and said, "My brothers, you know that a long time ago God chose me from among you to preach the message of Good News to the Gentiles, so that they could hear and believe. And God, who knows the hearts of men, showed his approval of the Gentiles by giving the Holy Spirit to them, just as he had to us. He made no difference between us and them; he purified their hearts because they believed. So then, why do you want to put God to the test now by laying a load on the backs of the believers which neither our ancestors nor we ourselves were able to carry? No! We believe and are saved by the grace of the Lord Jesus, just as they are."

The whole group was silent as they heard Barnabas and Paul report all the wonders and miracles that God had done through them among the Gentiles. When they finished speaking, James spoke up, "Listen to me, brothers! Simon has just explained how God first showed his care for the Gentiles by taking from among them a people to be all his own. The words of the prophets agree completely with this. As the scripture says, 'After this I will return, says the Lord, and I will raise David's fallen house. I will restore its ruins, and build it up again. And so all other people will seek the Lord, all the Gentiles whom I have called to be my own. So says the Lord, who made this known long ago.'

"It is my opinion," James went on, "that we should not trouble the Gentiles who are turning to God. Instead, we should write a letter telling them not to eat any food that is unclean because it has been offered to idols; to keep themselves from immorality; not to eat any animal that has been strangled, or any blood. For the Law of Moses has been read for a very long time in the synagogues every Sabbath, and his words are preached in every town."

Paul and Barnabas Separate

Some time later Paul said to Barnabas, "Let us go back and visit our brothers in every city where we preached the word of the Lord, and find out how they are getting along." Barnabas wanted to take John Mark with them, but Paul did not think it was right to take him, because he had not stayed with them to the end of their mission, but had turned back and left them in Pamphylia. They had a sharp argument between them, and separated from each other. Barnabas took Mark and sailed off for Cyprus, while Paul chose Silas and left, commended by the brothers to the care of the Lord's grace. He went through Syria and Cilicia, strengthening the churches.

Timothy Goes with Paul and Silas

Paul traveled on to Derbe and Lystra. A believer named Timothy lived there; his mother, also a believer, was Jewish, but his father was Greek. All the brothers in Lystra and Iconium spoke well of Timothy. Paul wanted to take Timothy along with him, so he circumcised him. He did so because all the Jews who lived in those places knew that Timothy's father was Greek. As they went through the towns they delivered to the believers the rules decided upon by the apostles and elders in Jerusalem, and told them to obey these rules. So the churches were made stronger in the faith and grew in numbers every day.

In Troas: Paul's Vision

They traveled through the region of Phrygia and Galatia, because the Holy Spirit did not let them preach the message in the province of Asia. When they reached the border of Mysia, they tried to go into the province of Bithynia, but the Spirit of Jesus did not allow them. So they traveled right on through Mysia and went down to Troas. Paul had a vision that night in which he saw a man of Macedonia standing and begging him, "Come over to Macedonia and help us!" As soon as Paul had this vision, we got ready to leave for Macedonia, because we decided that God had called us to preach the Good News to the people there.

In Philippi: the Conversion of Lydia

We left by ship from Troas and sailed straight across to Samothrace, and the next day to Neapolis. From there we went inland to Philippi, a city of the first district of Macedonia; it is also a Roman colony. We spent several days in that city. On the Sabbath day we went out of the city to the riverside, where we thought there would be a Jewish place for prayer. We sat down and talked to the women who gathered there. One of those who heard us was Lydia, from Thyatira, who was a dealer in purple goods. She was a woman who worshiped God, and the Lord opened her mind to pay attention to what Paul was saying. She and the people of her house were baptized. Then she invited us, "Come and stay in my house, if you have decided that I am a true believer in the Lord." And she persuaded us to go.

In Prison at Philippi

One day as we were going to the place of prayer, we were met by a slave girl who had an evil spirit in her that made her predict the future. She earned much money for her owners by telling fortunes. She followed Paul and us, shouting, "These men are servants of the Most High God! They announce to you how you can be saved!" She did this for many days, until Paul became so upset that he turned around and said to the spirit, "In the name of Jesus Christ I order you to come out of her!" The spirit went out of her that very moment. When her owners realized that their chance of making money was gone, they grabbed Paul and Silas and dragged them to the authorities in the public square. They brought them before the Roman officials and said, "These men are Jews, and they are causing trouble in our city. They are teaching customs that are against our law; we are Romans and cannot accept or practice them." The crowd joined the attack against them; the officials tore the clothes off Paul and Silas, and ordered them to be whipped. After a severe beating they were thrown into jail, and the jailer was ordered to lock them up tight. Upon receiving this order, the jailer threw them into the inner cell and fastened their feet between heavy blocks of wood.

About midnight Paul and Silas were praying and singing hymns to God, and the other prisoners were listening to them. Suddenly there was a violent earthquake, which shook the prison to its foundations. At once all the doors opened, and the chains fell off all the prisoners. The jailer woke up, and when he saw the prison doors open he thought that all the prisoners had escaped; so he pulled out his sword and was about to kill himself. But Paul shouted at the top of his voice, "Don't harm yourself! We are all here!"

The jailer called for a light, rushed in, and fell trembling at the feet of Paul and Silas. Then he led them out and asked, "What must I do, sirs, to be saved?"

"Believe in the Lord Jesus," they said, "and you will be saved—you and your family." Then they preached the word of the Lord to him and to all the others in his house. At that very hour of the night the jailer took them and washed off their wounds; and he and all his family were baptized at once. He took Paul and Silas up into his house and gave them some food to eat. He and his family were filled with joy because he now believed in God.

The next morning the Roman authorities sent police officers with the order, "Let those men go."

So the jailer told it to Paul, "The officials have sent an order for you and Silas to be released. You may leave, then, and go in peace.

But Paul said to the police officers, "We were not found guilty of any crime, yet they whipped us in public—and we are Roman citizens! Then they threw us in prison. And now they want to send us away secretly? Not at all! The Roman officials themselves must come here and let us out."

The police officers reported these words to the Roman officials; and when they heard that Paul and Silas were Roman citizens, they were afraid. So they went and apologized to them; then they led them out of the prison and asked them to leave the city. Paul and Silas left the prison and went to Lydia's house. There they met the brothers, spoke words of encouragement to them, and left.

In Thessalonica

They traveled on through Amphipolis and Apollonia, and came to Thessalonica, where there was a Jewish synagogue. According to his usual habit, Paul went to the synagogue. There during three Sabbath days he argued with the people from the Scriptures, explaining them and proving from them that the Messiah had to suffer, and rise from death. "This Jesus whom I announce to you," Paul said, "is the Messiah." Some of them were convinced and joined Paul and Silas; so did a large group of Greeks who worshiped God, and many of the leading women.

In Athens

But when the Jews in Thessalonica heard that Paul had preached the word of God in Berea also, they came there and started exciting and stirring up the mobs. At once the brothers sent Paul away to the coast; but both Silas and Timothy stayed in Berea. The men who were taking Paul went with him as far as Athens. Then they went back to Berea with instructions from Paul that Silas and Timothy join him as soon as possible.

While Paul was waiting in Athens for Silas and Timothy, he was greatly upset when he noticed how full of idols the city was. So he argued in the synagogue with the Jews and the Gentiles who worshiped God, and in the public square every day with the people who happened to come by. Certain Epicurean and Stoic teachers also debated with him. Some said, "What is this ignorant show-off trying to say?"

Others said, "He seems to be talking about foreign gods." They said this because Paul was preaching about Jesus and the resurrection. So they took Paul, brought him before the meeting of the Areopagus, and said, "We would like to know this new teaching that you are talking about. Some of the things we hear you say sound strange to us, and we would like to know what they mean." (For all the citizens of Athens and the foreigners who lived there liked to spend all their time telling and hearing the latest new thing.)

Paul stood up in front of the meeting of the Aeropagus and said, "Men of Athens! I see that in every way you are very religious. For as I walked through your city and looked at the places where you worship, I found also an altar on which is written, 'To an Unknown God.' That which you worship, then, even though you do not know it, is what I now proclaim to you. God, who made the world and everything in it, is Lord of heaven and earth, and does not live in temples made by men. Nor does he need anything that man can supply by working for him, since it is he himself who gives life and breath and everything else to all men. From the one man he created all races of men, and made them live over the whole earth. He himself fixed beforehand the exact times and the limits of the places where they would live. He did this so that they would look for him, and perhaps find him as they felt around for him. Yet God is actually not far from any one of us; as someone has said, 'In him we live and move and exist.' It is as some of your poets have said, 'We too are his children.' Since we are God's children, we should not suppose that his nature is anything like an image of gold or silver or stone, shaped by the art and skill of man. God has overlooked the times when men did not know, but now he commands all men everywhere to turn away from their evil ways. For he has fixed a day in which he will judge the whole world with justice, by means of a man he has chosen. He has given proof of this to everyone by raising that man from death!"

When they heard Paul speak about a raising from death, some of them made fun of him, but others said, "We want to hear you speak about this again." And so Paul left the meeting. Some men joined him and believed; among them was Dionysius, a member of the Areopagus, a woman named Damaris, and some others.

In Corinth

After this, Paul left Athens and went on to Corinth. There he met a Jew named Aquila, born in Pontus, who had just come from Italy with his wife Priscilla, because

Emperor Claudius had ordered all the Jews to leave Rome. Paul went to see them, and stayed and worked with them, because he earned his living by making tents, just as they did. He argued in the synagogue every Sabbath, trying to convince both Jews and Greeks.

When Silas and Timothy arrived from Macedonia, Paul gave his whole time to preaching the message, testifying to the Jews that Jesus is the Messiah. When they opposed him and said evil things about him, he protested by shaking the dust from his clothes and saying to them, "If you are lost, you yourselves must take the blame for it! I am not responsible. From now on I will go to the Gentiles." So he left them and went to live in the house of a Gentile named Titius Justus, who worshiped God; his house was next to the synagogue.

The Return to Antioch

Paul stayed on in Corinth with the brothers for many days, then left them and sailed off with Priscilla and Aquila for Syria. Before sailing he made a vow in Cenchreae and had his head shaved. They arrived in Ephesus, where Paul left Priscilla and Aquila. He went into the synagogue and argued with the Jews. They asked him to stay with them a long time, but he would not consent. Instead, he told them as he left, "If it is the will of God, I will come back to you." And so he sailed from Ephesus.

When he arrived at Caesarea he went to Jerusalem and greeted the church, and then went to Antioch.

To Macedonia and Greece

After spending some time there he left. He went through the region of Galatia and Phrygia, strengthening all the believers.

He went through those regions and encouraged the people with many messages. Then he came to Greece, where he stayed three months. He was getting ready to go to Syria when he discovered that the Jews were plotting against him; so he decided to go back through Macedonia. Sopater, the son of Pyrrhus, from Berea, went with him; so did Aristarchus and Secundus, from Thessalonica; Gaius, from Derbe; Timothy; and Tychicus and Trophimus, from the province of Asia. They went ahead and waited for us in Troas. We sailed from Philippi after the Feast of Unleavened Bread, and five days later joined them in Troas, where we spent a week.

Paul's Last Visit in Troas
On Saturday evening we gathered together for the fellowship meal. Paul spoke to the people, and kept on speaking until midnight, since he was going to leave the next day. There were many lamps in the upstairs room where we were meeting. A young man named Eutychus was sitting in the window; and as Paul kept on talking, Eutychus got sleepier and sleepier, until he finally went sound asleep and fell from the third story to the ground. They picked him up, and he was dead. But Paul went down and threw himself on him and hugged him. "Don't worry," he said, "he is still alive!" Then he went back upstairs, broke bread, and ate. After talking with them for a long time until sunrise, Paul left. They took the young man home alive, and were greatly comforted.

We went on ahead to the ship and sailed off to Assos, where we were going to take Paul aboard. He had told us to do this, because he was going there by land. When he met us in Assos, we took him aboard and went on to Mitylene. We sailed from there and arrived off Chios the next day. A day later we came to Samos, and the following day we reached Miletus. Paul had decided to sail on by Ephesus, so as not to lose any time in the province of Asia. He was in a hurry to arrive in Jerusalem, if at all possible, by the day of Pentecost.

Paul's Farewell Speech to the Elders of Ephesus
Paul sent a message from Miletus to Ephesus, asking the elders of the church to meet him. When they arrived, he said to them, "You know how I spent the whole time I was with you, from the first day I arrived in the province of Asia. With all humility and many tears I did my work as the Lord's servant, through the hard times that came to me because of the plots of the Jews. You know that I did not hold back anything that would be of help to you as I preached and taught you in public and in your homes. To Jews and Gentiles alike I

gave solemn warning that they should turn from their sins to God, and believe in our Lord Jesus. And now, in obedience to the Holy Spirit, I am going to Jerusalem, not knowing what will happen to me there. I only know that in every city the Holy Spirit has warned me that prison and troubles wait for me. But I reckon my own life to be worth nothing to me, in order that I may complete my mission and finish the work that the Lord Jesus gave me to do, which is to declare the Good News of the grace of God.

"I have gone about among all of you, preaching the Kingdom of God. And now I know that none of you will ever see me again. So I solemnly declare to you this very day: if any of you should be lost, I am not responsible. For I have not held back from announcing to you the whole purpose of God. Keep watch over yourselves and over all the flock which the Holy Spirit has placed in your care. Be shepherds of the church of God, which he made his own through the death of his own Son. I know that after I leave, fierce wolves will come among you, and they will not spare the flock. The time will come when some men from your own group will tell lies to lead the believers away after them. Watch, then, and remember that with many tears, day and night, I taught every one of you for three years.

"And now I place you in the care of God and the message of his grace. He is able to build you up and give you the blessings he keeps for all his people. I have not coveted anyone's silver or gold or clothing. You yourselves know that with these hands of mine I have worked and provided everything that my companions and I have needed. I have shown you in all things that by working hard in this way we must help the weak, remembering the words that the Lord Jesus himself said, 'There is more happiness in giving than in receiving.'"

When Paul finished, he knelt down with them all and prayed. They were all crying as they hugged him and kissed him good-bye. They were especially sad at the words he had said that they would never see him again. And so they went with him to the ship.

Paul Visits James

When we arrived in Jerusalem the brothers welcomed us warmly. The next day Paul went with us to see James; and all the church elders were present. Paul greeted them and gave a complete report of everything that God had done among the Gentiles through his work. After hearing him, they all praised God. Then they said to Paul, "You can see how it is, brother. There are thousands of Jews who have become believers, and they are all very devoted to the Law. They have been told about you that you have been teaching all the Jews who live in Gentile countries to abandon the Law of Moses, telling them not to circumcise their children or follow the Jewish customs. They are sure to hear that you have arrived. What should be done, then? Do what we tell you. There are four men here who have taken a vow. Go along with them and join them in the ceremony of purification and pay their expenses; then they will be able to shave their heads. In this way everyone will know that there is no truth in any of the things that they have been told about you, but that you yourself live in accordance with the Law of Moses. But as to the Gentiles who have become believers, we have sent them a letter telling them we decided that they must not eat any food that has been offered to idols, or any blood, or any animal that has been strangled, and that they must keep themselves from immorality."

So Paul took the men and the next day performed the ceremony of purification with them. Then he went into the temple and gave notice of how many days it would be until the end of the period of purification, when the sacrifice for each one of them would be offered.

Paul Arrested in the Temple

When the seven days were about to come to an end, some Jews from the province of Asia saw Paul in the temple. They stirred up the whole crowd and grabbed Paul. "Men of Israel!" they shouted. "Help! This is the man who goes everywhere teaching everyone against the people of Israel, the Law of Moses, and this temple.

And now he has even brought some Gentiles into the temple and defiled this holy place!" (They said this because they had seen Trophimus from Ephesus with Paul in the city, and they thought that Paul had taken him into the temple.)

Confusion spread through the whole city, and the people all ran together, grabbed Paul, and dragged him out of the temple. At once the temple doors were closed. The mob was trying to kill Paul when a report was sent up to the commander of the Roman troops that all of Jerusalem was rioting. At once the commander took some officers and soldiers and rushed down to the crowd. When the people saw him with the soldiers, they stopped beating Paul. The commander went over to Paul, arrested him, and ordered him to be tied up with two chains. Then he asked, "Who is this man, and what has he done?" Some in the crowd shouted one thing, others something else. There was such confusion that the commander could not find out exactly what had happened; so he ordered his men to take Paul up into the fort. They got with him to the steps, and then the soldiers had to carry him because the mob was so wild. They were all coming after him and screaming, "Kill him!"

As they were about to take Paul into the fort, he spoke to the commander, "May I say something to you?"

"Do you speak Greek?" the commander asked. "Then you are not that Egyptian fellow who some time ago started a revolution and led four thousand armed terrorists out into the desert?"

Paul answered, "I am a Jew, born in Tarsus of Cilicia, a citizen of an important city. Please, let me speak to the people."

They were screaming, waving their clothes, and throwing dust up in the air. The Roman commander ordered his men to take Paul into the fort, and told them to whip him to find out why the Jews were screaming like this against him. But when they had tied him up to be whipped, Paul said to the officer standing there, "Is it lawful for you to whip a Roman citizen who hasn't even been tried for any crime?"

When the officer heard this, he went to the commander and asked him, "What are you doing? That man is a Roman citizen!"

So the commander went to Paul and asked him, "Tell me, are you a Roman citizen?"

"Yes," answered Paul.

The commander said, "I became one by paying a large amount of money."

"But I am one by birth," Paul answered.

At once the men who were going to question Paul drew back from him; and the commander was afraid when he realized that Paul was a Roman citizen, and that he had put him in chains.

The commander wanted to find out for sure what the Jews were accusing Paul of; so the next day he had Paul's chains taken off and ordered the chief priests and the whole Council to meet. Then he took Paul, and made him stand before them.

Paul Before the Council
When Paul saw that some of the group were Sadducees and that others were Pharisees, he called out in the Council, "My brothers! I am a Pharisee, the son of Pharisees. I am on trial here because I hope that the dead will rise to life!"

As soon as he said this, the Pharisees and Sadducees started to quarrel, and the group was divided. (For the Sadducees say that people will not rise from death, and that there are no angels or spirits; but the Pharisees believe in all three.) The shouting became louder, and some of the teachers of the Law who belonged to the party of the Pharisees stood up and protested strongly, "We cannot find a thing wrong with this man! Perhaps a spirit or an angel really did speak to him!"

The argument became so violent that the commander was afraid that Paul would be torn to pieces by them. So he ordered his soldiers to go down into the group and get Paul away from them, and take him into the fort.

The following night the Lord stood by Paul and said, "Courage! You have given your witness to me here in Jerusalem, and you must do the same in Rome also."

The next morning some Jews met together and made a plan. They took a vow that they would not eat or drink anything until they had killed Paul. There were more than forty of them who planned this together. Then they went to the chief priests and elders and said, "We have taken a solemn vow together not to eat a thing until we kill Paul. Now then, you and the Council send word to the Roman commander to bring Paul down to you, pretending that you want to get more accurate information about him. But we will be ready to kill him before he ever gets here."

But the son of Paul's sister heard of the plot; so he went and entered the fort and told it to Paul. Then Paul called one of the officers and said to him, "Take this young man to the commander; he has something to tell him."

The commander said, "Don't tell anyone that you have reported this to me." And he sent the young man away.

Then the commander called two of his officers and said, "Get two hundred soldiers ready to go to Caesarea, together with seventy horsemen and two hundred spearmen, and be ready to leave by nine o'clock tonight. Provide some horses for Paul to ride, and get him safely through to Governor Felix."

Paul Accused by the Jews

Five days later the High Priest Ananias went to Caesarea with some elders and a lawyer named Tertullus. They appeared before Governor Felix and made their charges against Paul. Tertullus was called and began to accuse Paul as follows:

"Your Excellency! Your wise leadership has brought us a long period of peace, and many necessary reforms are being made for the good of our country. We welcome this everywhere at all times, and we are deeply grateful to you. I do not want to take up too much of your time, however, so I beg you to be kind and listen to our brief account. We found this man to be a dangerous nuisance; he starts riots among the Jews all over the world, and is a leader of the party of the Nazarenes. He also tried to defile the temple, and we arrested him.

[We planned to judge him according to our own Law, but the commander Lysias came in and with great violence took him from us. Then Lysias gave orders that his accusers should come before you.] If you question this man, you yourself will be able to learn from him all the things that we are accusing him of." The Jews joined in the accusation and said that all this was true.

The Governor then motioned to Paul to speak, and Paul said,

"I know that you have been a judge over this nation for many years, and so I am happy to defend myself before you. As you can find out for yourself, it was no more than twelve days ago that I went up to Jerusalem to worship. The Jews did not find me arguing with anyone in the temple, nor did they find me stirring up the people, either in the synagogues or anywhere else in the city. Nor can they give you proof of the accusations they now bring against me."

Then Felix, who was well informed about the Way, brought the hearing to a close. "I will decide your case," he told them, "when the commander Lysias arrives." He ordered the officer in charge of Paul to keep him under guard, but to give him some freedom and allow his friends to provide for his needs.

After some days Felix came with his wife Drusilla, who was Jewish. He sent for Paul and listened to him as he talked about faith in Christ Jesus. But as Paul went on discussing about goodness, self-control, and the coming Day of Judgment, Felix was afraid and said, "You may leave now. I will call you again when I get the chance." At the same time he was hoping that Paul would give him some money; and for this reason he would call for him often and talk with him.

After two years had passed, Porcius Festus took the place of Felix as Governor. Felix wanted to gain favor with the Jews, so he left Paul in prison.

Paul Appeals to the Emperor
Three days after Festus arrived in the province, he went from Caesarea to Jerusalem. There the chief priests and the Jewish leaders brought their charges against Paul. They begged Festus to do them the favor of having Paul

come to Jerusalem, because they had made a plot to kill him on the way. Festus answered, "Paul is being kept a prisoner in Caesarea, and I myself will be going back there soon. Let your leaders go to Caesarea with me and accuse the man, if he has done anything wrong."

Festus spent another eight or ten days with them, and then went to Caesarea. On the next day he sat down in the judgment court, and ordered Paul to be brought in. When Paul arrived, the Jews who had come from Jerusalem stood around him and started making many serious charges against him, which they were not able to prove. But Paul defended himself, "I have done nothing wrong against the Law of the Jews, or the temple, or the Roman Emperor."

Festus wanted to gain favor with the Jews, so he asked Paul, "Would you be willing to go to Jerusalem and be tried on these charges before me there?"

Paul said, "I am standing before the Emperor's own judgment court, where I should be tried. I have done no wrong to the Jews, as you yourself well know. If I have broken the law and done something for which I deserve the death penalty, I do not ask to escape it. But if there is no truth in the charges they bring against me, no one can hand me over to them. I appeal to the Emperor."

Then Festus, after conferring with his advisers, answered, "You have appealed to the Emperor, so to the Emperor you will go."

Paul Before Agrippa and Bernice

Some time later King Agrippa and Bernice came to Caesarea to pay a visit of welcome to Festus. After they had been there several days, Festus explained Paul's situation to the king, "There is a man here who was left a prisoner by Felix; and when I went to Jerusalem, the Jewish chief priests and elders brought charges against him and asked me to condemn him. But I told them that the Romans are not in the habit of handing over any man accused of a crime before he has met his accusers face to face, and has the chance of defending himself against the accusation. When they came here, then, I lost no time, but on the very next day I sat in the judgment court and ordered the man to be brought in.

THE PLIGHT AND STRUGGLE OF THE BELIEVERS 219

His opponents stood up, but they did not accuse him of any of the evil crimes that I thought they would. All they had were some arguments with him about their own religion and about a man named Jesus, who has died; but Paul claims that he is alive. I was undecided about how I could get information on these matters, so I asked Paul if he would be willing to go to Jerusalem and be tried there on these charges. But Paul appealed; he asked to be kept under guard and let the Emperor decide his case. So I gave orders for him to be kept under guard until I could send him to the Emperor."

Agrippa said to Festus, "I would like to hear this man myself."

"You will hear him tomorrow," Festus answered.

The next day Agrippa and Bernice came with great pomp and ceremony, and entered the audience hall with the military chiefs and the leading men of the city. Festus gave the order and Paul was brought in.

Paul Defends Himself Before Agrippa

Agrippa said to Paul, "You have permission to speak on your own behalf." Paul stretched out his hand and defended himself as follows:

"Why do you Jews find it impossible to believe that God raises the dead?

"I myself thought that I should do everything I could against the name of Jesus of Nazareth. That is what I did in Jerusalem. I received authority from the chief priests and put many of God's people in prison; and when they were sentenced to death, I also voted for it. Many times I had them punished in all the synagogues, and tried to make them deny their faith. I was so furious with them that I even went to foreign cities to persecute them.

"It was for this purpose that I went to Damascus with the authority and orders from the chief priests. It was on the road at midday, your Majesty, that I saw a light much brighter than the sun shining from the sky around me and the men traveling with me. All of us fell to the ground, and I heard a voice say to me in the Hebrew language, 'Saul, Saul! Why are you persecuting me? You hurt yourself by hitting back, like an ox kicking against its owner's stick.' 'Who are you, Lord?' I asked. And the Lord said: 'I am Jesus, whom you persecute.'

"And so, King Agrippa, I did not disobey the vision I had from heaven. First in Damascus and in Jerusalem, and then in the whole country of the Jews and among the Gentiles, I preached that they must repent of their sins and turn to God, and do the things that would show they had repented. It was for this reason that the Jews seized me while I was in the temple, and tried to kill me. But to this very day I have been helped by God, and so I stand here giving my witness to all, to the small and great alike. What I say is the very same thing the prophets and Moses said was going to happen: that the Messiah must suffer and be the first one to rise from death, to announce the light of salvation to the Jews and to the Gentiles."

As Paul defended himself in this way, Festus shouted at him, "You are mad, Paul! Your great learning is driving you mad!"

Paul answered, "I am not mad, your Excellency! The words I speak are true and sober. King Agrippa! I can speak to you with all boldness, because you know about these things. I am sure that you have taken notice of every one of them, for this thing has not happened hidden away in a corner. King Agrippa, do you believe the prophets? I know that you do!"

Agrippa said to Paul, "In this short time do you think you will make me a Christian?"

"Whether a short time or a long time," Paul answered, "my prayer to God is that you and all the rest of you who are listening to me today might become what I am—except, of course, for these chains!"

Then the King, the Governor, Bernice, and all the others got up, and after leaving they said to each other, "This man has not done anything for which he should die or be put in prison." And Agrippa said to Festus, "This man could have been released if he had not appealed to the Emperor."

Paul Sails for Italy
When it was decided that we should sail to Italy, they handed Paul and some other prisoners over to Julius, an

officer in the Roman army regiment called "The Emperor's Regiment." We went aboard a ship from Adramyttium, which was ready to leave for the seaports of the province of Asia, and sailed away. Aristarchus, a Macedonian from Thessalonica, was with us. We crossed over the sea of Cilicia and Pamphylia, and came to Myra, in Lycia. There the officer found a ship from Alexandria that was going to sail for Italy, so he put us aboard.

We sailed slowly for several days, and with great difficulty finally arrived off the town of Cnidus. The wind would not let us go any farther in that direction, so we sailed down the sheltered side of the island of Crete, passing by Cape Salmone. We kept close to the coast, and with great difficulty came to a place called Safe Harbors, not far from the town of Lasea.

We spent a long time there, until it became dangerous to continue the voyage, because by now the day of Atonement was already past. So Paul gave them this advice, "Men, I see that our voyage from here on will be dangerous; there will be great damage to the cargo and to the ship, and loss of life as well." But the army officer was convinced by what the captain and the owner of the ship said, and not by what Paul said. The harbor was not a good one to spend the winter in; so most of the men were in favor of putting out to sea and trying to reach Phoenix, if possible. It is a harbor in Crete that faces southwest and northwest, and they could spend the winter there.

The Storm at Sea

A soft wind from the south began to blow, and the men thought that they could carry out their plan; so they pulled up the anchor and sailed as close as possible along the coast of Crete. But soon a very strong wind—the one called "Northeaster"—blew down from the island. It hit the ship, and since it was impossible to keep the ship headed into the wind, we gave up trying and let it be carried along by the wind. For many days we could not see the sun or the stars, and the wind kept on blowing very hard. We finally gave up all hope of being saved.

After the men had gone a long time without food, Paul stood before them and said, "Men, you should have listened to me and not have sailed from Crete; then we would have avoided all this damage and loss. But now I beg you, take courage! Not one of you will lose his life; only the ship will be lost. For last night an angel of the God to whom I belong and whom I worship came to me and said, 'Don't be afraid, Paul! You must stand before the Emperor; and God, in his goodness, has given you the lives of all those who are sailing with you.' And so, men, take courage! For I trust in God that it will be just as I was told. But we will be driven ashore on some island."

It was the fourteenth night, and we were being driven by the storm on the Mediterranean. About midnight the sailors suspected that we were getting close to land.

When day came, the sailors did not recognize the coast, but they noticed a bay with a beach and decided that, if possible, they would run the ship aground there. So they cut off the anchors and let them sink in the sea, and at the same time they untied the ropes that held the steering oars. Then they raised the sail at the front of the ship so that the wind would blow the ship forward, and headed for shore. But the ship hit a sandbank and went aground; the front part of the ship got stuck and could not move, while the back part was being broken to pieces by the violence of the waves.

The soldiers made a plan to kill all the prisoners, so that none of them would swim ashore and escape. But the army officer wanted to save Paul, so he stopped them from doing this. Instead, he ordered all the men who could swim to jump overboard first and swim ashore; the rest were to follow, holding on to the planks or to some broken pieces of the ship. And this was how we all got safely ashore.

In Malta
When we were safely ashore, we learned that the island was called Malta. The natives there were very friendly to us. It had started to rain and was cold, so they built a fire and made us all welcome. Paul gathered up a bundle of sticks and was putting them on the fire when a

snake came out, on account of the heat, and fastened itself to his hand. The natives saw the snake hanging on Paul's hand and said to one another, "This man must be a murderer, but Fate will not let him live, even though he escaped from the sea." But Paul shook the snake off into the fire without being harmed at all. They were waiting for him to swell up or suddenly fall down dead. But after waiting for a long time and not seeing anything unusual happening to him, they changed their minds and said, "He is a god!"

From Malta to Rome
After three months we sailed away on a ship from Alexandria, called "The Twin Gods," which had spent the winter in the island.

When we arrived in Rome, Paul was allowed to live by himself with a soldier guarding him.

For two years Paul lived there in a place he rented for himself, and welcomed all who came to see him. He preached about the Kingdom of God and taught about the Lord Jesus Christ, speaking with all boldness and freedom.

Twelve

THE FOLLOWERS OF CHRIST PREACH THE GOOD NEWS

Prayer of Thanksgiving
From Paul, a servant of Christ Jesus, and an apostle chosen and called by God to preach his Good News.

And so I write to all of you in Rome whom God loves and has called to be his own people:

May God our Father and the Lord Jesus Christ give you grace and peace.

First, I thank my God, through Jesus Christ, for all of you; because the whole world is hearing of your faith. God can prove that what I say is true—the God whom I serve with all my heart by preaching the Good News about his Son. God knows that I always remember you every time I pray. I ask that God, in his good will, may at last make it possible for me to visit you now. For I want very much to see you in order to share a spiritual blessing with you, to make you strong. What I mean is that both you and I will be helped at the same time, you by my faith and I by your faith.

You must remember this, my brothers: many times I have planned to visit you, but something has always kept me from doing so. I want to win converts among you, too, as I have among other Gentiles. For I have an obligation to all peoples, to the civilized and to the savage, to the educated and to the ignorant. So then, I am eager to preach the Good News to you also who live in Rome.

The Power of the Gospel

I have complete confidence in the gospel; it is God's power to save all who believe, first the Jews and also the Gentiles. For the gospel reveals how God puts men right with himself: it is through faith, from beginning to end. As the scripture says, "He who is put right with God through faith shall live."

The Guilt of Mankind

God's wrath is revealed coming down from heaven upon all the sin and evil of men whose evil ways prevent the truth from being known. God punishes them, because what men can know about God is plain to them. God himself made it plain to them. Ever since God created the world, his invisible qualities, both his eternal power and his divine nature, have been clearly seen. Men can perceive them in the things that God has made. So they have no excuse at all! They know God, but they do not give him the honor that belongs to him, nor do they thank him. Instead, their thoughts have become complete nonsense and their empty minds are filled with darkness.

How God Puts Men Right

God puts men right through their faith in Jesus Christ. God does this to all who believe in Christ, because there is no difference at all: all men have sinned and are far away from God's saving presence. But by the free gift of God's grace they are all put right with him through Christ Jesus, who sets them free. God offered him so that by his death he should become the means by which men's sins are forgiven, through their faith in him. God did this in order to demonstrate his righteousness. In the past, he was patient and overlooked men's sins; but now in the present time he deals with men's sins, to demonstrate his righteousness. In this way God shows that he himself is righteous and that he puts right everyone who believes in Jesus.

What, then, can we boast about? Nothing! And what is the reason for this? Is it that we obey the Law? No, but that we believe. For we conclude that a man is put right with God only through faith, and not by doing what the Law commands.

Right with God

Now that we have been put right with God through faith, we have peace with God through our Lord Jesus Christ. He has brought us, by faith, into this experience of God's grace, in which we now live. We rejoice, then, in the hope we have of sharing God's glory! And we also rejoice in our troubles, because we know that trouble produces endurance, endurance brings God's approval, and his approval creates hope. This hope does not disappoint us, because God has poured out his love into our hearts by means of the Holy Spirit, who is God's gift to us.

For when we were still helpless, Christ died for the wicked, at the time that God chose. It is a difficult thing for someone to die for a righteous person. It may be that someone might dare to die for a good person. But God has shown us how much he loves us; it was while we were still sinners that Christ died for us! By his death we are now put right with God; how much more, then, will we be saved by him from God's wrath.

Life in the Spirit

But you do not live as your human nature tells you to; you live as the Spirit tells you to—if, in fact, God's Spirit lives in you. Whoever does not have the Spirit of Christ does not belong to him. But if Christ lives in you, although your bodies are going to die because of sin, yet the Spirit is life for you because you have been put right with God. If the Spirit of God, who raised Jesus from death, lives in you, then he who raised Christ from death will also give life to your mortal bodies by the presence of his Spirit in you.

So then, my brothers, we have an obligation, but not to live as our human nature wants us to. For if you live according to your human nature, you are going to die; but if, by the Spirit, you kill your sinful actions, you will live. Those who are led by God's Spirit are God's sons.

For the Spirit that God has given you does not make you a slave and cause you to be afraid; instead, the Spirit makes you God's sons, and by the Spirit's power we cry to God, "Father! my Father!" God's Spirit joins himself to our spirits to declare that we are God's children. Since we are his children, we will possess the blessings he keeps for his people, and we will also possess with Christ what God has kept for him; for if we share Christ's suffering, we will also share his glory.

The Future Glory
I consider that what we suffer at this present time cannot be compared at all with the glory that is going to be revealed to us. All of creation waits with eager longing for God to reveal his sons. For creation was condemned to become worthless, not of its own will, but because God willed it to be so. Yet there was this hope, that creation itself would one day be set free from its slavery to decay, and share the glorious freedom of the children of God. For we know that up to the present time all of creation groans with pain like the pain of childbirth. But not just creation alone; we who have the Spirit as the first of God's gifts, we also groan within ourselves as we wait for God to make us his sons and set our whole being free. For it was by hope that we were saved; but if we see what we hope for, then it is not really hope. For who hopes for something that he sees? But if we hope for what we do not see, we wait for it with patience.

In the same way the Spirit also comes to help us, weak that we are. For we do not know how we ought to pray; the Spirit himself pleads with God for us, in groans that words cannot express. And God, who sees into the hearts of men, knows what the thought of the Spirit is; because the Spirit pleads with God on behalf of his people and in accordance with his will.

We know that in all things God works for good with those who love him, those whom he has called according to his purpose. Those whom God had already chosen he had also set apart to become like his Son, so that the Son would be the first among many brothers. And so God called those that he had set apart; and those that he called he also put right with himself; and with those that he put right with himself he also shared his glory.

God's Love in Christ Jesus

Faced with all this, what can we say? If God is for us, who can be against us? He did not even keep back his own Son, but offered him for us all! He gave us his Son—will he not also freely give us all things? Who will accuse God's chosen people? God himself declares them not guilty! Can anyone, then, condemn them? Christ Jesus is the one who died, or rather, who was raised to life and is at the right side of God. He pleads with God for us! Who, then, can separate us from the love of Christ? Can trouble do it, or hardship, or persecution, or hunger, or poverty, or danger, or death? As the scripture says, "For your sake we are in danger of death the whole day long; we are treated like sheep that are going to be slaughtered." No, in all these things we have complete victory through him who loved us! For I am certain that nothing can separate us from his love: neither death nor life; neither angels nor other heavenly rulers or powers; neither the present nor the future; neither the world above nor the world below—there is nothing in all creation that will ever be able to separate us from the love of God which is ours through Christ Jesus our Lord.

God and His Chosen People

What I say is true; I belong to Christ and I do not lie. My conscience, ruled by the Holy Spirit, also assures me that I am not lying. How great is my sorrow, how endless the pain in my heart for my people, my own flesh and blood! For their sake I could wish that I myself were under God's curse and separated from Christ. They are God's chosen people; he made them his sons and shared his glory with them; he made his covenants with them and gave them the Law; they have the true worship; they have received God's promises; they are descended from the patriarchs, and Christ, as a human being, belongs to their race. May God, who rules over all, be praised forever!

I am not saying that the promise of God has failed; because not all the people of Israel are the chosen people of God. Neither are all Abraham's descendants the children of God. God said to Abraham, "The descendants of Isaac will be counted as yours." This means that the children born in the natural way are not the children of God; instead, the children born as a result of God's promise are regarded as the true descendants.

And the same is true of what God has done. He wanted to show his wrath and to make his power known. So he was very patient in enduring those who were the objects of his wrath, who were ready to be destroyed. And he wanted also to reveal his rich glory, which was poured out on us who are the objects of his mercy, those of us whom he has prepared to receive his glory. For we are the ones whom he called, not only from among the Jews but also from among the Gentiles.

Salvation Is for All

My brothers, how I wish with all my heart that my own people might be saved! How I pray to God for them! I can be a witness for them that they are deeply devoted to God. But their devotion is not based on true knowledge. They have not known the way in which God puts men right with himself, and have tried to set up their own way; and so they did not submit themselves to God's way of putting men right. For Christ has brought the Law to an end, so that everyone who believes is put right with God. This includes everyone, because there is no difference between Jews and Gentiles; God is the same Lord of all, and richly blesses all who call to him. As the scripture says, "Everyone who calls on the name of the Lord will be saved."

But how can they call to him, if they have not believed? And how can they believe, if they have not heard the message? And how can they hear, if the message is not proclaimed? And how can the message be proclaimed, if the messengers are not sent out? As the scripture says, "How wonderful is the coming of those who bring good news!" But they have not all accepted the Good News. Isaiah himself said, "Lord, who believed our message?" So then, faith comes from hearing the message and the message comes through preaching Christ.

God's Mercy on Israel

I ask, then: Did God reject his own people? Certainly not! I myself am an Israelite, a descendant of Abraham, a member of the tribe of Benjamin. God has not rejected his people, whom he chose from the beginning. You know what the scripture says in the passage where Elijah pleads with God against Israel: "Lord, they have killed your prophets and torn down your altars; I am the only one left, and they are trying to kill me." What answer did God give him? "I have kept for myself seven thousand men who have not worshiped the false god Baal." It is the same way now at this time: there is a small number of those whom God has chosen, because of his mercy. His choice is based on his mercy, not on what they have done. For if God's choice were based on what men do, then his mercy would not be true mercy.

What then? The people of Israel did not find what they were looking for. It was the small group that God chose who found it; the rest grew deaf to God's call. As the scripture says, "God made them dull of heart and mind; to this very day they cannot see with their eyes or hear with their ears." And David says, "May they be caught and trapped at their feasts; may they fall, may they be punished! May their eyes be closed so that they cannot see; and make them bend under their troubles at all times."

I ask, then: When the Jews stumbled, did they fall to their ruin? By no means! Because they sinned, salvation has come to the Gentiles, to make the Jews jealous of them. The sin of the Jews brought rich blessings to the world, and their spiritual poverty brought rich blessings to the Gentiles. How much greater the blessings will be, then, when the complete number of Jews is included!

The Salvation of the Gentiles

I am speaking now to you Gentiles: as long as I am an apostle to the Gentiles I will take pride in my work. Perhaps I can make the people of my own race jealous, and so be able to save some of them. For when they were rejected, the world was made friends with God. What will it be, then, when they are accepted? It will be life for the dead!

For God has made all men prisoners of disobedience, that he might show mercy to them all.

How great are God's riches! How deep are his wisdom and knowledge! Who can explain his decisions? Who can understand his ways? As the scripture says, "Who knows the mind of the Lord? Who is able to give him advice? Who has ever given him anything, so that he had to pay it back?" For all things were created by him, and all things exist through him and for him. To God be the glory forever!

Life in God's Service

So then, my brothers, because of God's great mercy to us, I make this appeal to you: Offer yourselves as a living sacrifice to God, dedicated to his service and pleasing to him. This is the true worship that you should offer. Do not conform outwardly to the standards of this world, but let God transform you inwardly by a complete change of your mind. Then you will be able to know the will of God—what is good, and is pleasing to him, and is perfect.

Ask God to bless those who persecute you; yes, ask him to bless, not to curse. Be happy with those who are happy, weep with those who weep. Have the same concern for all alike. Do not be proud, but accept humble duties. Do not think of yourselves as wise.

If someone does evil to you, do not pay him back with evil. Try to do what all men consider to be good. Do everything possible, on your part, to live at peace with all men. Never take revenge, my friends, but instead let God's wrath do it. For the scripture says, "I will take revenge, I will pay back, says the Lord." Instead, as the scripture says: "If your enemy is hungry, feed him; if he is thirsty, give him to drink; for by doing this you will heap burning coals on his head." Do not let evil defeat you; instead, conquer evil with good.

Duties Toward the State Authorities

Everyone must obey the state authorities, because no authority exists without God's permission, and the existing authorities have been put there by God.

This is also the reason that you pay taxes, because the authorities are working for God when they fulfil their duties. Pay, then, what you owe them; pay them your personal and property taxes, and show respect and honor for them all.

Duties Toward One Another

Be in debt to no one—the only debt you should have is to love one another. Whoever loves his fellow-man has obeyed the Law. The commandments, "Do not commit adultery; do not murder; do not steal; do not covet"— all these, and any others besides, are summed up in the one command, "Love your fellow-man as yourself." Whoever loves his fellow-man will never do him wrong. To love, then, is to obey the whole Law.

You must do this, because you know what hour it is: the time has come for you to wake up from your sleep. For the moment when we will be saved is closer now than it was when we first believed. The night is nearly over, day is almost here. Let us stop doing the things that belong to the dark, and take up the weapons for fighting in the light. Let us conduct ourselves properly, as people who live in the light of day; no orgies or drunkenness, no immorality or indecency, no fighting or jealousy. But take up the weapons of the Lord Jesus Christ, and stop giving attention to your sinful nature, to satisfy its desires.

Do Not Judge Your Brother

The man who will eat anything is not to despise the man who doesn't; while the one who eats only vegetables is not to pass judgment on the one who eats anything, because God has accepted him. Who are you to judge the servant of someone else? It is his own Master who will decide whether he succeeds or fails. And he will succeed, because the Lord is able to make him succeed.

Every one of us, then, will have to give an account of himself to God.

So then, let us stop judging one another. Instead, this is what you should decide: not to do anything that would make your brother stumble, or fall into sin. My union with the Lord Jesus makes me know for certain that nothing is unclean of itself; but if a man believes that something is unclean, then it becomes unclean for him. If you hurt your brother because of something you eat, then you are no longer acting from love. Do not let the food that you eat ruin the man for whom Christ died! Do not let what you regard as good acquire a bad name. For God's Kingdom is not a matter of eating and drinking, but of the righteousness, peace, and joy that the Holy Spirit gives.

Please Others, Not Yourselves

We who are strong in the faith ought to help the weak to carry their burdens. We should not please ourselves. Instead, each of us should please his brother for his own good, in order to build him up in the faith. For Christ did not please himself. Instead, as the scripture says, "The insults spoken by those who insulted you have fallen on me." Everything written in the Scriptures was written to teach us, in order that we might have hope through the patience and encouragement the Scriptures give us. And may God, the source of patience and encouragement, enable you to have the same point of view among yourselves by following the example of Christ Jesus, so that all of you together, with one voice, may praise the God and Father of our Lord Jesus Christ.

The Gospel to the Gentiles

Accept one another, then, for the glory of God, as Christ has accepted you. Because I tell you that Christ became a servant of the Jews to show that God is faithful, to make God's promises to the patriarchs come true, and also to enable the Gentiles to praise God for his mercy. As the scripture says, "And so I will give thanks to you among the Gentiles, I will sing praises to your name." Again it says, "Rejoice, Gentiles, with God's chosen people!" And again, "Praise the Lord, all Gentiles; praise him, all peoples!" And again, Isaiah says, "A descendant of Jesse will come; he will be raised to rule the Gentiles, and they will put their hope in him."

May God, the source of hope, fill you with all joy and peace by means of your faith in him, so that your hope will continue to grow by the power of the Holy Spirit.

A Request from Paul
I urge you, brothers, by our Lord Jesus Christ and by the love that the Spirit gives: join me in praying fervently to God for me. Pray that I may be kept safe from the unbelievers in Judea, and that my service in Jerusalem may be acceptable to God's people there. And so I will come to you full of joy, if it is God's will, and enjoy a refreshing visit with you. May God, our source of peace, be with all of you.

Questions About Marriage
From Paul, who by the will of God was called to be an apostle of Christ Jesus, and from our brother Sosthenes—

To the church of God which is in Corinth, to all who are called to be God's holy people, who belong to him in union with Christ Jesus, together with all people everywhere who call on the name of our Lord Jesus Christ, their Lord and ours:

May God our Father and the Lord Jesus Christ give you grace and peace.

Now, to deal with the matters you wrote about. A man does well not to marry. But because there is so much immorality, every man should have his own wife, and every woman should have her own husband. A man should fulfill his duty as a husband and a woman should fulfil her duty as a wife, and each should satisfy the other's needs. The wife is not the master of her own body, but the husband is; in the same way the husband is not the master of his own body, but the wife is. Do not deny yourselves to each other, unless you first agree to do so for a while, in order to spend your time in prayer; but then resume normal marital relations, to keep you from giving in to Satan's temptation because of your lack of self-control.

I tell you this not as an order, but simply as a permission. Actually I would prefer that all were as I am; but each one has the special gift that God has given him, one man this gift, another man that.

Now, I say this to the unmarried and to the widows: it would be better for you to continue to live alone, as I do. But if you cannot restrain your desires, go on and marry—it is better to marry than to burn with passion.

For married people I have a command, not my own but the Lord's: a wife must not leave her husband; if she does, she must remain single or else be reconciled to her husband; and a husband must not divorce his wife.

Questions About the Unmarried and the Widows

Now, the matter about the unmarried: I do not have a command from the Lord, but I give my opinion as one who by the Lord's mercy is worthy of trust.

Considering the present distress, I think it is better for a man to stay as he is. Do you have a wife? Then don't try to get rid of her. Are you unmarried? Then don't look for a wife. But if you do marry, you haven't committed a sin; and if an unmarried woman marries, she hasn't committed a sin. But I would rather spare you the everyday troubles that such people will have.

What I mean, brothers, is this: there is not much time left, and from now on married men should live as though they were not married; those who weep, as though they were not sad; those who laugh, as though they were not happy; those who buy, as though they did not own what they bought; those who deal in worldly goods, as though they were not fully occupied with them. For this world, as it is now, will not last much longer.

I would like you to be free from worry. An unmarried man concerns himself with the Lord's work, because he is trying to please the Lord; but a married man concerns himself with worldly matters, because he wants to please his wife, and so he is pulled in two directions. An unmarried woman or a virgin concerns herself with the Lord's work, because she wants to be dedicated both in body and spirit; but a married woman concerns herself with worldly matters, because she wants to please her husband.

I am saying this because I want to help you. I am not trying to put restrictions on you. Instead, I want you to do what is right and proper, and give yourselves completely to the Lord's service without any reservation.

The Question About Food Offered to Idols

Now, the matter about food offered to idols.

It is true, of course, that "all of us have knowledge," as they say. Such knowledge, however, puffs a man up with pride; but love builds up.

Be careful, however, and do not let your freedom of action make those who are weak in the faith fall into sin. Suppose a man whose conscience is weak in this matter sees you, who have "knowledge," eating in the temple of an idol; will not this encourage him to eat food offered to idols? And so this weak man, your brother for whom Christ died, will perish because of your "knowledge"! And in this way you will be sinning against Christ by sinning against your brothers and wounding their weak conscience. So then, if food makes my brother sin, I will never eat meat again, so as not to make my brother fall into sin.

Rights and Duties of an Apostle

Surely you know that in a race all the runners take part in it, but only one of them wins the prize. Run, then, in such a way as to win the prize. Every athlete in training submits to strict discipline; he does so in order to be crowned with a wreath that will not last; but we do it for one that will last forever. That is why I run straight for the finish line; that is why I am like a boxer, who does not waste his punches. I harden my body with blows and bring it under complete control, to keep from being rejected myself after having called others to the contest.

Warning Against Idols

I want you to remember, brothers, what happened to our ancestors who followed Moses. They were all under the protection of the cloud, and all passed safely through the Red Sea. In the cloud and in the sea they were all baptized as followers of Moses. All ate the same spiritual bread, and all drank the same spiritual drink. They drank from that spiritual rock that went along with them; and that rock was Christ himself. But even then God was not pleased with most of them, and so their dead bodies were scattered over the desert.

Now, all these things are examples for us, to warn us not to desire evil things, as they did, nor to worship idols, as some of them did. As the scripture says, "The people sat down to eat and drink, and got up to dance." We must not commit sexual immorality, as some of them did—and in one day twenty-three thousand of them fell dead. We must not put the Lord to the test, as some of them did—and they were killed by the snakes. You must not complain, as some of them did—and they were destroyed by the Angel of Death.

All these things happened to them as examples for others, and they were written down as a warning for us. For we live at the time when the end is about to come.

Whoever thinks he is standing up had better be careful that he does not fall. Every temptation that has come your way is the kind that normally comes to people. But God keeps his promise, and he will not allow you to be tempted beyond your power to resist; at the time you are tempted he will give you the strength to endure it, and so provide you with a way out.

So then, my dear friends, keep away from the worship of idols. I speak to you as a sensible people; judge for yourselves what I say. The cup of blessing for which we give thanks to God: do we not share in the blood of Christ when we drink from this cup? And the bread we break: do we not share in the body of Christ when we eat this bread? Because there is the one bread, all of us, though many, are one body, because we all share the same loaf.

Consider the Hebrew people; those who eat what is offered in sacrifice share in the altar's service to God. What do I mean? That an idol or the food offered to it really amounts to anything? No! What I am saying is that what is sacrificed on pagan altars is offered to demons, not to God. And I do not want you to be partners with demons. You cannot drink from the Lord's cup and also from the cup of demons; you cannot eat at the Lord's table and also at the table of demons. Or do we want to make the Lord jealous? Do we think that we are stronger than he?

"We are allowed to do anything," so they say. Yes, but not everything is good. "We are allowed to do anything"—but not everything is helpful. No one should be looking out for his own interests, but for the interests of others.

The Lord's Supper
In the following instructions, however, I do not praise you; because your church meetings actually do more harm than good. In the first place, I have been told that there are opposing groups in your church meetings; and this I believe is partly true. (No doubt there must be divisions among you so that the ones who are in the right may be clearly seen.) When you meet together as a group, you do not come to eat the Lord's Supper. For as you eat, each one goes ahead with his own meal, so that some are hungry while others get drunk. Don't you have your own homes in which to eat and drink? Or would you rather despise the church of God and put to shame the people who are in need? What do you expect me to say to you about this? Should I praise you? Of course I do not praise you!

For from the Lord I received the teaching that I passed on to you: that the Lord Jesus, on the night he was betrayed, took the bread, gave thanks to God, broke it, and said, "This is my body, which is for you. Do this in memory of me." In the same way, he took the cup after the supper and said, "This cup is God's new covenant, sealed with my blood. Whenever you drink it, do it in memory of me." For until the Lord comes, you proclaim his death whenever you eat this bread and drink from this cup.

It follows, then, that if anyone eats the Lord's bread or drinks from his cup in a way that dishonors him, he is guilty of sin against the Lord's body and blood. So then, everyone should examine himself first, and then eat the bread and drink from the cup. For if he does not recognize the meaning of the Lord's body when he eats the bread and drinks from the cup, he brings judgment on himself as he eats and drinks.

Love
Set your hearts, then, on the more important gifts.

Best of all, however, is the following way.

I may be able to speak the languages of men and even of angels, but if I have not love, my speech is no more than a noisy gong or a clanging bell. I may have the gift of inspired preaching; I may have all knowledge and understand all secrets; I may have all the faith needed to move mountains—but if I have not love, I am nothing. I may give away everything I have, and even give up my body to be burned—but if I have not love, it does me no good.

Love is patient and kind; love is not jealous, or conceited, or proud; love is not ill-mannered, or selfish, or irritable; love does not keep a record of wrongs; love is not happy with evil, but is happy with the truth. Love never gives up; its faith, hope, and patience never fail.

Love is eternal. There are inspired messages, but they are temporary; there are gifts of speaking in strange tongues, but they will cease; there is knowledge, but it will pass. For our gifts of knowledge and of inspired messages are only partial; but when what is perfect comes, then what is partial will disappear.

When I was a child, my speech, feelings, and thinking

were all those of a child; now that I am a man, I have no more use for childish ways. What we see now is like the dim image in a mirror; then we shall see face to face. What I know now is only partial; then it will be complete, as complete as God's knowledge of me.

Meanwhile these three remain: faith, hope, and love; and the greatest of these is love.

The Resurrection of Christ
And now I want to remind you, brothers, of the Good News which I preached to you, which you received, and on which your faith stands firm. That is the gospel, the message that I preached to you. You are saved by the gospel if you hold firmly to it—unless it was for nothing that you believed.

I passed on to you what I received, which is of the greatest importance: that Christ died for our sins, as written in the Scriptures; that he was buried, and was raised to life on the third day, as written in the Scriptures; that he appeared to Peter, and then to all twelve apostles. Then he appeared to more than five hundred of his followers at once, most of whom are still alive, although some have died. Then he appeared to James, and then to all the apostles.

Last of all he appeared also to me—even though I am like one who was born in a most unusual way. For I am the least of all the apostles—I do not even deserve to be called an apostle, because I persecuted God's church. But by God's grace I am what I am, and the grace that he gave me was not without effect. On the contrary, I have worked harder than all the other apostles, although it was not really my own doing, but God's grace working with me. So then, whether it came from me or from them, this is what we all preach, this is what you believe.

Our Resurrection
Now, since our message is that Christ has been raised from death, how can some of you say that the dead will not be raised to life? If that is true, it means that Christ was not raised; and if Christ has not been raised from

death, then we have nothing to preach and you have nothing to believe. If our hope in Christ is good for this life only, and no more, then we deserve more pity than anyone else in all the world.

But the truth is that Christ has been raised from death, as the guarantee that those who sleep in death will also be raised. For just as death came by means of a man, in the same way the rising from death comes by means of a man. For just as all men die because of their union to Adam, in the same way all will be raised to life because of their union to Christ. But each one in his proper order: Christ, the first of all; then those who belong to Christ, at the time of his coming.

The Resurrection Body

Someone will ask, "How can the dead be raised to life? What kind of body will they have?" You fool! When you plant a seed in the ground it does not sprout to life unless it dies. And what you plant in the ground is a bare seed, perhaps a grain of wheat, or of some other kind, not the full-bodied plant that will grow up. God provided that seed with the body he wishes; he gives each seed its own proper body.

And the flesh of living beings is not all the same kind of flesh; men have one kind of flesh, animals another, birds another, and fish another.

And there are heavenly bodies and earthly bodies; there is a beauty that belongs to heavenly bodies, and another kind of beauty that belongs to earthly bodies. The sun has its own beauty, the moon another beauty, and the stars a different beauty; and even among stars there are different kinds of beauty.

This is how it will be when the dead are raised to life. When the body is buried it is mortal; when raised, it will be immortal. When buried, it is ugly and weak; when raised, it will be beautiful and strong. When buried, it is a physical body; when raised, it will be a spiritual body. There is, of course, a physical body, so there has to be a spiritual body. For the scripture says, "The first man, Adam, was created a living being"; but the last Adam is the life-giving Spirit. It is not the spiritual that comes first, but the physical, and then the spiritual. The first Adam was made of the dust of the earth; the second Adam came from heaven. Those who belong to the earth are like the one who was made of earth; those who are of heaven are like the one who came from heaven. Just as we wear the likeness of the man made of earth, so we will wear the likeness of the Man from heaven.

What I mean, brothers, is this: what is made of flesh and blood cannot share in God's Kingdom, and what is mortal cannot possess immortality.

Listen to this secret: we shall not all die, but in an instant we shall all be changed, as quickly as the blinking of an eye, when the last trumpet sounds. For when it sounds, the dead will be raised immortal beings, and we shall all be changed. For what is mortal must clothe itself with what is immortal; what will die must clothe itself with what cannot die. So when what is mortal has been clothed with what is immortal, and when what will die has been clothed with what cannot die, then the scripture will come true: "Death is destroyed; victory is complete! Where, Death, is your victory? Where, Death, is your power to hurt?" Death gets its power to hurt from sin, and sin gets its power from the Law. But thanks be to God who gives us the victory through our Lord Jesus Christ!

So then, my dear brothers, stand firm and steady. Keep busy always in your work for the Lord, since you know that nothing you do in the Lord's service is ever without value.

Spiritual Treasure in Clay Pots

We are often troubled, but not crushed; sometimes in doubt, but never in despair; there are many enemies, but we are never without a friend; and though badly hurt at times, we are not destroyed. At all times we carry in our mortal bodies the death of Jesus, so that his life also may be seen in our bodies. Throughout our lives we are always in danger of death for Jesus' sake, in order that his life may be seen in this mortal body of ours.

For this reason we never become discouraged. Even though our physical being is gradually decaying, yet our spiritual being is renewed day after day. And this small and temporary trouble we suffer will bring us a tremendous and eternal glory, much greater than the trouble. For we fix our attention, not on things that are seen, but on things that are unseen. What can be seen lasts only for a time; but what cannot be seen lasts forever.

For we know that when this tent we live in—our body here on earth—is torn down, God will have a house in heaven for us to live in, a home he himself made, which will last forever. And now we sigh, so great is our desire to have our home which is in heaven put on over us; by being clothed with it we shall not be found without a body. While we live in this earthly tent we groan with a feeling of oppression; it is not that we want to get rid of our earthly body, but that we want to have the heavenly one put on over us, so that what is mortal will be swallowed up by life.

Paul Defends His Ministry

I, Paul, make a personal appeal to you—I who am said to be meek and mild when I am with you, but bold toward you when I am away from you. I beg of you, by the gentleness and kindness of Christ: Do not force me to be bold with you when I come; for I am sure I can be bold with those who say that we act from worldly motives. It is true that we live in the world; but we do not fight from worldly motives. The weapons we use in our fight are not the world's weapons, but God's powerful weapons, with which to destroy strongholds. We destroy false arguments; we pull down every proud obstacle that is raised against the knowledge of God; we take every thought captive and make it obey Christ. And after you have proved your complete loyalty, we will be ready to punish any act of disloyalty.

I wish you would tolerate me, even when I am a bit foolish. Please do! I am jealous for you just as God is; you are like a pure virgin whom I have promised in marriage to one man only, who is Christ. I am afraid that your minds will be corrupted and that you will abandon your full and pure devotion to Christ—in the same way that Eve was deceived by the snake's clever lies. For you gladly tolerate anyone who comes to you and preaches a different Jesus, not the one we preached; and you accept a spirit and a gospel completely different from the Spirit and the gospel you received from us!

I do not think that I am the least bit inferior to those very special "apostles" of yours! Perhaps I am an amateur in speaking, but certainly not in knowledge; we have made this clear to you at all times and in all conditions.

Paul's Sufferings as an Apostle
You tolerate anyone who orders you around, or takes advantage of you, or traps you, or looks down on you, or slaps you in the face. I am ashamed to admit it: we were too timid to do that!

But if anyone dares to boast of something—I am talking like a fool—I will be just as daring. Are they Hebrews? So am I. Are they Israelites? So am I. Are they Abraham's descendants? So am I. Are they Christ's servants? I sound like a madman—but I am a better servant than they are! I have worked much harder, I have been in prison more times, I have been whipped much more, and I have been near death more often. Five times I was given the thirty-nine lashes by the Jews; three times I was whipped by the Romans, and once I was stoned; I have been in three shipwrecks, and once I spent twenty-four hours in the water. In my many travels I have been in danger from floods and from robbers, in danger from fellow Jews and from Gentiles; there have been dangers in the cities, dangers in the wilds, dangers on the high seas, and dangers from false friends. There has been work and toil; often I have gone without sleep; I have been hungry and thirsty; I have often been without enough food, shelter, or clothing. And, not to mention other things, every day I am under the pressure of my concern for all the churches. When someone is weak, then I feel weak too; when someone is led into sin, I am filled with distress.

If I must boast, I will boast of things that show how weak I am. The God and Father of the Lord Jesus—blessed be his name forever!—knows that I am not lying. When I was in Damascus, the governor under King Aretas placed guards at the city gates to arrest me. But I was let down in a basket, through an opening in the wall, and escaped from him.

Paul's Visions and Revelations

I have to boast, even though it doesn't do any good. But I will now talk about visions and revelations given me by the Lord. I know a certain Christian man who fourteen years ago was snatched up to the highest heaven (I do not know whether this actually happened, or whether he had a vision—only God knows). I repeat, I know that this man was snatched to Paradise (again, I do not know whether this actually happened, or whether it was a vision—only God knows), and there he heard things which cannot be put into words, things that human lips may not speak. So I will boast of this man—but I will not boast about myself, except the things that show how weak I am. If I wanted to boast, I would not be a fool, because I would be telling the truth. But I will not boast, because I do not want anyone to have a higher opinion of me than he has from what he has seen me do and heard me say.

But to keep me from being puffed up with pride because of the many wonderful things I saw, I was given a painful physical ailment, which acts as Satan's messenger to beat me and keep me from being proud. Three times I prayed to the Lord about this, and asked him to take it away. His answer was, "My grace is all you need; for my power is strongest when you are weak." I am most happy, then, to be proud of my weaknesses, in order to feel the protection of Christ's power over me. I am content with weaknesses, insults, hardships, persecutions, and difficulties for Christ's sake. For when I am weak, then I am strong.

Paul's Concern for the Corinthians

I am acting like a fool—but you have made me do it. You are the ones who ought to show your approval of me. For even if I am nothing, I am in no way inferior to those very special "apostles" of yours. The things that prove that I am an apostle were done with all patience among you; there were signs and wonders and miracles. How were you treated any worse than the other churches, except that I did not bother you for help? Please forgive me for being so unfair!

This is now the third time that I am ready to come to visit you—and I will not make any demands on you. It is you I want, not your money. After all, children should not have to provide for their parents, but parents should provide for their children. I will be glad to spend all I have, and myself as well, in order to help you. Will you love me less because I love you so much?

Paul's Farewell

And now, brothers, good-bye! Strive for perfection; listen to my appeals; agree with one another, and live in peace. And the God of love and peace will be with you.

Greet one another with a brotherly kiss.

All God's people send you their greetings.

The grace of the Lord Jesus Christ, the love of God, and the fellowship of the Holy Spirit be with you all.

The One Gospel

From Paul, whose call to be an apostle did not come from man or by means of man, but from Jesus Christ and God the Father, who raised him from death. All the brothers who are here join me in sending greetings to the churches of Galatia:

May God our Father and the Lord Jesus Christ give you grace and peace.

In order to set us free from this present evil age, Christ gave himself for our sins, in obedience to the will of our God and Father. To God be the glory forever and ever!

I am surprised at you! In no time at all you are deserting the one who called you by the grace of Christ, and are going to another gospel. Actually, there is no "other gospel," but I say it because there are some people who are upsetting you and trying to change the gospel of Christ. But even if we, or an angel from heaven, should preach to you a gospel that is different from the one we preached to you, may he be condemned to hell! We have said it before, and now I say it again: if anyone preaches to you a gospel that is different from the one you accepted, may he be condemned to hell!

Does this sound as if I am trying to win men's approval? No! I want God's approval! Am I trying to be popular with men? If I were still trying to do so, I would not be a servant of Christ.

How Paul Became an Apostle

Let me tell you, my brothers, that the gospel I preach was not made by man. I did not receive it from any man, nor did anyone teach it to me. Instead, it was Jesus Christ himself who revealed it to me.

You have been told of the way I used to live when I was devoted to the Jewish religion, how I persecuted without mercy the church of God and did my best to destroy it. I was ahead of most fellow Jews of my age in my practice of the Jewish religion. I was much more devoted to the traditions of our ancestors.

But God, in his grace, chose me even before I was born, and called me to serve him. And when he decided to reveal his Son to me, so that I might preach the Good News about him to the Gentiles, I did not go to anyone for advice, nor did I go to Jerusalem to see those who were apostles before me. Instead, I went at once to Arabia, and then I returned to Damascus. It was three years later that I went to Jerusalem to get information from Peter, and I stayed with him for two weeks. I did not see any other apostle except James, the Lord's brother.

What I write is true. I am not lying, so help me God!

Afterward I went to places in Syria and Cilicia. At that time the members of the Christian churches in Judea did not know me personally. They knew only what others said, "The man who used to persecute us is now preaching the faith that he once tried to destroy!" And so they praised God because of me.

Paul and the Other Apostles

Fourteen years later I went back to Jerusalem with Barnabas; I also took Titus along with me. I went because God revealed to me that I should go. In a private meeting with the leaders, I explained to them the gospel message that I preach to the Gentiles. I did not want my work in the past or in the present to go for nothing. My companion Titus, even though he is Greek, was not forced to be circumcised.

On the contrary, they saw that God had given me the task of preaching the gospel to the Gentiles, just as he had given Peter the task of preaching the gospel to the Jews. For by God's power I was made an apostle to the Gentiles, just as Peter was made an apostle to the Jews. James, Peter, and John, who seemed to be the leaders, recognized that God had given me this special task; so they shook hands with Barnabas and me. As partners we all agreed that we would work among the Gentiles and they among the Jews. All they asked was that we should remember the needy in their group, the very thing I have worked hard to do.

Paul Rebukes Peter at Antioch

When Peter came to Antioch, I opposed him in public, because he was clearly wrong. Before some men who had been sent by James arrived there, Peter had been eating with the Gentile brothers. But after these men arrived, he drew back and would not eat with them, because he was afraid of those who were in favor of circumcising the Gentiles. The other Jewish brothers started acting like cowards, along with Peter; and even Barnabas was swept along by their cowardly action. When I saw that they were not walking a straight path in line with the truth of the gospel, I said to Peter, in front of them all, "You are a Jew, yet you have been living like a Gentile, not like a Jew. How, then, can you try to force Gentiles to live like Jews?"

Indeed, we are Jews by birth, and not Gentile sinners. Yet we know that a man is put right with God only through faith in Jesus Christ, never by doing what the Law requires. We, too, have believed in Christ Jesus in order to be put right with God through our faith in Christ, and not by doing what the Law requires. For no man is put right with God by doing what the Law requires. So far as the Law is concerned, however, I am dead—killed by the Law itself—in order that I might live for God. I have been put to death with Christ on his cross, so that it is no longer I who live, but it is Christ who lives in me. This life that I live now, I live by faith in the Son of God, who loved me and gave his life for me. I do not reject the grace of God. If a man is put right with God through the Law, it means that Christ died for nothing!

Preserve Your Freedom
Freedom is what we have—Christ has set us free! Stand, then, as free men, and do not allow yourselves to become slaves again.

Listen! I, Paul, tell you this: if you allow yourselves to be circumcised, it means that Christ is of no use to you at all. Once more I warn any man who allows himself to be circumcised that he is obliged to obey the whole Law. Those of you who try to be put right with God by obeying the Law have cut yourselves off from Christ. You are outside God's grace.

Final Warning and Greeting
See what big letters I make as I write to you now with my own hand! Those who want to show off and brag about external matters are the ones who are trying to force you to be circumcised. They do it, however, only that they may not be persecuted for the cross of Christ. Even those who practice circumcision do not obey the Law; they want you to be circumcised so they can boast that you submitted to this physical ceremony. As for me, however, I will boast only of the cross of our Lord Jesus Christ; for by means of his cross the world is dead to me, and I am dead to the world. It does not matter at all whether or not one is circumcised. What does matter

is being a new creature. As for those who follow this rule in their lives, may peace and mercy be with them—with them and with all God's people!

To conclude: let no one give me any more trouble, because the scars I have on my body show that I am the slave of Jesus.

May the grace of our Lord Jesus Christ be with you all, my brothers.

The Life and Faith of the Thessalonians
From Paul, Silas, and Timothy—

To the people of the church in Thessalonica, who belong to God the Father and the Lord Jesus Christ:

May grace and peace be yours.

We always thank God for you all, and always mention you in our prayers. For we remember before our God and Father how you put your faith into practice, how your love made you work so hard, and how your hope in our Lord Jesus Christ is firm. We know, brothers, that God loves you and has chosen you to be his own. For we brought the Good News to you, not with words only, but also with power and the Holy Spirit, and with complete conviction of its truth. You know how we lived when we were with you; it was for your own good.

Paul's Work in Thessalonica
You yourselves know, brothers, that our visit to you was not a failure. You know how we had already been mistreated and insulted in Philippi before we came to you in Thessalonica. Yet our God gave us courage to tell you the Good News that comes from him, even though there was much opposition. Surely you remember, brothers, how we worked and toiled! We worked day and night so we would not be any trouble to you as we preached to you the Good News from God.

You are our witnesses, and so is God: our conduct toward you who believe was pure, right, and without fault. You know that we treated each one of you just as a father treats his own children. We encouraged you, we comforted you, and we kept urging you to live the kind of life that pleases God, who calls you to share his own Kingdom and glory.

And for this other reason, also, we always give thanks to God. When we brought you God's message, you heard it and accepted it, not as man's message but as God's message, which indeed it is. For God is at work in you who believe. You, my brothers, had the same things happen to you that happened to the churches of God in Judea, to the people there who belong to Christ Jesus. You suffered the same persecutions from your own countrymen that they suffered from the Jews, who killed the Lord Jesus and the prophets, and persecuted us. How displeasing they are to God! How hostile they are to all men! They even tried to stop us from preaching to the Gentiles the message that would bring them salvation. This is the last full measure of the sins they had always committed. And now God's wrath has at last fallen upon them!

Paul's Desire to Visit Them Again

As for us, brothers, when we were separated from you for a little while—not in our thoughts, of course, but only in body—how we missed you and how hard we tried to see you again! We wanted to go back to you. I, Paul, tried to go back more than once, but Satan would not let us. After all, it is you—you, no less than others!—who are our hope, our joy, and our reason for boasting of our victory in the presence of our Lord Jesus when he comes. Indeed, you are our pride and our joy!

Finally, we could not bear it any longer. So we decided to stay on alone in Athens while we sent Timothy, our brother who works with us for God in preaching the Good News about Christ. We sent him to strengthen you and help your faith, so that none of you should turn back because of these persecutions. You yourselves know that such persecutions are part of God's will for us. For while we were still with you, we told you ahead of time that we were going to be persecuted; and, as you well know, that is exactly what happened. That is why I had to send Timothy. I could not bear it any longer, so I sent him to find out about your faith. Surely it could not be that the Devil had tempted you, and all our work had been for nothing!

Now Timothy has come back to us from you, and he has brought the welcome news about your faith and love. He has told us that you always think well of us, and that you want to see us just as much as we want to see you. So, in all our trouble and suffering we have been encouraged about you, brothers. It was your faith that encouraged us, because now we really live if you stand firm in your life in the Lord.

The Lord's Coming
Brothers, we want you to know the truth about those who have died, so that you will not be sad, as are those who have no hope. We believe that Jesus died and rose again; so we believe that God will bring with Jesus those who have died believing in him.

This is the Lord's teaching that we tell you: we who are alive on the day the Lord comes will not go ahead of those who have died. There will be the shout of command, the archangel's voice, the sound of God's trumpet, and the Lord himself will come down from heaven. Those who have died believing in Christ will rise to life first; then we who are living at that time will all be gathered up along with them in the clouds to meet the Lord in the air. And so we will always be with the Lord. So then, cheer each other up with these words.

You are Chosen for Salvation
Concerning the coming of our Lord Jesus Christ and our being gathered together to be with him: I beg you, brothers, do not be so easily confused in your thinking or upset by the claim that the Day of the Lord has come. Perhaps this was said by someone prophesying, or by someone preaching. Or it may have been said that we wrote this in a letter.

Don't you remember? I told you all this while I was with you.

So then, brothers, stand firm and hold on to those truths which we taught you, both in our preaching and in our letter.

May our Lord Jesus Christ himself, and God our Father, who loved us and in his grace gave us eternal courage and a good hope, fill your hearts with courage and make you strong to do and say all that is good.

Thirteen

"LET US COME NEAR TO GOD"

Spiritual Blessings in Christ
From Paul, who by God's will is an apostle of Christ Jesus—

To God's people who live in Ephesus, those who are faithful in their life in Christ Jesus:

May God our Father and the Lord Jesus Christ give you grace and peace.

Let us give thanks to the God and Father of our Lord Jesus Christ! For he has blessed us, in our union with Christ, by giving us every spiritual gift in the heavenly world. Before the world was made, God had already chosen us to be his in Christ, so that we would be holy and without fault before him. Because of his love, God had already decided that through Jesus Christ he would bring us to himself as his sons—this was his pleasure and purpose. Let us praise God for his glorious grace, for the free gift he gave us in his dear Son!

For by the death of Christ we are set free, that is, our sins are forgiven. How great is the grace of God, which he gave to us in such large measure! In all his wisdom and insight God did what he had purposed, and made known to us the secret plan he had already decided to complete by means of Christ. God's plan, which he will complete when the time is right, is to bring all creation together, everything in heaven and on earth, with Christ as head.

From Death to Life
In the past you were spiritually dead because of your disobedience and sins. At that time you followed the

world's evil way; you obeyed the ruler of the spiritual powers in space, the spirit who now controls the people who disobey God. Actually all of us were like them, and lived according to our natural desires, and did whatever suited the wishes of our own bodies and minds. Like everyone else, we too were naturally bound to suffer God's wrath.

But God's mercy is so abundant, and his love for us is so great, that while we were spiritually dead in our disobedience he brought us to life with Christ. It is by God's grace that you have been saved. In our union with Christ Jesus he raised us up with him to rule with him in the heavenly world.

Paul's Work for the Gentiles

So then, you Gentiles are not foreigners or strangers any longer; you are now fellow-citizens with God's people, and members of the family of God. You, too, are built upon the foundation laid by the apostles and prophets, the cornerstone being Christ Jesus himself. He is the one who holds the whole building together and makes it grow into a sacred temple in the Lord.

I am less than the least of all God's people; yet God gave me this privilege of taking to the Gentiles the Good News of the infinite riches of Christ. I beg you, then, do not be discouraged because I am suffering for you; it is all for your benefit.

For this reason, then, I fall on my knees before the Father, from whom every family in heaven and on earth receives its true name. I ask God, from the wealth of his glory, to give you power through his Spirit to be strong in your inner selves, and that Christ will make his home in your hearts, through faith. I pray that you may have your roots and foundations in love, so that you, together with all God's people, may have the power to understand how broad and long and high and deep is Christ's love. Yes, may you come to know his love—although it can never be fully known—and so be completely filled with the perfect fulness of God.

To him who is able to do so much more than we can ever ask for, or even think of, by means of the power working in us: to God be the glory in the church and in Christ Jesus, for all time, forever and ever!

The Unity of the Body
I urge you, then—I who am a prisoner because I serve the Lord: live a life that measures up to the standard God set when he called you. Be humble, gentle, and patient always. Show your love by being helpful to one another. Do your best to preserve the unity which the Spirit gives, by the peace that binds you together. There is one body and one Spirit, just as there is one hope to which God has called you. There is one Lord, one faith, one baptism; there is one God and Father of all men, who is Lord of all, works through all, and is in all.

Wives and Husbands
Submit yourselves to one another, because of your reverence for Christ.

Wives, submit yourselves to your husbands, as to the Lord. For a husband has authority over his wife in the same way that Christ has authority over the church; and Christ is himself the Savior of the church, his body. And so wives must submit themselves completely to their husbands, in the same way that the church submits itself to Christ.

Husbands, love your wives in the same way that Christ loved the church and gave his life for it. He did this to dedicate the church to God, by his word, after making it clean by the washing in water, in order to present the church to himself, in all its beauty, pure and faultless, without spot or wrinkle, or any other imperfection. Men ought to love their wives just as they love their own bodies. A man who loves his wife loves himself. (No one ever hates his own body. Instead, he feeds it and takes care of it, just as Christ does the church; for we are members of his body.) As the scripture says, "For this reason, a man will leave his father and mother, and unite with his wife, and the two will become one." There is a great truth revealed in this scripture, and I understand it applies to Christ and the church. But it also applies to you: every husband must love his wife as himself, and every wife must respect her husband.

Children and Parents
Children, it is your Christian duty to obey your parents, for this is the right thing to do. "Honor your father and mother" is the first commandment that has a promise added: "so that all may be well with you, and you may live a long time in the land."

Parents, do not treat your children in such a way as to make them angry. Instead, raise them with Christian discipline and instruction.

Slaves and Masters
Slaves, obey your human masters, with fear and trembling; and do it with a sincere heart, as though you were serving Christ. Do this not only when they are watching you, to gain their approval; but with all your heart do what God wants, as slaves of Christ. Do your work as slaves cheerfully, then, as though you served the Lord, and not merely men. Remember that the Lord will reward every man, whether slave or free, for the good work he does.

Masters, behave in the same way toward your slaves; and stop using threats. Remember that you and your slaves belong to the same Master in heaven, who judges everyone by the same standard.

Final Greetings
May God the Father and the Lord Jesus Christ give peace and love to all the brothers, with faith. May God's grace be with all those who love our Lord Jesus Christ with undying love.

Paul's Prayer for His Readers
From Paul and Timothy, servants of Christ Jesus—

To all God's people living in Philippi who are in union with Christ Jesus, and to the church leaders and helpers:

May God our Father and the Lord Jesus Christ give you grace and peace.

I thank my God for you every time I think of you; and every time I pray for you all, I pray with joy, because of the way in which you have helped me in the work of the gospel, from the very first day until now. And so I am sure of this: that God, who began this good work in you, will carry it on until it is finished in the Day of Christ Jesus. You are always in my heart! And so it is only right for me to feel this way about you. For you have all shared with me in this privilege that God has given me, both now that I am in prison and also while I was free to defend and firmly establish the gospel. God knows that I tell the truth when I say that my deep feeling for you all comes from the heart of Christ Jesus himself.

This is my prayer for you: I pray that your love will keep on growing more and more, together with true knowledge and perfect judgment, so that you will be able to choose what is best. Then you will be free from all impurity and blame on the Day of Christ.

Christ's Humility and Greatness
Don't do anything from selfish ambition, or from a cheap desire to boast; but be humble toward each other, never thinking you are better than others. And look out for each other's interests, not just for your own. The attitude you should have is the one that Christ Jesus had: He always had the very nature of God, but he did not think that by force he should try to become equal with God. Instead, of his own free will he gave it all up, and took the nature of a servant. He became like man, and appeared in human likeness. He was humble and walked the path of obedience to death—his death on the cross. For this reason God raised him to the highest place above, and gave him the name that is greater than any other name. And so, in honor of the name of Jesus, all beings in heaven, on earth, and in the world below will fall on their knees, and all will openly proclaim that Jesus Christ is the Lord, to the glory of God the Father.

The True Righteousness
Watch out for those who do evil things, those dogs, men who insist on cutting the body. For we, not they,

are the ones who have received the true circumcision, because we worship God by his Spirit, and rejoice in our life in Christ Jesus. We do not put any trust in external ceremonies. I could, of course, put my trust in such things. If anyone thinks he can trust in external ceremonies, I have even more reason to feel that way. I was circumcised when I was a week old. I am an Israelite by birth, of the tribe of Benjamin, a pure-blooded Hebrew. So far as keeping the Jewish Law is concerned, I was a Pharisee, and I was so zealous that I persecuted the church. So far as a man can be righteous by obeying the commands of the Law, I was without fault. But all those things that I might count as profit I now reckon as loss, for Christ's sake. Not only those things; I reckon everything as complete loss for the sake of what is so much more valuable, the knowledge of Christ Jesus my Lord. For his sake I have thrown everything away; I consider it all as mere garbage, so that I might gain Christ, and be completely united with him. No longer do I have a righteousness of my own, the kind to be gained by obeying the Law. I now have the righteousness that is given through faith in Christ, the righteousness that comes from God, and is based on faith. All I want is to know Christ and to experience the power of his resurrection; to share in his sufferings and become like him in his death, in the hope that I myself will be raised from death to life.

Running Toward the Goal

I do not claim that I have already succeeded or have already become perfect. I keep going on to try to win the prize for which Christ Jesus has already won me to himself. Of course, brothers, I really do not think that I have already won it; the one thing I do, however, is to forget what is behind me and do my best to reach what is ahead. So I run straight toward the goal in order to win the prize, which is God's call through Christ Jesus to the life above.

All of us who are spiritually mature should have this same attitude. If, however, some of you have a different attitude, God will make this clear to you. However that may be, let us go forward according to the same rules we have followed until now.

Keep on imitating me, my brothers. We have set the right example for you, so pay attention to those who follow it. I have told you this many times before, and now I repeat it, with tears: there are many whose lives make them enemies of Christ's death on the cross. They are going to end up in hell, because their god is their bodily desires, they are proud of what they should be ashamed of, and they think only of things that belong to this world. We, however, are citizens of heaven, and we eagerly wait for our Savior to come from heaven, the Lord Jesus Christ. He will change our weak mortal bodies and make them like his own glorious body, using that power by which he is able to bring all things under his rule.

Prayer of Thanksgiving
From Paul, who by God's will is an apostle of Christ Jesus, and from our brother Timothy—

To God's people in Colossae, those who are our faithful brothers in Christ:

May God our Father give you grace and peace.

We always give thanks to God, the Father of our Lord Jesus Christ, when we pray for you. Then you will be able to live as the Lord wants, and always do what pleases him. Your lives will be fruitful in all kinds of good works, and you will grow in your knowledge of God. May you be made strong with all the strength which comes from his glorious might, so that you may be able to endure everything with patience. And give thanks, with joy, to the Father, who has made you fit to have your share of what God has reserved for his people in the kingdom of light. He rescued us from the power of darkness and brought us safe into the kingdom of his dear Son, by whom we are set free, that is, our sins are forgiven.

The Person and Work of Christ
Christ is the visible likeness of the invisible God. He is the firstborn Son, superior to all created things. For by him God created everything in heaven and on earth, the

seen and the unseen things, including spiritual powers, lords, rulers, and authorities. God created the whole universe through him and for him. He existed before all things, and in union with him all things have their proper place. He is the head of his body, the church; he is the source of the body's life; he is the first-born Son who was raised from death, in order that he alone might have the first place in all things. For it was by God's own decision that the Son has in himself the full nature of God. Through the Son, then, God decided to bring the whole universe back to himself. God made peace through his Son's death on the cross, and so brought back to himself all things, both on earth and in heaven.

At one time you were far away from God and were his enemies because of the evil things you did and thought. But now, by means of the physical death of his Son, God has made you his friends, in order to bring you, holy, pure, and faultless, into his presence. You must, of course, continue faithful on a firm and sure foundation, and not allow yourselves to be shaken from the hope you gained when you heard the gospel. It is of this gospel that I, Paul, became a servant—this gospel which has been preached to everybody in the world.

Fulness of Life in Christ

Since you have accepted Christ Jesus as Lord, live in union with him. Keep your roots deep in him, build your lives on him, and become ever stronger in your faith, as you were taught. And be filled with thanksgiving.

See to it, then, that no one makes a captive of you with the worthless deceit of human wisdom, which comes from the teachings handed down by men, and from the ruling spirits of the universe, and not from Christ. For the full content of divine nature lives in Christ, in his humanity, and you have been given full life in union with him. He is supreme over every spiritual ruler and authority.

In union with him you were circumcised, not with the circumcision that is made by men, but with Christ's own circumcision, which consists of being freed from the power of this sinful body. For when you were baptized, you were buried with Christ, and in baptism you were also raised with Christ through your faith in the active power of God, who raised him from death. You were at one time spiritually dead because of your sins, and because you were Gentiles without the Law. But God has now brought you to life with Christ; God forgave us all our sins. He canceled the unfavorable record of our debts, with its binding rules, and did away with it completely by nailing it to the cross. And on that cross Christ freed himself from the power of the spiritual rulers and authorities; he made a public spectacle of them by leading them as captives in his victory procession.

Dying and Living with Christ
You have died with Christ and are set free from the ruling spirits of the universe. Why, then, do you live as though you belonged to this world? Why do you obey such rules as "Don't handle this," "Don't taste that," "Don't touch the other"? All these things become useless, once they are used. They are only man-made rules and teachings. Of course they appear to have wisdom in their forced worship of angels, and false humility, and severe treatment of the body; but they have no real value in controlling physical passions.

You have been raised to life with Christ. Set your hearts, then, on the things that are in heaven, where Christ sits on his throne at the right side of God. Keep your minds fixed on things there, not on things here on earth. For you have died, and your life is hidden with Christ in God. Your real life is Christ, and when he appears, then you too will appear with him and share his glory!

The Old Life and the New
You must put to death, then, the earthly desires at work in you, such as immorality, indecency, lust, evil passions, and greed (for greediness is a form of idol worship). Because of such things God's wrath will come upon those who do not obey him. And you yourselves at one time used to live according to such desires, when your life was dominated by them.

But now you must get rid of all these things: anger,

passion, and hateful feelings. No insults or obscene talk must ever come from your lips. Do not lie to one another, because you have put off the old self with its habits, and have put on the new self. This is the new man which God, its creator, is constantly renewing in his own image, to bring you to a full knowledge of himself. As a result, there are no Gentiles and Jews, circumcised and uncircumcised, barbarians, savages, slaves, or free men, but Christ is all. Christ is in all.

You are the people of God; he loved you and chose you for his own. So then, you must put on compassion, kindness, humility, gentleness, and patience. Be helpful to one another, and forgive one another, whenever any of you has a complaint against someone else. You must forgive each other in the same way that the Lord has forgiven you. And to all these add love, which binds all things together in perfect unity. The peace that Christ gives is to be the judge in your hearts; for to this peace God has called you together in the one body. And be thankful. Christ's message, in all its richness, must live in your hearts. Teach and instruct each other with all wisdom. Sing psalms, hymns, and sacred songs; sing to God, with thanksgiving in your hearts. Everything you do or say, then, should be done in the name of the Lord Jesus, as you give thanks through him to God the Father.

Final Greetings
Give our best wishes to the brothers in Laodicea, and to Nympha and the church that meets in her house. After you read this letter, make sure that it is read also in the church at Laodicea. At the same time, you are to read the letter Laodicea will send you. And tell Archippus, "Be sure to finish the task you were given in the Lord's service."

With my own hand I write this: *Greetings from Paul.* Do not forget my chains!

May God's grace be with you.

Warnings Against False Teaching
From Paul, an apostle of Christ Jesus by order of God our Savior and Christ Jesus our hope—

To Timothy, my true son in the faith:

May God the Father and Christ Jesus our Lord give you grace, mercy, and peace.

I want you to stay in Ephesus, just as I urged you when I was on my way to Macedonia. Some people there are teaching false doctrines, and you must order them to stop. Tell them to give up those legends and those long lists of names of ancestors, because these only produce arguments; they do not serve God's plan, which is known by faith. The purpose of this order is to arouse the love that comes from a pure heart, a clear conscience, and a genuine faith. Some men have turned away from these and have lost their way in foolish discussions. They want to be teachers of God's law, but they do not understand their own words or the matters about which they speak with so much confidence.

We know that the Law is good, if it is used as it should be used. It must be remembered, of course, that laws are made, not for good people, but for lawbreakers and criminals, for the godless and sinful, for those who are not religious or spiritual, for men who kill their fathers or mothers, for murderers, for the immoral, for sexual perverts, for kidnappers, for those who lie and give false testimony or do anything else contrary to the true teaching. That teaching is found in the gospel that was entrusted to me to announce, the Good News from the glorious and blessed God.

Church Worship

First of all, then, I urge that petitions, prayers, requests, and thanksgivings be offered to God for all men; for kings and all others who are in authority, that we may live a quiet and peaceful life, in entire godliness and proper conduct. This is good and it pleases God our Savior, who wants all men to be saved and to come to know the truth. For there is one God, and there is one who brings God and men together, the man Christ Jesus, who gave himself to redeem all men. That was the proof, at the right time, that God wants all men to be saved, and this is why I was sent as an apostle and teacher of the Gentiles, to proclaim the message of faith and truth. I am not lying, I am telling the truth!

I want men everywhere to pray, men who are dedicated to God and can lift up their hands in prayer without anger or argument.

I also want women to be modest and sensible about their clothes and to dress properly; not with fancy hair styles, or with gold ornaments or pearls or expensive dresses, but with good deeds, as is proper for women who claim to be religious. Women should learn in silence and all humility. I do not allow women to teach or to have authority over men; they must keep quiet. For Adam was created first, and then Eve.

Leaders in the Church

This is a true saying: If a man is eager to be a church leader he desires an excellent work. A church leader must be a man without fault; he must have one wife, be sober, self-controlled, and orderly; he must welcome strangers in his home; he must be able to teach; he must not be a drunkard or a violent man, but gentle and peaceful; he must not love money; he must be able to manage his own family well, and make his children obey him with all respect. For if a man does not know how to manage his own family, how can he take care of the church of God? He must not be a man who has been recently converted; else he will swell up with pride and be condemned, as the Devil was. He should be a man who is respected by the people outside the church, so that he will not be disgraced and fall into the Devil's trap.

False Teachers

The Spirit says clearly that some men will abandon the faith in later times; they will obey lying spirits and follow the teachings of demons. These teachings come from the deceit of men who are liars, and whose consciences are dead, as if burnt with a hot iron. Such men teach that it is wrong to marry and to eat certain foods. But God created these foods to be eaten, after a prayer of thanks, by those who are believers and have come to know the truth. Everything that God has created is good; nothing is to be rejected, but all is to be received with a prayer of thanks; because the word of God and the prayer make it acceptable to God.

Personal Instructions
But you, man of God, avoid all these things. Strive for righteousness, godliness, faith, love, endurance, and gentleness. Run your best in the race of faith, and win eternal life for yourself; for it was to this life that God called you when you made your good profession of faith before many witnesses. Before God, who gives life to all things, and before Christ Jesus, who made the good profession before Pontius Pilate, I command you: Obey the commandment and keep it pure and faultless, until the Day our Lord Jesus Christ will appear. His appearing will be brought about at the right time by God, the blessed and only Ruler, the King of kings, and the Lord of lords. He alone is immortal; he lives in the light that no one can approach. No one has ever seen him, no one can ever see him. To him be honor and eternal might!

Thanksgiving and Encouragement
I give thanks to God, whom I serve with a clear conscience, as my ancestors did. I thank him as I remember you always in my prayers, night and day. I remember your tears, and I want to see you very much, so that I may be filled with joy. I remember the sincere faith you have, the kind of faith that your grandmother Lois and your mother Eunice also had. I am sure that you have it also. For this reason I remind you to keep alive the gift that God gave to you when I laid my hands on you.

Hold to the true words that I taught you, as the example for you to follow, and stay in the faith and love that are ours in union with Christ Jesus. Keep the good things that have been entrusted to you, through the power of the Holy Spirit, who lives in us.

A Loyal Soldier of Christ Jesus
As for you, my son, be strong through the grace that is ours in union with Christ Jesus. Take the words that you heard me preach in the presence of many witnesses, and give them into the keeping of men you can trust, men who will be able to teach others also.

Take your part in suffering, as a loyal soldier of Christ Jesus. A soldier in active service wants to please his commanding officer, and so does not get mixed up in the affairs of civilian life. An athlete who runs in a race cannot win the prize unless he obeys the rules.

Last Instructions

But as for you, continue in the truths that you were taught and firmly believe. You know who your teachers were, and you remember that ever since you were a child you have known the Holy Scriptures, which are able to give you the wisdom that leads to salvation through faith in Christ Jesus. All Scripture is inspired by God and is useful for teaching the truth, rebuking error, correcting faults, and giving instruction for right living, so that the man who serves God may be fully qualified and equipped to do every kind of good work.

I solemnly urge you in the presence of God and of Christ Jesus, who will judge all men, living and dead: because of his coming and of his Kingdom, I command you to preach the message, to insist upon telling it, whether the time is right or not; to convince, reproach, and encourage, teaching with all patience. The time will come when men will not listen to the true teaching, but will follow their own desires, and will collect for themselves more and more teachers who will tell them what they are itching to hear. They will turn away from listening to the truth and give their attention to legends. But you must keep control of yourself in all circumstances; endure suffering, do the work of a preacher of the Good News, and perform your whole duty as a servant of God.

As for me, the hour has come for me to be sacrificed; the time is here for me to leave this life. I have done my best in the race, I have run the full distance, I have kept the faith. And now the prize of victory is waiting for me, the crown of righteousness which the Lord, the righteous Judge, will give me on that Day—and not only to me, but to all those who wait with love for him to appear.

Personal Words

Do your best to come to me soon. Demas fell in love with this present world and has deserted me; he has gone off to Thessalonica. Crescens went to Galatia, and Titus to Dalmatia. Only Luke is with me. Get Mark and bring him with you, because he can help me in the work. I sent Tychicus to Ephesus. When you come, bring my coat that I left in Troas with Carpus; bring the books too, and especially the ones made of parchment.

The Lord be with your spirit.

God's grace be with you all.

Titus' Work in Crete

From Paul, a servant of God and an apostle of Jesus Christ.

I was chosen and sent to help the faith of God's chosen people and lead them to the truth taught by our religion, which is based on the hope for eternal life. God, who does not lie, promised us this life before the beginning of time, and at the right time he revealed it in his message. This was entrusted to me, and I proclaim it by order of God our Savior.

I write to Titus, my true son in the faith that we share:

May God the Father and Christ Jesus our Savior give you grace and peace.

I left you in Crete for you to put in order the things that still needed doing, and to appoint church elders in every town. Remember my instructions: an elder must be without fault; he must have only one wife, and his children must be believers and not have the reputation of being wild or disobedient. For since he is in charge of God's work, the church leader should be without fault. He must not be arrogant or quick-tempered, or a drunkard, or violent, or greedy. He must be hospitable and love what is good. He must be self-controlled, upright, holy, and disciplined. He must hold firmly to the message which can be trusted and which agrees with the doctrine. In this way he will be able to encourage others with the true teaching, and also show the error of those who are opposed to it.

For there are many who rebel and deceive others with their nonsense, especially the converts from Judaism. It is necessary to stop their talking, because they are upsetting whole families by teaching what they should not, for the shameful purpose of making money.

Sound Doctrine

But you must teach what is required by sound doctrine. Tell the older men to be sober, sensible, and self-controlled; to be sound in their faith, love, and endurance. In the same way tell the older women to behave as women who live a holy life should. They must not be slanderers, or slaves to wine. They must teach what is good, in order to train the younger women to love their husbands and children, to be self-controlled and pure, and to be good housewives, who obey their husbands, so that no one will speak evil of the message from God.

In the same way urge the young men to be self-controlled. You yourself, in all things, must be an example in good works. Be sincere and serious in your teaching. Use sound words that cannot be criticized, so that your enemies may be put to shame by not having anything bad to say about us.

For God has revealed his grace for the slavation of all men. That grace instructs us to give up ungodly living and worldly passions, and to live self-controlled, upright, and godly lives in this world, as we wait for the blessed Day we hope for, when the glory of our great God and Savior Jesus Christ will appear. He gave himself for us, to rescue us from all wickedness and make us a pure people who belong to him alone and are eager to do good.

Philemon's Love and Faith

From Paul, a prisoner for the sake of Christ Jesus, and from our brother Timothy—

To our friend and fellow worker Philemon, and the church that meets in your house, and our sister Apphia, and our fellow soldier Archippus:

May God our Father and the Lord Jesus Christ give you grace and peace.

Every time I pray, brother Philemon, I mention you

and give thanks to my God. For I hear of your love for all God's people and the faith you have in the Lord Jesus. My prayer is that our fellowship with you as believers will bring about a deeper understanding of every blessing which we have in our life in Christ. Your love, dear brother, has brought me great joy and much encouragement! You have cheered the hearts of all God's people.

A request for Onesimus
For this reason I could be bold enough, as your brother in Christ, to order you to do what should be done. But love compels me to make a request instead. I do this even though I am Paul, the ambassador of Christ Jesus and at present also a prisoner for his sake. So I make a request to you on behalf of Onesimus, who is my own son in Christ; for while in prison I have become his spiritual father. At one time he was of no use to you, but now he is useful both to you and to me.

I am sending him back to you now, and with him goes my heart. I would like to keep him here with me, while I am in prison for the gospel's sake, so that he could help me in your place. However, I do not want to force you to help me; rather, I would like for you to do it of your own free will. So I will not do a thing unless you agree.

It may be that Onesimus was away from you for a short time so that you might have him back for all time. And now he is not just a slave, but much more than a slave; he is a dear brother in Christ. How much he means to me! And how much more he will mean to you, both as a slave and as a brother in the Lord!

So, if you think of me as your partner, welcome him back just as you would welcome me. If he has done you any wrong, or owes you anything, charge it to my account. Here, I will write this with my own hand: *I, Paul, will pay you back.* (I should not have to remind you, of course, that you owe your very life to me.) So, my brother, please do me this favor, for the Lord's sake; cheer up my heart, as a brother in Christ!

I am sure, as I write this, that you will do what I ask—in fact I know that you will do even more. At the same time, get a room ready for me, because I hope that God will answer the prayers of all of you and give me back to you.

Final Greetings
Epaphras, who is in prison with me for the sake of Christ Jesus, sends you his greetings, and so do my fellow workers Mark, Aristarchus, Demas, and Luke.

May the grace of the Lord Jesus Christ be with you all.

God's World Through His Son
In the past God spoke to our ancestors many times and in many ways through the prophets, but in these last days he has spoken to us through his Son. He is the one through whom God created the universe, the one whom God has chosen to possess all things at the end. He shines with the brightness of God's glory; he is the exact likeness of God's own being, and sustains the universe with his powerful word. After he had made men clean from their sins, he sat down in heaven at the right side of God, the Supreme Power.

The Son was made greater than the angels, just as the name that God gave him is greater than theirs.

The Great Salvation
That is why we must hold on all the more firmly to the truths we have heard, so that we will not be carried away. The message given by the angels was shown to be true, and anyone who did not follow it or obey it received the punishment he deserved. How, then, shall we escape if we pay no attention to such a great salvation? The Lord himself first announced this salvation, and those who heard him proved to us that it is true. At the same time God added his witness to theirs by doing signs of power, wonders, and many kinds of miracles. He also distributed the gifts of the Holy Spirit according to his will.

A Rest for God's People
So then, as the Holy Spirit says, "If you hear God's voice today, do not be stubborn as you were when you

rebelled against God, as you were that day in the desert when you put him to the test. There your ancestors put me to the test and tried me, says God, even though they saw what I did for forty years. For that reason I was angry with those people and said. 'They are always disloyal, and refuse to obey my commands.' I was angry and made a solemn promise: 'They shall never come in and rest with me!'"

My brothers, be careful that no one among you has a heart so bad and unbelieving that he will turn away from the living God. Instead, in order that none of you be deceived by sin and become stubborn, you must help one another every day, as long as the "Today" in the scripture applies to us. For we are all partners with Christ, if we hold on firmly to the end the confidence we had at the beginning.

This is what the scripture says: "If you hear God's voice today, do not be stubborn as you were when you rebelled against God."

Who heard God's voice and rebelled against him? All the people who were led out of Egypt by Moses. With whom was God angry for forty years? With the people who sinned, who fell down dead in the desert. When God made his solemn promise, "They shall never come in and rest with me"—of whom was he speaking? Of those who rebelled. We see, then, that they were not able to go in because they did not believe.

Let us, then, do our best to go in and rest with God. We must not, any of us, disobey as they did and fail to go in.

The word of God is alive and active. It is sharper than any double-edged sword. It cuts all the way through, to where soul and spirit meet, to where joints and marrow come together. It judges the desires and thoughts of men's hearts. There is nothing that can be hid from God. Everything in all creation is exposed and lies open before his eyes; and it is to him that we must all give account of ourselves.

Let us, then, hold firmly to the faith we profess. For we have a great high priest who has gone into the very presence of God—Jesus, the Son of God. Our high priest is not one who cannot feel sympathy with our weaknesses. On the contrary, we have a high priest who was tempted in every way that we are, but did not sin.

Jesus the Great High Priest

Every high priest is chosen from his fellow-men and appointed to serve God on their behalf, to offer gifts and sacrifices for sins. Since he himself is weak in many ways, he is able to be gentle with those who are ignorant and make mistakes. And because he is himself weak, he must offer sacrifices not only for the sins of the people but also for his own sins. No one chooses for himself the honor of being a high priest. It is only by God's call that a man is made a high priest—just as Aaron was called.

In the same way, Christ did not take upon himself the honor of being a high priest. Instead, God said to him, "You are my Son; today I have become your Father." He also said in another place, "You will be a priest forever, in the priestly order of Melchizedek."

In his life on earth Jesus made his prayers and requests with loud cries and tears to God, who could save him from death. Because he was humble and devoted, God heard him. But even though he was God's Son he learned to be obedient by means of his sufferings. When he was made perfect, he became the source of eternal salvation for all those who obey him, and God declared him to be high priest, in the priestly order of Melchizedek.

The Priest Melchizedek

This Melchizedek was king of Salem and a priest of the Most High God. As Abraham was coming back from the battle in which he killed the kings, Melchizedek met him and blessed him. Abraham gave him one tenth of all he had taken. (The first meaning of Melchizedek's name is "King of Righteousness." And because he was king of Salem, his name also means "King of Peace.") There is no record of Melchizedek's father or mother, or of any of his ancestors; no record of his birth or of his death. He is like the Son of God; he remains a priest forever.

You see, then, how great he was. Abraham, the patriarch, gave him one tenth of all he got in the battle.

It was on the basis of the Levitical priesthood that the Law was given to the people of Israel. Now, if the work of the Levitical priests had been perfect, there would have been no need for a different kind of priest to appear, one who is in the priestly order of Melchizedek, not in Aaron's order. For when the priesthood is changed, there also has to be a change of the law. And our Lord, of whom these things are said, belonged to a different tribe; and no member of his tribe ever served as a priest at the altar. It is well known that he was born a member of the tribe of Judah; and Moses did not mention this tribe when he spoke of priests.

There is another difference: those other priests were many because they died and could not continue their work. But Jesus lives on forever, and his work as priest does not pass on to someone else. And so he is able, now and always, to save those who come to God through him, because he lives forever to plead with God for them.

Jesus, then, is the High Priest that meets our needs. He is holy; he has no fault or sin in him; he has been set apart from sinful men and raised above the heavens. He is not like other high priests; he does not need to offer sacrifices every day, for his own sins first, and then for the sins of the people. He offered one sacrifice, once and for all, when he offered himself. The Law of Moses appoints men who are imperfect to be high priests; but God's promise with the vow, which came later than the Law, appoints the Son, who has been made perfect forever.

Jesus Our High Priest

Here is the whole point of what we are saying: we have such a high priest as this, who sits at the right of the throne of the Divine Majesty in heaven. He serves as high priest in the Most Holy Place, that is, in the real tent which was put up by the Lord, not by man.

This is how those things were arranged. The priests go into the outside tent every day to perform their duties; but only the High Priest goes into the inside tent, and he does so only once a year. He takes blood with him which he offers to God on behalf of himself and for the sins which the people have committed without knowing they were sinning.

But Christ has already come as the High Priest of the good things that are already here. The tent in which he serves is greater and more perfect; it is not made by men, that is, it is not a part of this created world. When Christ went through the tent and entered once and for all into the Most Holy Place, he did not take the blood of goats and calves to offer as sacrifice; rather, he took his own blood and obtained eternal salvation for us. The blood of goats and bulls and the ashes of the burnt calf are sprinkled on the people who are ritually unclean, and make them clean by taking away their ritual impurity. Since this is true, how much more is accomplished by the blood of Christ! Through the eternal Spirit he offered himself as a perfect sacrifice to God. His blood will make our consciences clean from useless works, so that we may serve the living God.

For this reason Christ is the one who arranges a new covenant, so that those who have been called by God may receive the eternal blessings that God has promised. This can be done because there has been a death which sets men free from the wrongs they did while they were under the first covenant.

For Christ did not go into a holy place made by men, a copy of the real one. He went into heaven itself, where he now appears on our behalf in the presence of God. The Jewish High Priest goes into the Holy Place every year with the blood of an animal. But Christ did not go in to offer himself many times; for then he would have had to suffer many times ever since the creation of the world. Instead, he has now appeared once and for all, when all ages of time are nearing the end, to remove sin through the sacrifice of himself. Everyone must die once, and after that be judged by God. In the same manner, Christ also was offered in sacrifice once to take away the sins of many. He will appear a second time, not to deal with sin, but to save those who are waiting for him.

Let Us Come Near to God
We have, then, brothers, complete freedom to go into the Most Holy Place by means of the death of Jesus. He opened for us a new way, a living way, through the curtain—that is, through his own body. We have a great priest in charge of the house of God. Let us come near to God, then, with a sincere heart and a sure faith, with hearts that have been made clean from a guilty conscience, and bodies washed with pure water. Let us hold on firmly to the hope we profess, because we can trust God to keep his promise. Let us be concerned with one another, to help one another to show love and to do good. Let us not give up the habit of meeting together, as some are doing. Instead, let us encourage one another, all the more since you see that the Day of the Lord is coming near.

For there is no longer any sacrifice that will take away sins if we purposely go on sinning after the truth has been made known to us. Instead, all that is left is to be afraid of what will happen: the Judgment and the fierce fire which will destroy those who oppose God!

Remember how it was with you in the past. In those days, after God's light had shone on you, you suffered many things, yet were not defeated by the struggle. You were at times publicly insulted and mistreated, and at other times you were ready to join those who were being treated in this way. You shared the sufferings of prisoners, and when all your belongings were seized you endured your loss gladly, because you knew that you still had for yourselves something much better, which would last forever. Do not lose your courage, then, because it brings with it a great reward.

We are not people who turn back and are lost. Instead, we have faith and are saved.

Faith
To have faith is to be sure of the things we hope for, to be certain of the things we cannot see. It was by their faith that the men of ancient times won God's approval.

It is by faith that we understand that the universe was

created by God's word, so that what can be seen was made out of what cannot be seen.

It was faith that made Abel offer to God a better sacrifice than Cain's. Through his faith he won God's approval as a righteous man, because God himself approved his gifts. By means of his faith Abel still speaks, even though he is dead.

It was faith that kept Enoch from dying. Instead, he was taken up to God, and nobody could find him, because God had taken him up. The scripture says that before Enoch was taken up he had pleased God. No man can please God without faith. For whoever comes to God must have faith that God exists and rewards those who seek him.

It was faith that made Noah hear God's warnings about things in the future that he could not see. He obeyed God, and built an ark in which he and his family were saved. In this way he condemned the world, and received from God the righteousness that comes by faith.

It was faith that made Abraham obey when God called him, and go out to a country which God had promised to give him. He left his own country without knowing where he was going. By faith he lived in the country that God had promised him, as though he were a foreigner. He lived in tents with Isaac and Jacob, who received the same promise from God. For Abraham was waiting for the city which God had designed and built, the city with permanent foundations.

It was faith that made Abraham able to become a father even though he was too old and Sarah herself was unable to have children. He trusted God to keep his promise. Though he was practically dead, for this one man there came as many descendants as there are stars in the sky, as many as the numberless grains of sand on the seashore.

It was in faith that all these persons died. They did not receive the things God had promised, but from a long way off they saw and welcomed them, and admitted openly that they were foreigners and refugees on earth. Those who say such things make it clear that they are looking for a country of their own. They did not think back to the country they had left; if they had, they would have had the chance to return. Instead, it was a better country they longed for, the heavenly country. And so God is not ashamed to have them call him their God, because he has prepared a city for them.

It was faith that made Joseph, when he was about to die, speak of the departure of the Israelites from Egypt, and leave instructions about what should be done with his body.

It was faith that made the parents of Moses hide him for three months after he was born. They saw that he was a beautiful child, and they were not afraid to disobey the king's order.

It was faith that made Moses, when he was grown, refuse to be called the son of Pharaoh's daughter. He preferred to suffer with God's people rather than to enjoy sin for a little while. He reckoned that to suffer scorn for the Messiah was worth far more than all the treasures of Egypt; because he kept his eyes on the future reward.

It was faith that made Moses leave Egypt without being afraid of the King's anger; he would not turn back, as though he saw the invisible God. It was faith that made him establish the Passover and order the blood sprinkled on the doors, so that the Angel of Death would not kill the firstborn sons of the Israelites.

It was faith that enabled the Israelites to cross the Red Sea as if on dry land; when the Egyptians tried to do it, the water swallowed them up.

It was faith that made the walls of Jericho fall down, after the Israelites had marched around them for seven days. It was faith that kept the harlot Rahab from being killed with those who disobeyed God, because she gave the spies a friendly welcome.

Should I go on? There isn't enough time for me to speak of Gideon, Barak, Samson, Jephthah, David, Samuel, and the prophets. Through faith they fought whole countries and won. They did what was right and received what God had promised. They shut the mouths of lions, put out fierce fires, escaped being killed by the sword. They were weak but became strong; they were mighty in battle and defeated the armies of foreigners. Through faith women received their dead raised back to life.

Others, refusing to accept freedom, died under torture in order to be raised to a better life. Some were mocked and whipped, and others were tied up and put in prison. They were stoned, they were sawn in two, they were killed with the sword. They went around clothed in skins of sheep or goats, poor, persecuted, and mistreated. The world was not good enough for them! They wandered like refugees in the deserts and hills, living in caves and holes in the ground.

What a record all of these have won by their faith! Yet they did not receive what God had promised, because God had decided on an even better plan for us. His purpose was that they would be made perfect only with us.

God Our Father

As for us, we have this large crowd of witnesses around us. Let us rid ourselves, then, of everything that gets in the way, and the sin which holds on to us so tightly, and let us run with determination the race that lies before us. Let us keep our eyes fixed on Jesus, on whom our faith depends from beginning to end. He did not give up because of the cross! On the contrary, because of the joy that was waiting for him, he thought nothing of the disgrace of dying on the cross, and is now seated at the right side of God's throne.

Think of what he went through, how he put up with so much hatred from sinful men! So do not let yourselves become discouraged and give up. For in your struggle against sin you have not yet had to fight to the point of being killed.

How to Please God

The priests who serve in the Jewish tent have no right to eat of the sacrifice on our altar. The Jewish High Priest brings the blood of the animals into the Most Holy Place to offer it as a sacrifice for sins; but the bodies of the animals are burned outside the camp. For this reason Jesus also died outside the city gate, in order to cleanse the people from sin with his own blood. Let us, then, go to him outside the camp and share his shame. For there is no permanent city for us here on earth; we are looking for the city which is to come.

Prayer
God has raised from the dead our Lord Jesus, who is the Great Shepherd of the sheep because of his death, by which the eternal covenant is sealed. May the God of peace provide you with every good thing you need in order to do his will, and may he, through Jesus Christ, do in us what pleases him. And to Christ be the glory forever and ever!

Fourteen

THE BETTER PART

Faith and Wisdom
From James, a servant of God and of the Lord Jesus Christ:

Greetings to all God's people, scattered over the whole world.

My brothers! Consider yourselves fortunate when all kinds of trials come your way, because you know that when your faith succeeds in facing such trials, the result is the ability to endure. Be sure that your endurance carries you all the way, without failing, so that you may be perfect and complete, lacking nothing.

Happy is the man who remains faithful under trials, because when he succeeds in passing the test he will receive as his reward the life which God has promised to those who love him.

Do not fool yourselves by just listening to his word. Instead, put it into practice. Whoever listens to the word but does not put it into practice is like a man who looks in a mirror and sees himself as he is. He takes a good look at himself and then goes away, and at once forgets what he looks like. But whoever looks closely into the perfect law that sets men free, who keeps on paying attention to it, and does not simply listen and then forget it, but puts it into practice—that person will be blessed by God in what he does.

Warning Against Prejudice
My brothers! As believers in our Lord Jesus Christ, the Lord of glory, you must never treat people in different ways, according to their outward appearance. Suppose a

rich man wearing a gold ring and fine clothes comes to your meeting, and a poor man in ragged clothes also comes. If you show more respect to the well-dressed man and say to him, "Have this best seat here," but say to the poor man, "Stand, or sit down here on the floor by my feet," then you are guilty of creating distinctions among yourselves and of making judgments based on evil motives.

The Tongue

My brothers! Not many of you should become teachers, because you know that we teachers will be judged with greater strictness than others. All of us often make mistakes. The person who never makes a mistake in what he says is perfect, able also to control his whole being. We put a bit into the mouth of a horse to make it obey us, and we are able to make it go where we want. Or think of a ship: big as it is, and driven by such strong winds, it can be steered by a very small rudder, and goes wherever the pilot wants it to go. So it is with the tongue: small as it is, it can boast about great things.

Just think how large a forest can be set on fire by a tiny flame! And the tongue is like a fire. It is a world of wrong, occupying its place in our bodies and spreading evil through our whole being. It sets on fire the entire course of our existence with the fire that comes to it from hell itself. Man is able to tame, and has tamed, all other creatures—wild animals and birds, reptiles and fish. But no man has ever been able to tame the tongue. It is evil and uncontrollable, full of deadly poison.

Warning Against Judging a Brother

Do not criticize one another, my brothers. Whoever criticizes his brother, or judges him, criticizes the Law and judges it. If you judge the Law, then you are no longer one who obeys the Law, but one who judges it. God is the only lawgiver and judge. He alone can save and destroy. Who do you think you are, to judge your fellow-man?

Warning Against Boasting

Now listen to me, you that say, "Today or tomorrow we will travel to a certain city, where we will stay a year, and go into business and make a lot of money." You don't even know what your life tomorrow will be! You are like a thin fog, which appears for a moment and then disappears. What you should say is this. "If the Lord is willing, we will live and do this or that." But now you are proud, and you boast; all such boasting is wrong.

So then, the person who does not do the good he knows he should do is guilty of sin.

Warning to the Rich

And now, you rich people, listen to me! Weep and wail over the miseries that are coming upon you! Your riches have rotted away, and your clothes have been eaten by moths. Your gold and silver are covered with rust, and this rust will be a witness against you, and eat up your flesh like fire. You have piled up riches in these last days. You have not paid the wages to the men who work in your fields. Hear their complaints! The cries of those who gather in your crops have reached the ears of God, the Lord Almighty. Your life here on earth has been full of luxury and pleasure. You have made yourselves fat for the day of slaughter. You have condemned and murdered the innocent man, and he does not resist you.

Patience and Prayer

Be patient, then, my brothers, until the Lord comes. See how the farmer is patient as he waits for his hand to produce precious crops. He waits patiently for the autumn and spring rains. You also must be patient. Keep your hopes high, for the day of the Lord's coming is near.

Is anyone among you in trouble? He should pray. Is anyone happy? He should sing praises. Is there anyone who is sick? He should call the church elders, who will pray for him and rub oil on him in the name of the

Lord. This prayer, made in faith, will heal the sick man; the Lord will restore him to health, and the sins he has committed will be forgiven. So then, confess your sins to one another, and pray for one another, so that you will be healed. The prayer of a good man has a powerful effect. Elijah was the same kind of person that we are. He prayed earnestly that there would be no rain, and no rain fell on the land for three and a half years. Once again he prayed, and the sky poured out its rain and the earth produced its crops.

My brothers! If one of you wanders away from the truth, and another one brings him back again, remember this: whoever turns a sinner back from his wrong way will save that sinner's soul from death, and bring about the forgiveness of many sins.

A Living Hope

From Peter, apostle of Jesus Christ—

To God's chosen people who live as refugees scattered throughout the provinces of Pontus, Galatia, Cappadocia, Asia, and Bithynia. You were chosen according to the purpose of God the Father, and were made a holy people by his Spirit, to obey Jesus Christ and be cleansed by his blood.

May grace and peace be yours in full measure.

Let us give thanks to the God and Father of our Lord Jesus Christ! Because of his great mercy, he gave us new life by raising Jesus Christ from the dead. This fills us with a living hope, and so we look forward to possess the rich blessings that God keeps for his people. He keeps them for you in heaven, where they cannot decay or spoil or fade away. They are for you, who through faith are kept safe by God's power for the salvation which is ready to be revealed at the end of time.

Be glad about this, even though it may now be necessary for you to be sad for a while because of the many kinds of trials you suffer. Their purpose is to prove that your faith is genuine. Even gold, which can be destroyed, is tested by fire; and so your faith, which is much more precious than gold, must also be tested, that it may endure. Then you will receive praise and glory and honor on the Day when Jesus Christ is revealed.

The Living Stone and the Holy Nation

Come to the Lord, the living stone rejected as worthless by men, but chosen as valuable by God. Come as living stones, and let yourselves be used in building the spiritual temple, where you will serve as holy priests to offer spiritual and acceptable sacrifices to God through Jesus Christ. For the scripture says, "I chose a valuable stone, which now I place for the cornerstone in Zion; and whoever believes in him will never be disappointed." This stone is of great value for you that believe; but for those who do not believe: "The very stone which the builders rejected turned out to be the most important stone." And another scripture says, "This is the stone that will make people stumble, the rock that will make them fall." They stumbled because they did not believe in the word; such was God's will for them.

But you are the chosen race, the King's priests, the holy nation, God's own people, chosen to proclaim the wonderful acts of God, who called you from the darkness into his own marvelous light. At one time you were not God's people, but now you are his people; at one time you did not know God's mercy, but now you have received his mercy.

Slaves of God

I appeal to you, my friends, as strangers and refugees in this world! Do not give in to bodily passions, which are always at war against the soul. Your conduct among the heathen should be so good that when they accuse you of being evildoers they will have to recognize your good deeds, and so praise God on the Day of his coming.

Submit yourselves, for the Lord's sake, to every human authority: to the Emperor, who is the supreme authority, and to the governors, who have been sent by him to punish the evildoers and praise those who do good. For God's will is this: he wants you to silence the ignorant talk of foolish men by the good things you do. Live as free men; do not use your freedom, however, to cover up any evil, but live as God's slaves. Respect all men, love your fellow believers, fear God, and respect the Emperor.

The Example of Christ's Suffering

You servants must submit yourselves to your masters and show them complete respect, not only to those who are kind and considerate, but also to those who are harsh. God will bless you for this, if you endure the pain of undeserved suffering because you are conscious of his will. For what credit is there if you endure the beatings you deserve for having done wrong? But if you endure suffering even when you have done right, God will bless you for it. It was to this that God called you; because Christ himself suffered for you and left you an example, so that you would follow his steps. He committed no sin; no one ever heard a lie come from his lips. When he was insulted he did not answer back with an insult; when he suffered he did not threaten, but placed his hopes in God, the righteous Judge. Christ himself carried our sins in his body to the cross, so that we might die to sin and live for righteousness. By his wounds you have been healed. You were like sheep that had lost their way; but now you have been brought back to follow the Shepherd and Keeper of your souls.

Suffering for Doing Right

As the scripture says, "Whoever wants to enjoy life and wishes to see good times, must keep from speaking evil and stop telling lies. He must turn away from evil and do good; he must seek peace and pursue it. For the Lord keeps his eyes on the righteous and always listens to their prayers; but he turns against those who do evil."

Who will harm you if you are eager to do what is good? But even if you should suffer for doing what is right, how happy you are! Do not be afraid of men, and do not worry. But have reverence for Christ in your hearts, and make him your Lord. Be ready at all times to answer anyone who asks you to explain the hope you have in you.

Suffering as a Christian

My dear friends, do not be surprised at the painful test you are suffering, as though something unusual were happening to you. Rather be glad that you are sharing

Christ's sufferings, so that you may be full of joy when his glory is revealed. Happy are you if you are insulted because you are Christ's followers; this means that the glorious Spirit, the Spirit of God, is resting on you. None of you should suffer because he is a murderer, or a thief, or a criminal, or tries to manage other people's business. But if you suffer because you are a Christian, don't be ashamed of it, but thank God that you bear Christ's name.

The Flock of God
I appeal to the church elders among you, I who am an elder myself. I am a witness of Christ's sufferings, and I will share in the glory that will be revealed. I appeal to you: be shepherds of the flock that God gave you, and look after it willingly, as God wants you to, and not unwillingly. Do your work, not for mere pay, but from a real desire to serve. Do not try to rule over those who have been given into your care, but be examples to the flock. And when the Chief Shepherd appears, you will receive the glorious crown which will never lose its brightness.

God's Call and Choice
So then, my brothers, try even harder to make God's call and his choice of you a permanent experience; if you do so, you will never fall away. In this way you will be given the full right to enter the eternal Kingdom of our Lord and Savior Jesus Christ.

For this reason I will always remind you of these matters, even though you already know them and are firmly fixed in the truth you have received. I think it only right for me to stir up your memory of these matters, as long as I am still alive. I know that I shall soon put off this mortal body, as our Lord Jesus Christ plainly told me. I will do my best, then, to provide a way for you to remember these matters at all times after my death.

Eyewitnesses of Christ's Glory
We have not depended on made-up legends in making known to you the mighty coming of our Lord Jesus

Christ. With our own eyes we saw his greatness. We were there when he was given honor and glory by God the Father, when the voice came to him from the Supreme Glory, saying, "This is my own dear Son, with whom I am well pleased!" We ourselves heard this voice coming from heaven, when we were with him on the sacred mountain.

So we are even more confident of the message proclaimed by the prophets. You will do well to pay attention to it, because it is like a lamp shining in a dark place, until the Day dawns and the light of the morning star shines in your hearts. Above all else, however, remember this: no one can explain, by himself, a prophecy in the Scriptures. For no prophetic message ever came just from the will of man, but men were carried along by the Holy Spirit as they spoke the message that came from God.

The Word of Life

We write to you about the Word of life, which has existed from the very beginning: we have heard it, and we have seen it with our eyes; yes, we have seen it, and our hands have touched it. When this life became visible, we saw it; so we speak of it and tell you about the eternal life which was with the Father and was made known to us. What we have seen and heard we tell to you also, so that you will join with us in the fellowship that we have with the Father and with his Son Jesus Christ.

The New Command

I write you this, my children, so that you will not sin; but if anyone does sin, we have Jesus Christ, the righteous, who pleads for us with the Father. And Christ himself is the means which our sins are forgiven, and not our sins only, but also the sins of all men.

If we obey God's commands, then we are sure that we know him.

Whoever says that he is in the light, yet hates his brother, is in the darkness to this very hour. Whoever loves his brother stays in the light, and so there is nothing in him that will cause someone else to sin. But whoever hates his brother is in the darkness; he walks in it and does not know where he is going, because the darkness has made him blind.

Do not love the world or anything that belongs to the world. If you love the world, you do not have the love for the Father in you. Everything that belongs to the world—what the sinful self desires, what people see and want, and everything in this world that people are so proud of—none of this comes from the Father; it all comes from the world. The world and everything in it that men desire is passing away; but he who does what God wants lives forever.

Children of God
See how much the Father has loved us! His love is so great that we are called God's children—and so, in fact, we are. This is why the world does not know us: it has not known God. My dear friends, we are now God's children, but it is not yet clear what we shall become. But we know that when Christ appears, we shall become like him, because we shall see him as he really is. Everyone who has this hope in Christ keeps himself pure, just as Christ is pure.

Love One Another
So do not be surprised, my brothers, if the people of the world hate you. We know that we have left death and come over into life; we know it because we love our brothers. Whoever does not love is still in death. Whoever hates his brother is a murderer; and you know that a murderer does not have eternal life in him. This is how we know what love is: Christ gave his life for us. We too, then, ought to give our lives for our brothers! If a man is rich and sees his brother in need, yet closes his heart against his brother, how can he claim that he has love for God in his heart? My children! Our love should not be just words and talk; it must be true love, which shows itself in action.

God Is Love
Dear friends! Let us love one another, because love comes from God. Whoever loves is a child of God and knows God. Whoever does not love does not know

God, because God is love. This is how God showed his love for us: he sent his only Son into the world that we might have life through him. This is what love is: it is not that we have loved God, but that he loved us and sent his Son to be the means by which our sins are forgiven.

Dear friends, if this is how God loved us, then we should love one another.

Our Victory over the World

For our love for God means that we obey his commands. And his commands are not too hard for us, because every child of God is able to defeat the world. This is how we win the victory over the world: with our faith. Who can defeat the world? Only he who believes that Jesus is the Son of God.

Jesus Christ is the one who came; he came with the water of his baptism and the blood of his death. He came not only with the water, but with both the water and the blood. And the Spirit himself testifies that this is true, because the Spirit is truth. There are three witnesses, the Spirit, the water, and the blood; and all three agree. We believe the witness that men give; the witness that God gives is much stronger, and this is the witness that God has given about his Son. So whoever believes in the Son of God has this witness in his heart; but whoever does not believe God has made a liar out of him, because he has not believed what God has said as a witness about his Son. This, then, is the witness: God has given us eternal life, and this life is in his Son. Whoever has the Son has this life; whoever does not have the Son of God does not have life.

Truth and Love

Many deceivers have gone out over the world, men who do not declare that Jesus Christ came as a human being. Such a person is a deceiver and the Enemy of Christ. Watch yourselves, then, so that you will not lose what you have worked for, but will receive your reward in full.

Anyone who does not stay with the teaching of Christ, but goes beyond it, does not have God. Whoever does stay with the teaching has both the Father and the Son. If anyone comes to you, then, who does not bring this teaching, do not welcome him in your home; do not even say, "Peace be with you." For anyone who wishes him peace becomes his partner in the evil thing he does.

Final Words
My dear friend, do not imitate what is bad, but imitate what is good. Whoever does good belongs to God; whoever does what is bad has not seen God.

I have so much to tell you, but I do not want to do it with pen and ink. I hope to see you soon, and then we will talk personally.

Peace be with you.

All your friends send greetings. Greet all our friends personally.

False Teachers
From Jude, a servant of Jesus Christ, and the brother of James—

To those who have been called by God, who live in the love of God the Father and the protection of Jesus Christ:

May mercy, peace, and love be yours in full measure.

My dear friends! I was doing my best to write to you about the salvation we share in common, when I felt the need of writing you now to encourage you to fight on for the faith which once and for all God has given to his people. For some godless men have slipped in unnoticed among us, who distort the message about the grace of our God to excuse their immoral ways, and reject Jesus Christ, our only Master and Lord. Long ago the Scriptures predicted this condemnation they have received.

Warnings and Instructions
But remember, my friends! Remember what you were told in the past by the apostles of our Lord Jesus Christ. They said to you, "When the last days come, men will appear who will make fun of you, men who follow their own godless desires." These are the men who cause divisions, who are controlled by their natural desires, who do not have the Spirit. But you, my friends, keep on

building yourselves up on your most sacred faith. Pray in the power of the Holy Spirit, and keep yourselves in the love of God, as you wait for our Lord Jesus Christ in his mercy to give you eternal life.

Show mercy toward those who have doubts: save them, by snatching them out of the fire. Show mercy also, mixed with fear, to others as well, but hate their very clothes, stained by their sinful lusts.

Prayers of Praise
To him who is able to keep you from falling and bring you faultless and joyful before his glorious presence—to the only God our Savior, through Jesus Christ our Lord, be glory, majesty, might, and authority, from all ages past, and now, and forever and ever!

Fifteen

"A REVELATION OF THINGS THAT WERE, ARE, AND WILL BE"

Prologue
This book is about what Jesus Christ revealed, which God gave him, to show to God's servant what must happen very soon. Christ made these things known to his servant John by sending his angel to him, and John has told all that he has seen. This is his report concerning the message from God and the truth revealed by Jesus Christ. Happy is the one who reads this book, and happy are those who listen to the words of this prophetic message and obey what is written in this book! For the time is near when all this will happen.

Greetings to the Seven Churches
From John to the seven churches in the province of Asia:

Grace and peace be yours from God, who is, who was, and who is to come, and from the seven spirits in front of his throne, and from Jesus Christ, the faithful witness, the firstborn Son who was raised from death, who is also the ruler of the kings of earth.

He loves us, and by his death he has freed us from our sins and made us a kingdom of priests to serve his God and Father. To Jesus Christ be the glory and power forever and ever!

Look, he is coming with the clouds! Everyone will see him, including those who pierced him. All peoples of earth will mourn over him. Certainly so!

"I am the Alpha and the Omega," says the Lord God Almighty, who is, who was, and who is to come.

A Vision of Christ

I am John, your brother, and in union with Jesus I share with you in suffering, and in his Kingdom, and in enduring. I was put on the island named Patmos because I had proclaimed God's word and the truth that Jesus revealed. On the Lord's day the Spirit took control of me, and I heard a loud voice, that sounded like a trumpet, speaking behind me. It said, "Write down what you see, and send the book to these seven churches: in Ephesus, Smyrna, Pergamum, Thyatira, Sardis, Philadelphia, and Laodicea."

I turned around to see who was talking to me. There I saw seven gold lampstands. Among them stood a being who looked like a man, wearing a robe that reached to his feet, and a gold band around his chest. His hair was white as wool or as snow, and his eyes blazed like fire; his feet shone like brass melted in the furnace and then polished, and his voice sounded like a mighty waterfall. He held seven stars in his right hand, and a sharp two-edged sword came out of his mouth. His face was as bright as the midday sun. When I saw him, I fell down at his feet like a dead man. He placed his right hand on me and said, "Don't be afraid! I am the first and the last. I am the living one! I was dead, but look, I am alive forever and ever. I have authority over death and the world of the dead. Write, then, the things you see, both the things that are now, and the things that will happen afterward. Here is the secret meaning of the seven stars that you see in my right hand, and of the seven gold lampstands: the seven stars are the angels of the seven churches, and the seven lampstands are the seven churches."

The Message to Ephesus

"To the angel of the church in Ephesus write:

"This is the message from the one who holds the seven stars in his right hand, who walks among the seven gold lampstands. I know what you have done; I know how hard you have worked and how patient you have been. I know that you cannot tolerate evil men, and that you have tested those who say they are apostles but are not, and have found out that they are liars. You are patient, you have suffered troubles for my sake, and you have not given up. But here is what I have against you: you do not love me now as you did at first. Remember how far you have fallen! Turn from your sins and do what you did at first. If you don't turn from your sins, I will come to you and take your lampstand from its place."

The Message to Smyrna
"To the angel of the church in Smyrna write:

"This is the message from the one who is the first and the last, who died and lived again. I know your troubles; I know that you are poor—but really you are rich! I know the evil things said against you by those who claim to be Jews, but are not; they are a group that belongs to Satan! Do not be afraid of anything you are about to suffer. Listen! The Devil will put you to the test by having some of you thrown into prison; your troubles will last ten days. Be faithful to me, even if it means death, and I will give you the crown of life.

"If you have ears, then, listen to what the Spirit says to the churches!

"Those who win the victory will not be hurt by the second death."

The Message to Pergamum
"To the angel of the church in Pergamum write:

"This is the message from the one who has the sharp two-edged sword. I know where you live, there where Satan has his throne. You are true to me, and you did not abandon your faith in me even during the time when Antipas, a faithful witness for me, was killed there where Satan lives. But here are a few things I have against you: there with you are some who follow the teaching of Balaam, who taught Balak how to cause the people of Israel to sin by eating food that had been offered to idols, and by committing immorality. In the same way, you also have people among you who follow the teaching of the Nicolaitans."

The Message to Thyatira
"To the angel of the church in Thyatira write:

"This is the message from the Son of God, whose eyes blaze like fire, whose feet shine like polished brass. I know what you do. I know your love, your faithfulness, your service, and your patience. I know that you are doing more now than you did at first. But here is what I have against you: you tolerate that woman Jezebel, who calls herself a messenger of God. She teaches and misleads my servants into committing immorality and eating food that has been offered to idols.

"But the rest of you in Thyatira have not followed this evil teaching; you have not learned what the others call 'the deep secrets of Satan.' I say to you that I will not put any other burden on you. But you must hold firmly to what you have until I come."

The Message to Sardis
"To the angel of the church in Sardis write:

"This is the message from the one who has the seven spirits of God and the seven stars. I know what you are doing; I know that you have the reputation of being alive, even though you are dead! So wake up, and strengthen what you still have, before it dies completely. For I find that what you have done is not yet perfect in the sight of my God."

The Message to Philadelphia
"To the angel of the church in Philadelphia write:

"This is the message from the one who is holy and true, who holds the key that belonged to David, who opens so that none can close, who closes so that none can open.

"I am coming soon. Keep safe what you have, so that no one will rob you of your victory prize."

The Message to Laodicea
"To the angel of the church in Laodicea write:

"This is the message from the Amen, the faithful and true witness, who is the origin of all that God has created. I know what you have done; I know that you are

"A REVELATION OF THINGS THAT WERE, ARE,

neither cold nor hot. How I wish you were either one or the other! But because you are barely warm, neither hot nor cold, I am going to spit you out of my mouth! 'I am rich and well off,' you say, 'I have all I need.' But you do not know how miserable and pitiful you are! You are poor, naked, and blind.

"If you have ears, then, listen to what the Spirit says to the churches!"

Worship in Heaven

At this point I had another vision, and saw an open door in heaven.

And the voice that sounded like a trumpet, which I had heard speaking to me before, said, "Come up here, and I will show you what must happen after this." At once the Spirit took control of me. There in heaven was a throne, with someone sitting on it. His face gleamed like such precious stones as jasper and carnelian; all around the throne there was a rainbow the color of an emerald. In a circle around the throne were twenty-four other thrones, on which were seated twenty-four elders dressed in white and wearing gold crowns. From the throne came flashes of lightning, sounds, and peals of thunder. There were seven lighted torches burning before the throne; these are the seven spirits of God. In front of the throne there was what looked like a sea of glass, clear as crystal.

Surrounding the throne, on each of its sides, were four living creatures covered with eyes in front and in back. The first living creature looked like a lion; the second looked like a calf; the third had a face like a man's face; and the fourth looked like a flying eagle. Each one of the four living creatures had six wings, and they were covered over with eyes, inside and out. They never stop their singing day or night: "Holy, holy, holy, is the Lord God Almighty, who was, who is, and who is to come."

The four living creatures sing songs of glory and honor and thanks to the one who sits on the throne, and worship him who lives forever and ever. They throw their crowns before the throne and say, "Our Lord and God! You are worthy to receive glory, honor, and power. For you created all things, and by your will they were given existence and life."

The Scroll and the Lamb

I saw a scroll in the right hand of the one who sat on the throne; it was covered with writing on both sides, and was sealed with seven seals.

Then I saw a Lamb standing in the center of the throne, surrounded by the four living creatures and the elders. The Lamb appeared to have been killed. It had seven horns and seven eyes, which are the seven spirits of God that have been sent into all the world. The Lamb went and took the scroll from the right hand of the one who sat on the throne. As he did so, the four living creatures and the twenty-four elders fell down before the Lamb. Each had a harp, and gold bowls filled with incense, which are the prayers of God's people. They sang a new song: "You are worthy to take the scroll and to break open its seals. For you were killed, and by your death you bought men for God, from every tribe, language, nation, and race. You have made them a kingdom of priests to serve our God, and they shall rule on earth."

The Great Crowd

After this I looked, and there was a great crowd—no one could count all the people! They were from every race, tribe, nation, and language, and they stood in front of the throne and of the Lamb, dressed in white robes, and holding palm branches in their hands. They called out in a loud voice, "Our salvation comes from our God, who sits on the throne, and from the lamb!" All the angels stood around the throne, the elders, and the four living creatures. Then they fell down on their faces before the throne and worshiped God, saying, "Amen! Praise, glory, wisdom, thanks, honor, power, and might belong to our God forever and ever!"

One of the elders asked me, "Who are these people dressed in white robes, and where do they come from?"

"I don't know, sir. You do," I answered.

He said to me, "These are the people who have come safely through the great persecution. They washed their robes and made them white with the blood of the Lamb. That is why they stand before God's throne and serve him day and night in his temple. He who sits on the throne will protect them with his presence. Never again will they hunger or thirst; neither sun nor any scorching heat will burn them; because the Lamb, who is in the center of the throne, will be their shepherd, and he will guide them to springs of living water. And God will wipe away every tear from their eyes."

The Woman and the Dragon

Then a great mysterious sight appeared in the sky. There was a woman, whose dress was the sun and who had the moon under her feet and a crown of twelve stars on her head. She was soon to give birth, and the pains and suffering of childbirth made her cry out.

Another mysterious sight appeared in the sky. There was a huge red dragon with seven heads and ten horns, and a crown on each of his heads. With his tail he dragged a third of the stars out of the sky and threw them to earth. He stood in front of the woman who was about to give birth, in order to eat her child as soon as it was born. Then the woman gave birth to a son, who will rule over all nations with an iron rod. But the child was snatched away and taken to God and his throne. The woman fled to the desert, to a place God had prepared for her, where she will be taken care of for 1,260 days.

Then war broke out in heaven. Michael and his angels fought against the dragon, who fought back with his angels; but the dragon was defeated, and he and his angels were not allowed to stay in heaven any longer.

The Song of the Redeemed

Then I looked, and there was the Lamb standing on Mount Zion; with him were 144,000 people who have his name and his Father's name written on their foreheads. And I heard a voice from heaven that sounded like the roar of a mighty waterfall, like a loud peal of thunder. The voice I heard sounded like the music made by harpists playing their harps. The 144,000 stood facing the throne, the four living creatures, and the elders. They sang a new song which only they, who had been redeemed from the earth, could learn. They are the men who had kept themselves pure by not having sexual relations with women; they are virgins. They follow the Lamb wherever he goes. They have been redeemed from the rest of mankind and are the first ones to be offered to God and to the Lamb. They have never been known to lie; they are faultless.

Then I heard a voice from heaven saying, "Write this: Happy are the dead who from now on die in the service of the Lord!"

"Certainly so," answers the Spirit. "They will enjoy rest from their hard work, because the results of their service go with them."

The Wedding Feast of the Lamb
Then there came from the throne the sound of a voice, saying, "Praise our God, all his servants, and all men, both great and small, who fear him!" Then I heard what sounded like the voice of a great crowd, like the roar of a mighty waterfall, like loud peals of thunder. I heard them say, "Praise God! For the Lord, our Almighty God, is King! Let us rejoice and be glad; let us praise his greatness! For the time has come for the wedding of the Lamb, and his bride has prepared herself for it. She has been given clean shining linen to dress herself with." (The linen is the righteous deeds of God's people.)

Then the angel said to me, "Write this: Happy are those who have been invited to the wedding feast of the Lamb." And the angel added, "These are the true words of God"

The Final Judgment
Then I saw a large white throne and the one who sits on it. Earth and heaven fled from his presence, and were seen no more. And I saw the dead, great and small alike, standing before the throne. Books were opened, and then another book was opened, the book of the living. The dead were judged according to what they had done, as was written in the books. Then the sea gave up its dead. Death and the world of the dead also gave up

the dead they held. And all were judged according to what they had done. Then death and the world of the dead were thrown into the lake of fire. (This lake of fire is the second death.) Whoever did not have his name written in the book of the living was thrown into the lake of fire.

The New Heaven and the New Earth

Then I saw a new heaven and a new earth. The first heaven and the first earth disappeared, and the sea vanished. And I saw the Holy City, the new Jerusalem, coming down out of heaven from God, prepared and ready, like a bride dressed to meet her husband. I heard a loud voice speaking from the throne, "Now God's home is with men! He will live with them, and they shall be his people. God himself will be with them, and he will be their God. He will wipe away all tears from their eyes. There will be no more death, no more grief, crying, or pain. The old things have disappeared."

Then the one who sits on the throne said, "And now I make all things new!" He also said to me, "Write this, because these words are true and can be trusted." And he said, "It is done! I am the Alpha and the Omega, the beginning and the end. To anyone who is thirsty I will give a free drink of water from the spring of the water of life. Whoever wins the victory will receive this from me: I will be his God, and he will be my son. But the cowards, the traitors, and the perverts, the murderers and the immoral, those who practice magic and those who worship idols, and all liars—the place for them is the lake burning with fire and sulphur, which is the second death."

The New Jerusalem

One of the seven angels who had the seven bowls full of the seven last plagues came to me and said, "Come, and I will show you the Bride, the wife of the Lamb." The Spirit took control of me, and the angel carried me to the top of a very high mountain. He showed me Jerusalem, the Holy City, coming down out of heaven from God, shining with the glory of God. The city shone like a precious stone, like a jasper, clear as crystal. It had a great, high wall, with twelve gates, and with twelve angels in charge of the gates. On the gates were written the names of the twelve tribes of the people of Israel. There were three gates on each side: three on the east, three on the south, three on the north, and three on the west. The city's wall was built on twelve stones, on which were written the names of the twelve apostles of the Lamb.

The wall was made of jasper, and the city itself was made of pure gold, as clear as glass. The foundation stones of the city wall were adorned with all kinds of precious stones. The first foundation stone was jasper, the second sapphire, the third agate, the fourth emerald, the fifth onyx, the sixth carnelian, the seventh yellow quartz, the eighth beryl, the ninth topaz, the tenth chalcedony, the eleventh turquoise, the twelfth amethyst. The twelve gates were twelve pearls; each gate was made from a single pearl. The street of the city was of pure gold, transparent as glass.

I did not see a temple in the city, because its temple is the Lord God, the Almighty, and the Lamb. The city has no need of the sun or the moon to shine on it, because the glory of God shines on it, and the Lamb is its lamp. The peoples of the world will walk by its light, and the kings of the earth will bring their wealth into it. The gates of the city will stand open all day; they will never be closed, because there will be no night there. The greatness and the wealth of the nations will be brought into the city. But nothing that is impure will enter the city, nor anyone who does shameful things or tells lies. Only those whose names are written in the Lamb's book of the living will enter the city.

The angel also showed me the river of the water of life, sparkling like crystal, which comes from the throne of God and of the Lamb, and flows down the middle of the city's street. On each side of the river was the tree of life, which bears fruit twelve times a year, once every month; and its leaves are for the healing of the nations. Nothing that is under God's curse will be found in the city.

The throne of God and of the Lamb will be in the city, and his servants will worship him. They will see his face, and his name will be written on their foreheads. There shall be no more night, and they will not need lamps or sunlight, because the Lord God will be their light, and they will rule as kings forever and ever.

Epilogue
"I, Jesus, have sent my angel to announce these things to you in the churches. I am the descendant from the family of David; I am the bright morning star."

The Spirit and the Bride say, "Come!"

Everyone who hears this must also say, "Come!"

Come, whoever is thirsty; accept the water of life as a gift, whoever wants it.

I, John, solemnly warn everyone who hears the prophetic words of this book: if anyone adds anything to them, God will add to his punishment the plagues described in this book. And if anyone takes away anything from the prophetic words of this book, God will take away from him his share of the fruit of the tree of life, and his share of the Holy City, which are described in this book.

He who gives his testimony to all this, says, "Certainly so! I am coming soon!"

So be it. Come, Lord Jesus!

May the grace of the Lord Jesus be with all.

SCRIPTURAL REFERENCES

PART I. THE MESSIAH'S EARLY LIFE

PROLOGUE

The Word of Life, John 1:1-18
Introduction, Luke 1:1-4

CHAPTER ONE

The Dawn of the Good News
The Birth of John the Baptist Announced, Luke 1:5-25
The Birth of Jesus Announced, Luke 1:26-38
Mary Visits Elizabeth, Luke 1:39-45
Mary's Song of Praise, Luke 1:46-56
The Birth of John the Baptist, Luke 1:57-66
Zechariah's Prophecy, Luke 1:67-80
The Birth of Jesus Christ, Matthew 1:18-25; Luke 2:1-7
The Shepherds and the Angels, Luke 2:8-20
Jesus Is Named, Luke 2:21
Jesus Is Presented in the Temple, Luke 2:22-39
Visitors from the East, Matthew 2:1-12
The Escape to Egypt, Matthew 2:13-15
The Killing of the Children, Matthew 2:16-18
The Return from Egypt, Matthew 2:19-23
The Boy Jesus in the Temple, Luke 2:40-52

CHAPTER TWO

The Baptist Prepares the Way for the Son of God
The Preaching of John the Baptist, Matthew 3:1-10; Luke 3:10-14
The Baptism of Jesus, Matthew 3:13-17
The Temptation of Jesus, Matthew 4:1-11
John the Baptist's Message, John 1:19-34
The First Disciples of Jesus, John 1:35-51
The Wedding at Cana, John 2:1-12
Jesus Goes to the Temple, John 2:13-21
Jesus and Nicodemus, John 3:1-21
Jesus and the Baptist, John 3:22-30
He Who Comes from Heaven, John 3:31-36

CHAPTER THREE

The Early Ministry of Jesus
Jesus and the Woman of Samaria, John 4:1-42
Jesus Heals an Official's Son, John 4:43-54
The Healing at the Pool, John 5:1-18
The Authority of the Son, John 5:19-29
Witnesses to Jesus, John 5:30-47
Jesus Rejected at Nazareth, Luke 4:16-30
Jesus Calls Four Fishermen, Mark 1:14-20
A Man with an Evil Spirit, Mark 1:21-29, 35-39

CHAPTER FOUR

Jesus Speaks with Authority
The Sermon on the Mount, Matthew 5:1-48, 6:1-34, 7:1-29

CHAPTER FIVE

Miracles and Parables
Jesus Makes a Leper Clean, Matthew 8:1-4; Mark 1:45
Jesus Calls the First Disciples, Luke 5:1-11

SCRIPTURAL REFERENCES

Jesus Heals a Paralyzed Man, Mark 2:1-2; Luke 5:18-26
Jesus Calls Levi, Luke 5:27-32
The Question About Fasting, Luke 5:33-39
The Question About the Sabbath, Matthew 12:1-16
Jesus and Beelzebul, Luke 11:14-17; Mark 3:23-30
Jesus Chooses the Twelve Apostles, Luke 6:12-16; Mark 3:14-15
Jesus Teaches and Heals, Luke 6:17-49
Jesus Heals a Roman Officer's Servant, Matthew 8:5-13
Jesus Raises a Widow's Son, Luke 7:11-17
The Messengers from John the Baptist, Matthew 11:2-6; Luke 7:24-35
The Unbelieving Towns, Matthew 11:20-30
Jesus at the Home of Simon the Pharisee, Luke 7:36-50
Jesus and Beelzebul, Matthew 12:22-45
Jesus' Mother and Brothers, Matthew 12:46-50
Jesus Teaches in Parables, Mark 4:1-29; Matthew 13:31-33, 24-30, 34
The Parables Explained, Matthew 13:36-52; Mark 4:33-34
Jesus Calms a Storm, Mark 4:35-41
Jesus Heals a Man with Demons, Luke 8:26-39
Jairus' Daughter and the Woman Who Touched Jesus' Cloak, Mark 5:21-43
Jesus Heals Two Blind Men, Matthew 9:27-30
Jesus Has Pity for the People, Matthew 9:35-38
Jesus Sends Out the Twelve Disciples, Mark 6:6-11
The Mission of the Twelve, Matthew 10:5-42; Mark 6:12-13
The Death of John the Baptist, Mark 6:14-29; Luke 9:9
Jesus Feeds the Five Thousand, Mark 6:30-33; John 6:5-13
Jesus Walks on the Water, Matthew 14:22-33
Jesus the Bread of Life, John 6:22-71

CHAPTER SIX

Coming Events Cast Their Shadows
The Teaching of the Ancestors, Mark 7:1-13
The Things That Make a Person Unclean, Mark 7:14-23
A Woman's Faith, Matthew 15:21-28
Jesus Heals a Deaf and Dumb Man, Mark 7:31-37
Jesus Feeds the Four Thousand, Mark 8:1-21
Jesus Heals a Blind Man at Bethsaida, Mark 8:22-26
Peter's Declaration About Jesus, Matthew 16:13-20
Jesus Speaks About His Suffering and Death, Matthew 16:21-28
The Transfiguration, Mark 9:2-13
Jesus Heals a Boy with an Evil Spirit, Mark 9:14-25; Matthew 17:18-21; Mark 9:30-32
Who Is the Greatest? Mark 9:33-35; Luke 9:47-48
Payment of the Temple Tax, Matthew 17:24-27
Who Is Not Against Us Is for Us, Mark 9:38-41
Temptations to Sin, Mark 9:42-50
Be Merciful, Matthew 18:12-35
Jesus and His Brothers, John 7:1-9
Jesus at the Feast of Tabernacles, John 7:10-24
Is He the Messiah? John 7:25-36
Streams of Living Water, John 7:37-44; 8:1
The Woman Caught in Adultery, John 8:2-11
Jesus the Light of the World, John 8:12-59
Jesus Heals a Man Born Blind, John 9:1-41
Jesus the Good Shepherd, John 10:1-21
Jesus Rejected by the Jews, John 10:22-42

CHAPTER SEVEN

"To Search Out and to Save What Was Lost"
The Would-Be Followers of Jesus, Luke 9:51-62
Jesus Sends Out the Seventy-two, Luke 10:1-16
The Return of the Seventy-two, Luke 10:17-24

SCRIPTURAL REFERENCES

The Parable of the Good Samaritan, Luke 10:25-37
Jesus' Teaching on Prayer, Luke 11:1-13
True Happiness, Luke 11:27-54
Trust in God's Providence, Luke 12:1-40
The Faithful or the Unfaithful Servant, Luke 12:41-59
Turn from Your Sins or Die, Luke 13:1-9
Jesus Heals a Crippled Woman on the Sabbath, Luke 13:10-17
The Narrow Door, Luke 13:22-30
Jesus' Love for Jerusalem, Luke 13:31-35
Jesus Visits Martha and Mary, Luke 10:38-42
Jesus Heals a Sick Man, Luke 14:1-6
Humility and Hospitality, Luke 14:7-14
The Parable of the Great Feast, Luke 14:15-24
The Cost of Being a Disciple, Luke 14:25-33
The Lost Son, Luke 15:11-32
The Shrewd Manager, Luke 16:1-13
Some Sayings of Jesus, Luke 16:14-31
Sin, Luke 17:1-10
The Death of Lazarus, John 11:1-16
Jesus the Resurrection and the Life, John 11:17-37
Lazarus Brought to Life, John 11:38-44
The Plot Against Jesus, John 11:45-54
Jesus Makes Ten Lepers Clean, Luke 17:11-19
The Coming of the Kingdom, Luke 17:20-37
The Parable of the Widow and the Judge, Luke 18:1-8
The Parable of the Pharisee and the Tax Collector, Luke 18:9-14
Jesus Blesses Little Children, Mark 10:13-16
The Rich Man, Mark 10:17-22; Matthew 19:23-30
The Workers in the Vineyard, Matthew 20:1-16
Jesus Teaches About Divorce, Matthew 19:1-12
Jesus Speaks a Third Time About His Death, Mark 10:32-34
The Request of James and John, Mark 10:35-45
Jesus Heals a Blind Beggar, Luke 18:35-43

Jesus and Zacchaeus, Luke 19:1-10
The Parable of the Gold Coins, Luke 19:11-28

CHAPTER EIGHT

"And Now My Soul Is Distressed. What Am I to Say?"

The Triumphant Entry into Jerusalem, John 11:55-57; Mark 11:1-8; Luke 19:37-44; Matthew 21:10-11, 14-17
Jesus Curses the Fig Tree, Mark 11:12-14
Jesus Goes to the Temple, Mark 11:15-19
The Lesson from the Fig Tree, Mark 11:20-26
The Question About Jesus' Authority, Luke 20:1-8
The Parable of the Two Sons, Matthew 21:28-32
The Parable of the Tenants in the Vineyard, Matthew 21:33-46
The Pharisees Try to Trap Jesus, Matthew 22:15; Luke 20:20-23; Matthew 22:19-22; Luke 20:27-38; Mark 12:28-34
The Question About the Messiah, Luke 20:41-47
The Widow's Offering, Mark 12:41-44
Jesus Warns Against the Teachers of the Law and the Pharisees, Matthew 23:1-36
Jesus Speaks About His Death, John 12:20-36, 42-50
Portents of the Destruction of Jerusalem and the Second Coming, Mark 13:1-11; Luke 21:14-19; Matthew 24:11-15; Luke 21:20-21; Matthew 24:17-18; Luke 21:23; Mark 13:18-20; Matthew 24:23-31; Luke 21:28; Matthew 24:32-35; Luke 21:34-36; Mark 13:32-33; Matthew 24:37-42; Mark 13:34-37; Matthew 24:43-51; 25:1-46

CHAPTER NINE

Final Preaching of Jesus; His Betrayal and Arrest
Jesus Anointed at Bethany, John 12:1-6; Mark 14:6-9; John 12:9-11; Luke 22:1
Judas Agrees to Betray Jesus, Mark 14:1-2; Luke 22:3-6

Jesus Prepares to Eat the Passover Meal, Luke 22:7-13

The Lord's Supper, Luke 22:14-18; John 13:4-17; Luke 22:19; Matthew 26:27-29

Jesus Predicts His Betrayal, Mark 14:18; Luke 22:21-22; John 13:18-22; Mark 14:19-21; John 13:23-30

The New Commandment, John 13:31-35

Jesus Predicts Peter's Denial, John 13:36-38; Luke 22:31-34

The Argument About Greatness, Luke 22:24-30

Purse, Bag, and Sword, Luke 22:35-38

Final Discourses to His Apostles, John 14:1-31; 15:1-27; 16:1-33

Jesus Prays for His Disciples, John 17:1-26

The Agony in the Garden, Matthew 26:30-35; Mark 14:32-33; Luke 22:40-41; Matthew 26:37-39; Luke 22:43-44; Matthew 26:40-42; Luke 22:45-46; Matthew 26:44; Mark 14:36

The Betrayal and Arrest, Mark 14:40-43; John 18:4-9; Matthew 26:4-49; Luke 22:48; Mark 14:46; Luke 22:49; John 18:10; Luke 22:51; John 18:11; Matthew 26:52-56

CHAPTER TEN

The Trial of Jesus; His Crucifixion, Death, and Triumph

Jesus Before Annas, John 18:12-14

The High Priest Questions Jesus, John 18:19-24

Jesus Before the Council, Matthew 26:57-68

Peter Denies Jesus, Matthew 26:69-75

Jesus Before the Council, Luke 22:66-71

The Death of Judas, Matthew 27:1-10

Jesus Before Pilate, John 18:28-40; 19:6-12; Luke 23:3; Matthew 27:12-14; Luke 23:4-16

Jesus Sentenced to Death, Matthew 27:15-26

The Soldiers Made Fun of Jesus, Matthew 27:27-31

Jesus Nailed to the Cross, Luke 23:27-31; Mark 15:21-22

The Crucifixion and Death on the Cross, Matthew

27:34; Luke 23:32-34; John 19:19-24; Mark 15:29-30; Luke 23:36-37; Mark 15:31; Luke 23:39-43; John 19:25-27; Mark 15:33-34; John 19:28-30; Luke 23:46

Jesus' Side Pierced, John 19:31-37

The Burial of Jesus, Matthew 27:51-66

The Resurrection, Luke 24:1-7

Jesus Appears to Mary Magdalene, John 20:11-18; Mark 16:11; Luke 24:12

The Walk to Emmanus, Luke 24:13-35

Jesus Appears to His Disciples, Luke 24:36-43; John 20:21-23

Jesus and Thomas, John 20:24-29

Jesus Appears to Seven Disciples, John 21:1-14

Jesus and Peter, John 21:15-19

Jesus and the Other Disciple, John 21:20-23

Jesus Appears to the Eleven, Matthew 28:16-17; Mark 16:15-18; Matthew 28:18-20; Luke 24:44-49

Jesus Is Taken Up to Heaven, Luke 24:50; Acts 1:6-11

EPILOGUE

The Purpose of This Book, John 20:30-31; 21:25

PART II. THE REST OF THE NARRATIVE

CHAPTER ELEVEN

The Plight and Struggle of the Believers
Judas' Successor, Acts 1:12-26
The Coming of the Holy Spirit, Acts 2:1-13
Peter's Message, Acts 2:14-42
Life Among the Believers, Acts 2:43-47
The Lame Man Healed, Acts 3:1-10
Peter's Message in the Temple, Acts 3:11-19
Peter and John Before the Council, Acts 4:1-22
The Believers Pray for Boldness, Acts 4:23-31
All Things Together, Acts 4:32-37

Miracles and Wonders, Acts 5:14-16
The Seven Helpers, Acts 6:1-7
The Arrest of Stephen, Acts 6:8-15
Stephen's Speech, Acts 7:1-2, 44-53
The Stoning of Stephen, Acts 7:54-60
Saul Persecutes the Church, Acts 8:1-3
The Gospel Preached in Samaria, Acts 8:4-6, 8-22
The Conversion of Saul, Acts 9:1-19
Saul Preaches in Damascus, Acts 9:20-25
Saul in Jerusalem, Acts 9:26-30
Peter Set Free from Prison, Acts 11:27-30; 12:1-19
The Death of Herod, Acts 12:20-25
Barnabas and Saul Chosen and Sent, Acts 13:1-17, 32-39, 44-52
In Iconium, Acts 14:1-7
The Return to Antioch in Syria, Acts 14:19-28
The Meeting at Jerusalem, Acts 15:1-2, 7-21
Paul and Barnabas Separate, Acts 15:36-41
Timothy Goes with Paul and Silas, Acts 16:1-5
In Troas: Paul's Vision, Acts 16:6-10
In Philippi: the Conversion of Lydia, Acts 16:11-15
In Prison at Philippi, Acts 16:16-40
In Thessalonica, Acts, 17:1-4
In Athens, Acts 17:13-34
In Corinth, Acts 18:1-7
The Return to Antioch, Acts 18:18-22
To Macedonia and Greece, Acts 18:23; 20:2-6
Paul's Last Visit in Troas, Acts 20:7-16
Paul's Farewell Speech to the Elders of Ephesus, Acts 20:17-38
Paul Visits James, Acts 21:17-26
Paul Arrested in the Temple, Acts 21:27-39; 22:23-30
Paul Before the Council, Acts 23:6-17; 22-24
Paul Accused by the Jews, Acts 24:1-13, 22-27
Paul Appeals to the Emperor, Acts 25:1-12
Paul Before Agrippa and Bernice, Acts 25:13-23
Paul Defends Himself Before Agrippa, Acts 26:1, 8-15, 19-32

Paul Sails for Italy, Acts 27:1-2, 5-12
The Storm at Sea, Acts 27:13-15, 20-27, 39-44
In Malta, Acts 28:1-6
From Malta to Rome, Acts 28:11, 16, 30-31

CHAPTER TWELVE

The Followers of Christ Preach the Good News
Prayer of Thanksgiving, Romans 1:1, 7-15
The Power of the Gospel, Romans 1:16-17
The Guilt of Mankind, Romans 1:18-21
How God Puts Men Right, Romans 3:22-28
Right with God, Romans 5:1-9
Life in the Spirit, Romans 8:9-17
The Future Glory, Romans 8:18-30
God's Love in Christ Jesus, Romans 8:31-39
God and His Chosen People, Romans 9:1-8, 22-24
Salvation Is for All, Romans 10:1-4, 12-17
God's Mercy on Israel, Romans 11:1-12
The Salvation of the Gentiles, Romans 11:13-15, 32-36
Life in God's Service, Romans 12:1-2, 14-21
Duties Toward the State Authorities, Romans 13:1, 6-7
Duties Toward One Another, Romans 13:8-14
Do Not Judge Your Brother, Romans 14:3-4, 12-17
Please Others, Not Yourselves, Romans 15:1-6
The Gospel to the Gentiles, Romans 15:7-13
A Request from Paul, Romans 15:30-33
Questions About Marriage, 1 Corinthians 1:1-3; 7:1-11
Questions About the Unmarried and the Widows, I Corinthians 7:25-35
The Question About Food Offered to Idols, 1 Corinthians 8:1, 9-13
Rights and Duties of an Apostle, 1 Corinthians 9:24-27
Warning Against Idols, 1 Corinthians 10:1-24
The Lord's Supper, 1 Corinthians 11:17-29
Love, 1 Corinthians 12:31; 13:1-13

The Resurrection of Christ, 1 Corinthians 15:1-11
Our Resurrection, 1 Corinthians 15:12-14, 19-23
The Resurrection Body, 1 Corinthians 15:35-58
Spiritual Treasure in Clay Pots, 2 Corinthians 4:8-11, 16-18; 5:1-4
Paul Defends His Ministry, 2 Corinthians 10:1-6; 11:1-6
Paul's Sufferings as an Apostle, 2 Corinthians; 11:20-33
Paul's Visions and Revelations, 2 Corinthians 12:1-10
Paul's Concern for the Corinthians, 2 Corinthians 12:11-15
Paul's Farewell, 2 Corinthians 13:11-13
The One Gospel, Galatians 1:1-10
How Paul Became an Apostle, Galatians 1:11-24
Paul and the Other Apostles, Galatians 2:1-3, 7-10
Paul Rebukes Peter at Antioch, Galatians 2:11-16, 19-21
Preserve Your Freedom, Galatians 5:1-4
Final Warning and Greeting, Galatians 6:11-18
The Life and Faith of the Thessalonians, 1 Thessalonians 1:1-5
Paul's Work in Thessalonica, 1 Thessalonians 2:1-2, 9-16
Paul's Desire to Visit Them Again, 1 Thessalonians 2:17-20; 3:1-8
The Lord's Coming, 1 Thessalonians 4:13-18
You Are Chosen for Salvation, 2 Thessalonians 2:1-2, 5, 15-17

CHAPTER THIRTEEN

"Let Us Come Near to God"
Spiritual Blessings in Christ, Ephesians 1:1-10
From Death to Life, Ephesians 2:1-6
Paul's Work for the Gentiles, Ephesians, 2:19-21; 3:8, 13-21
The Unity of the Body, Ephesians 4:1-6
Wives and Husbands, Ephesians 5:21-33
Children and Parents, Ephesians 6:1-4

Slaves and Masters, Ephesians 6:5-9
Final Greetings, Ephesians 6:23-24
Paul's Prayer for His Readers, Philippians 1:1-10
Christ's Humility and Greatness, Philippians 2:3-11
The True Righteousness, Philippians 3:2-11
Running Toward the Goal, Philippians 3:12-21
Prayer of Thanksgiving, Colossians 1:1-3, 10-14
The Person and Work of Christ, Colossians 1:15-23
Fulness of Life in Christ, Colossians 2:6-15
Dying and Living with Christ, Colossians 2:20-23; 3:1-4
The Old Life and the New, Colossians 3:5-17
Final Greetings, Colossians 4:15-18
Warnings Against False Teaching, 1 Timothy 1:1-11
Church Worship, 1 Timothy 2:1-13
Leaders in the Church, 1 Timothy 3:1-7
False Teachers, 1 Timothy 4:1-5
Personal Instructions, 1 Timothy 6:11-16
Thanksgiving and Encouragement, 2 Timothy 1:3-6, 13-14
A Loyal Soldier of Christ Jesus, 2 Timothy 2:1-5
Last Instructions, 2 Timothy 3:14-17; 4:1-8
Personal Words, 2 Timothy 4:9-13, 22
Titus' Work in Crete, Titus 1:1-11
Sound Doctrine, Titus 2:1-8, 11-14
Philemon's Love and Faith, Philemon 1:1-7
A Request for Onesimus, Philemon 1:8-22
Final Greetings, Philemon 1:23-25
God's Word Through His Son, Hebrews 1:1-4
The Great Salvation, Hebrews 2:1-4
A Rest for God's People, Hebrews 3:7-19; 4:11-15
Jesus the Great High Priest, Hebrews 5:1-10
The Priest Melchizedek, Hebrews 7:1-4, 11-14, 23-28
Jesus Our High Priest, Hebrews 8:1-2; 9:6-7, 11-15, 24-28
Let Us Come Near to God, Hebrews 10:19-27, 32-35, 39
Faith, Hebrews 11:1-16, 22-40

God Our Father, Hebrews 12:1-4
How to Please God, Hebrews 13:10-14
Prayer, Hebrews 13:20-21

CHAPTER FOURTEEN

The Better Part
Faith and Wisdom, James 1:1-4, 12, 22-25
Warning Against Prejudice, James 2:1-4
The Tongue, James 3:1-8
Warning Against Judging a Brother, James 4:11-12
Warning Against Boasting, James 4:13-17
Warning to the Rich, James 5:1-6
Patience and Prayer, James 5:7-8, 13-20
A Living Hope, 1 Peter 1:1-7
The Living Stone and the Holy Nation, 1 Peter 2:4-10
Slaves of God, 1 Peter 2:11-17
The Example of Christ's Suffering, 1 Peter 2:18-25
Suffering for Doing Right, 1 Peter 3:10-15
Suffering as a Christian, 1 Peter 4:12-16
The Flock of God, 1 Peter 5:1-4
God's Call and Choice, 2 Peter, 1:10-15
Eyewitnesses of Christ's Glory, 2 Peter 1:16-21
The Word of Life, 1 John 1:1-3
The New Command, 1 John 2:1-3, 9-11, 15-17
Children of God, 1 John 3:1-3
Love One Another, 1 John 3:13-18
God Is Love, 1 John 4:7-11
Our Victory over the World, 1 John 5:3-12
Truth and Love, 2 John 1:7-11
Final Words, 3 John 1:11, 13-15
False Teachers, Jude 1:1-4
Warnings and Instructions, Jude 1:17-23
Prayer of Praise, Jude 1:24-25

CHAPTER FIFTEEN

"A Revelation of Things That Were, Are, and Will Be"
Prologue, Revelation 1:1-3
Greetings to the Seven Churches, Revelation 1:4-8

A Vision of Christ, Revelation 1:9-20
The Message to Ephesus, Revelation 2:1-5
The Message to Smyrna, Revelation 2:8-11
The Message to Pergamum, Revelation 2:12-15
The Message to Thyatira, Revelation 2:18-20, 24-25
The Message to Sardis, Revelation 3:1-2
The Message to Philadelphia, Revelation 3:7,11
The Message to Laodicea, Revelation 3:14-17, 22
Worship in Heaven, Revelation 4:1-11
The Scroll and the Lamb, Revelation 5:1, 6-10
The Great Crowd, Revelation 7:9-17
The Woman and the Dragon, Revelation 12:1-8
The Song of the Redeemed, Revelation 14:1-5, 13
The Wedding Feast of the Lamb, Revelation 19:5-9
The Final Judgment, Revelation 20:11-15
The New Heaven and the New Earth, Revelation 21:1-8
The New Jerusalem, Revelation 21:9-14, 18-27; 22:1-5
Epilogue, Revelation 22:16-21